Pat Shaw
1917 – 1977

His life
through the memories of his friends,
his music, dances and song

Brenda Godrich

edited by

Brenda Godrich

2010

Abbreviations used throughout this work –

CSH	Cecil Sharp House
EFDSS	English Folk Dance and Song Society
ED&S	English Dance and Song – the magazine of the EFDSS
FMJ	Folk Music Journal – the annual Journal of the EFDSS
RAH	Royal Albert Hall
VWML	Vaughan Williams Memorial Library – the Library of the EFDSS
CDSS	Country Dance and Song Society of America
CDS	Country Dance and Song – the magazine of the CDSS
NVS	Volksdansvereniging NVS – the Folk Dance Society of the Netherlands
DAWNS	Welsh Folk Dance Society newsletter

Published writings are shown by indented text. Words in italics are as written or spoken to the editor. Pat's works are in "bold" as are names of individual contributors when quoted direct. § before sentences in italics denotes an unattributed text.

Published by Nicolas Broadbridge

Copyright © Brenda Godrich

This edition first published 2010

ISBN 978 –0-9523924-2-2

Typeset in Bookman Old Style by Antony Heywood

Cover design by Compositions by Carn

Printed in the United Kingdom by
Ashford Colour Press Ltd, Gosport, Hants.

FOREWORD

This book would never have come into being but for the inspired idea of Hazel Moir and her great perseverance in gathering memories of Pat Shaw. Nor would it be in print save for the tremendous amount of work done by Brenda Godrich and her superlative dedication to this project, ably helped in the final stages of publication by Antony Heywood. I am most grateful to them and to all who contributed their memories.

This fascinating book will, I am sure, be greatly enjoyed by those privileged to have known Pat Shaw and will enable those who did not to gain an insight into his character and the wealth of his talents in music, dance, song and much more besides.

Marjorie Fennessy

ACKNOWLEDGEMENTS

A Short Biography
Thanks to Christopher Shuldham-Shaw for giving notes which are used in this section and particularly for allowing publication of his notes at the end.

Immediate Reactions to his Death / Pat in America / Pat in Holland
Thanks to the Country Dance and Song Society (www.cdss.org) for use of material from their magazine including Volume 16, April 1986. Pages 8-21 edited by David E. E. Sloane.

Pat the Academic
Thanks to Dr Emily Lyle of the School of Scottish Studies for her help with information concerning Pat and *The Greig-Duncan Folk Song Collection.*

Thanks to Ivor Allsop for permission to reproduce the letter from Pat Shaw concerning the Papa Stour Sword Dance.

Sing for Pleasure
Thanks to Jill Henderson for permission to quote from "Simi Jadech" and from James Wild's tribute to Pat Shaw at the launch of the book.

Pat through Song
Thanks to the English Folk Dance and Song Society for permission to quote from the Folk Music Journal and the English Dance and Song Magazine in this and other sections.

Pat's Musicianship
Thanks to Denis Smith for The Countryside Players' list of recital dates.

Pat in Shetland
Charles Simpson, Ewen & Clare Balfour and Christine Leask for help with contacts.
Angus Johnson and the team at the Shetland Archives.
Christine Leask and Cavy Johnson for reading through the final text.
Map on page 108 is reproduced by kind permission of © Collins Bartholomew Ltd 2008.

Pat in Holland
Reprints of Pat's Forewords and Introductions by permission of Volksdansvereniging NVS, hhtp://www.nvs-dance.nl.
Both "Holland as Seen in English Country Dance" (ISBN 90-805386-4-7) and "New Wine in Old Bottles" (ISBN 90-9009249-8) have been republished by the NVS. The former in 2002 and the latter in 2004 and again in 2010.

Pat in Wales
Dafydd Evans for translating the poem by Frances Môn Jones.
Hazel Moir for other translations and proof reading.
To the Welsh Folk Dance Society for permission for quotes from DAWNS – the Newsletter of the Welsh Folk Dance Society.

Pat in America
Hazel Moir for encouraging memories from people in America.
Fried de Metz Herman for allowing reproduction of her introduction to "Choice Morsels" and other pieces.
Country Dance and Song Society of America as above.
Sections reproduced from the Pinewoods Collections by kind permission of the Board of the Pinewoods Trust.

List of Publications
Thanks to Ivor Allsop for providing a list of publications in his possession.

Thanks are also due to –
The editor of Set & Turn Single, who first advertised the call for memories,
Pam Thornton for typing the initial responses,
Malcolm Taylor, Library Director and his staff at the Vaughan Williams Memorial Library, Cecil Sharp House,
… and to our proof readers, Hilary Blanford and Julian Hodgson.

Acknowledgements for photos are due to –
Han and Fien Daamen
David Fleming-Williams
Vic Godrich
Antony Heywood
Michael Isaacs
Ann Robertson
Christopher Shuldham-Shaw
Denis Smith
Keith and Maggie Uttley
Jan and Brian Willcocks

Over the years the origin of some photos has become uncertain so apologies for any omissions from this list.

Great thanks are due to Antony Heywood who undertook the task of putting the book into order for the printers. His precision and command of detail have been invaluable and certainly have added to the book's readability.

A final thank you to Marjorie Fennessy whose skill at finding wayward commas and spelling mistakes is enormous, whilst also ensuring that the facts herein are correct. And without whom the whole project would not have been so thorough.

CONTENTS

INTRODUCTION

Over many years of dancing in England, Wales, Holland and the USA Hazel Moir was frequently struck by the number of dancers who had stories to tell about Patrick Shuldham-Shaw. Eventually she came to the conclusion that these memories should be recorded so started to make enquiries wherever she danced and tried to persuade people to write down their recollections. Hazel also wrote many letters to people whose names she had been given as possible sources. In November 2004, Hazel sent a letter to the editor of "Set and Turn Single" magazine advertising this quest and, with this help, a wider area was covered.

The whole time Hazel was collecting memories, Marjorie Fennessy was extremely supportive and kept adding information from her vast collection of papers and other memorabilia about Pat and his work and from her vivid memory of events in his life. Since 1977, when Pat died, Marjorie has continued to work to ensure that Pat's memory and his work are recorded. She has always been a great help to Christopher Shuldham-Shaw when he has received requests regarding Pat's work and has been involved in various recordings of his music and dance books which have been produced in order to preserve his musical legacy.

In May 2008 Marjorie persuaded me to take the memories project forward and I have been working on the mass of material since then. This book will help future generations realise what was so special about this man whose dances will, I am sure, continue to be enjoyed for many years to come.

When initially gathering material together, the enormity of the task soon became clear, as did the fact that it would not do justice to the full breadth of the man to limit it to the memories that had been collected in the last three years, mainly from the dance world. Much was written about Pat at the time of his death – formal obituaries as well as pieces from his friends who were mourning such a loss both on a personal basis and to the wider folk world.

So, the scope has been widened to take in those obituaries, writings from the time of Pat's death in 1977, as well as memories gathered in the past three years. An attempt has been made to show, through these pieces, the enormous influence Pat had, not only on the Country Dance scene in England, Scotland, Wales, Shetland, the Netherlands and the USA, but also on the songs and music of these areas. The academic side of Patrick Shuldham-Shaw will be noted as will his contributions to various committees and the "Sing for Pleasure" movement.

As this project evolved, I had to continually remind myself that it was to be a collection of memories, not a biography. Sometimes there has been a great temptation to move from one to the other, and I can only hope that I have not ended up with something that satisfies neither category.

Many people and organisations have been enormously helpful in the completion of this project. Not least, of course, are all those who wrote their memories of this great man. Their names are in the list in chapter 19. The contributions came in all shapes and sizes – some names are included in the text, some not, as their pieces have been collated with others saying much the same things. § before sentences in italics denotes an unattributed text. These decisions have been mine and I hope that my choices will be accepted for what they are, I have named people who I think will be recognised by the current wider folk community or whose stories provide an extra depth because of their origination. I apologise for any errors of judgement on my part in this respect. The Shetland section has been the exception to this as, in Shetland, Pat Shaw is revered for reasons other than his dances. The communities there had not heard of our quest for written memories, so they were traced, visited and recorded.

I have tried to ensure that permissions have been given where written texts have been reproduced – any failures in this respect are mine.

It will be noted that the many versions of the name Patrick Shuldham-Shaw have been used throughout this book, mainly because Pat himself was not consistent in this respect. He added a P.S. to a letter written 15.2.1973 regarding his review of "The Scottish Folksinger".

For this sort of thing I prefer the shortened form of my name as given at the end of the review. My full name is such a mouthful and I really only use it for very official purposes.

Finally, although many times during the production of this work I have wanted to have my life back, I would like to thank Marjorie Fennessy for the opportunity it has given me to learn about this remarkable man and to thank her in a tangible way for the many years of the joy of dancing which she has given me.

Brenda Godrich
December 2009

Pat Shaw 1917 – 1977

1. Pat Shaw on Pat Shaw

It is appropriate that, if we are aiming for a picture of this remarkable man, we should start with his own autobiographical statement. Pat wrote this resumé of his life in 1968 after a recital in Lerwick, Shetland, in aid of the local hospital and frequently circulated it during his lifetime.

Full Name: Patrick Noel Shuldham-Shaw
Born: 24th December 1917
Died: Not yet anyway!

Pat on his father's knee

My father was an Irishman from County Kildare but spent thirty years in India as a tea planter.

My mother was a Devon woman, an indirect descendant of Sir Francis Drake, so my family claim. She was a professional singer, singing under her maiden name, Winifred Holloway. She was a pupil of Plunket Greene, and a very close personal friend of Cecil Sharp. She was one of the most active figures in the folk-song and folk-dance revival in England and on Cecil Sharp's death in 1924 became the honorary secretary of the Cecil Sharp Memorial Fund, which was founded to provide permanent headquarters for the English Folk Dance Society. After six years of hard plodding she raised over £30,000 and on Whitsun 1930 the building, Cecil Sharp House, was opened. My mother was too ill to be present at the opening (though I was dancing there as a small boy of twelve) and did not live long enough to see the finished building.

Pat as a baby

I myself was born in Stratford-upon-Avon, but all my childhood as far back as I can remember was spent in London and I look upon myself as a Londoner.

I was educated at St Aubyn's Rottingdean (1926-31, my prep school days) then at Harrow (1931-36) where I first developed a really passionate interest in music, being ably guided by the late Dr R. S. Thatcher (later warden at the Royal Academy of Music), who was then the director of music. After that I studied music at Cambridge (Queens' College, 1936-39), chiefly under Hubert Middleton and Professor E. J. Dent. In those days I was a fairly proficient oboe player and played in the University Musical Society Orchestra etc. and I used to sing regularly in the University Madrigal Society. I had a few singing lessons in those days but as I have had to unlearn nearly all I was taught, I prefer not to give the name of my teacher. Although I took a keen interest in all forms of music, as I still do, I always had a profound love of the folk music on which I was brought up and while at Cambridge I started

Pat on boat with mother and father all sitting next to each other

Picture opposite is of Pat's mother Winifred Holloway

Pat at St Aubyn's

Pat at Harrow

getting to know as much as I could about the folk music of other nations. I started dancing (English folk dancing) at the age of six and at the age of thirteen, the committee of the English Folk Dance Society passed a special grace allowing me to become a member, although five years under age. As for singing I can't remember at what age I started to sing – I can't remember not singing!

On leaving Cambridge in 1939, I worked for a short period as Midland area organiser for the English Folk Dance Society until I joined the National Fire Service (NFS) in Birmingham (later in Cardiff) early in 1942. During my whole time in the NFS I kept my interest in both folk song and dance, doing as much as possible of both in the limited leisure I had. I gave a folk song recital in Cardiff in aid of the NFS Benevolent Fund which was very successful.

In 1946 when I was released from the NFS I decided that I was going to take up singing professionally – specializing in the singing of folk songs of all nationalities in their correct languages. (Languages have always been a keen secondary interest to music for me.) I was ill for some time after coming out of the service but started working at my singing on my own. As a result of a holiday trip to Shetland Isles I found there was a whole mine of uncollected folk music there, and I decided to go there on a collecting trip. In 1947 I spent five months collecting folk music – mostly fiddle tunes but some songs as well – in the Shetlands. There is still much more to be had and I propose spending another two months up there this year to continue the work.

As a result of my collecting work and my general enthusiasm for folk music I was invited to attend the meeting of the International Folk Music Council in September 1947, during which I was privileged to sing some English folk songs to the whole meeting and give a short talk on my findings in the Shetland Isles – which proved of particular interest to the Scandinavian members of the conference. Since then I have accepted the invitation to be one of the "Correspondents" of the International Folk Music Council – the Correspondents consisting mainly of all the folk music collectors in the various countries.

I had felt for some time that I wanted help with my singing, but was doubtful to whom to go, as I felt that a real understanding of folk music was essential in my teacher. By chance I mentioned my problem to Edric Connor, who was also attending the conference, and he very kindly offered to take me on as a pupil, if I was prepared to take the risk of being his first pupil. Since then I have been doing very little public work, only some radio performances, and have been working hard at the technical problems. Having now discovered that I am the possessor of a far larger voice than I had ever before suspected, I want to broaden my repertoire to include songs of all kinds, although I shall never lose my passionate interest in folk music and I still intend to spend some time every year collecting folk music wherever I find it. My programmes vary considerably according to the circumstances, from a completely international programme to songs from one particular country, usually Great Britain. The one thing I firmly believe in is to do as little talking as possible and to let the music speak for itself.

Another subject that I am acutely interested in is folk song arrangement. In this I do not favour any particular style as long as the arrangement grows naturally out of the tune and is not something forced on it. I have arranged a number of folk songs myself and hope one day, if the various

Punting in Cambridge

copyright difficulties can be surmounted, to get some of them published. As regards serious composition I do occasionally put pen to paper and have composed about twenty songs – not in the folk style at all, though the influence of folk music may be discernable.

Lack of time and opportunity has caused me to give up the oboe. As a relaxation I play for English, Scottish and American traditional dances on the piano-accordion. I took up this instrument, to the disgust of my serious-minded friends, while in the Shetlands and now I regard it as my passport and ice breaker anywhere on my collecting trips. I have played pretty well continuously from 10 p.m. till after 5 a.m. for dances in the Shetlands! I play with gusto if without anything else. From time to time I amuse myself by composing jigs and reels, etc. for various friends. One set of three marches in the Scottish style has been privately recorded and over 500 copies sold.

My other activities include running two miles every morning when it is possible; a lively interest in cooking (and I think I may say I have a flare for it), which I regard as a truly traditional art; and collecting pipes (I have a collection of over a hundred of all sorts of shapes and sizes, one of the best of its kind in the country I believe). Also my collection of published folk music (which my mother collected plus a good deal I have added myself) is possibly the finest private library of its kind in the country.

Finally one predominant interest, lying at the back of most of my other interests, is in my fellow human beings of all races and nationalities. My future aim as a singer is to get the folk songs (and other songs) of my own country appreciated

and known abroad and at home where they are almost unknown, and to help my own fellow countrymen to understand the music of other peoples. In this way, small as it is, I hope to try to get people to care for what is best in other people. In fact in my own small way I want to carry out the ideals of the International Folk Music Council.

Reproduced from the Country Dance and Song magazine No. 16, April 1986 in an edition which included a Special Section on Pat Shaw.

Pat conducting a singing session in Holland

2. PAT SHAW AND THE
ENGLISH COUNTRY DANCE

In 1966, ED&S, the magazine of the EFDSS, published the following in which Pat Shaw gave his philosophy regarding English Country Dance. It gives us an insight into why Pat felt that his work of creating new dances and reinterpreting the published dances was a natural progression in the life of the dance – despite the fact that "the establishment" of the time disapproved.

PAT SHAW answers questions put to him by HUGH RIPPON in the first of a series of three interviews which discuss the history and development of the English Country Dance and its music from the Seventeenth Century to the present day.

Pat Shaw, can you give me a brief outline of the development of the English country dance from, say, the time of John Playford onwards?

That is a terrific question. First of all we want to remind ourselves that the dances in the Playford collection are of various kinds. Many of the earliest from the first edition, which were obviously in existence for probably a hundred years before, are of a very simple peasant type, and they became fashionable in higher circles, providing a great deal of relaxation after the rather stiff and starchy court dances of the period. Then also side by side with them, as the editions of Playford went on, you get the creations of the dancing masters of the period, and these are very varied. Some of them are very simple and very sociable, full of fun, and sometimes with odd bits of play-acting and a game element. On the other hand you get others where the attention is much more focussed on patterns and intricacies. As time went on the set dances, which you find in the earlier Playford editions, tended to drop out and by about 1730 the repertoire consisted almost entirely of longways duple minors and triple minors. But there was considerable originality in many of these earlier longways dances: you don't meet with a lot of repetition, you do occasionally find the same dance with a different tune given a different title, but on the whole, each dance was a very individual entity. And this seems to have gone on up to about 1750. After that there was a great change. I'm not sure what brought this about, but the dances started losing their individuality; they became mere sequences of well-known figures put together in more or less any order, and there was less definite connection between the pattern of the dance and its tune. This tendency went on right into the 1800s. The last great dancing master to publish much was Thomas Wilson early in the 19th century, and he gives in most of his books three or even four alternatives to every tune, and even there, although some of his dances attain a much higher level of interest than usual for the period, there doesn't seem to be a great connection between a dance and its tune and the figures seem fairly arbitrary. After that the longways, which had ruled more or less supreme, gradually gave way to cotillions and quadrilles. The waltz of course came in, but even the waltz was used in a longways formation at times. I suppose people got a bit tired of the longways formation and turned to the squares that had come in from

France. The two forms of dance went on through the earlier part of the 19th century side by side. Then other European forms of dance came in.

There was a time when the polka was the rage, and of course the set got split up gradually into couples; thus towards the end of the 19th century the emphasis was very much on couple dances. From longways sets to square sets to couples, and of course in the last few years the tendency has been more towards dancing on one's own, primitive fashion, so we seem to have gone right back to square one.

Who else published collections of dances besides John Playford and when?

I think the first in the field after John Playford was Walsh. I believe there were no serious laws of copy-right at that time and publishers used to pinch each others' material left, right and centre, and in the various Walsh collections you get many of the same dances described word for word in the same way. The descriptions were probably not Playford's at all, but by whatever dancing master he got them from. That is why you find the same movement described in different dances in different ways. Then from 1730 onwards the publishers get thicker and thicker on the ground. Wright's collection is another in the 1730s or 1740s. Then you get Rutherford, Johnson, Thompson, all starting about 1750. We do quite a lot of Thompson's dances these days although people may not realise it. All the dances in the Apted book are from Thompson's collections for various years. It's called the Apted book simply because it was found in the possession of a Mrs. Apted. Then you get Preston, Skillern and Cahusac and hosts of others towards the end of the century.

What about these so called French longways dances, some of which you have published?

You're thinking of Feuillet and John Essex. The thing is, that the longways country dance, even if it didn't completely originate in England is in the main an English development. It was introduced into polite society in France by Madame La Dauphine (whoever she was) and it became rather the rage there, from all accounts. From France it spread out into a great many parts of Europe going right up to Denmark and you can find in old Danish collections dances that are quite obviously English in their tunes and in their figures. When this became popular in France, naturally the dancing masters had to keep abreast of the times and teach what was the fashion, and one particular man, Feuillet, wrote a thesis on the English country dance, and published quite a number of dances which were, he says, the most popular and the most beautiful to be found in England to which he added one or two of his own and of other French dancing masters of the period. This was published in 1706. Now this proved so popular that a man called John Essex did what really amounts to a translation of all the text and the descriptions of steps and hand holds, etc., but giving a rather different selection of dances at the end.

This was published in 1710. The interesting thing about these two collections is that the dances are not described verbally, as they are in Playford and all the other collections, but that they're drawn out in the form of diagrams, and so, when you get a dance occurring both in Playford and in Feuillet or John Essex, it's interesting to compare the two because the diagrams show quite clearly the pattern of many figures which may be subject to some doubt when interpreting them from verbal descriptions only. It's from these sources that we have got complete black-and-white evidence as to how siding was done for instance.

Is it true that by the 1800s there were about 10,000 English country dances in print?

Yes, this is probably true. I've never counted them, but one has to remember that many of those from earlier collections would by 1800 be very inaccessible to the ordinary person. I doubt if 10,000 were really readily available to people at any one time, but I'm quite sure that that number of country dances had been published by the early 1800s. But you must remember this, that if you examine them you will find duplication of actual dance patterns over and over again, exactly the same sequence of figures occurring many times to different tunes.

Why were they called country dances?

The usual explanation is that they weren't country dances in that they came from the country and had a rural origin, but simply that they were contrary dances. The French use the word "contre dance" and the Americans to this day call them "contras". Because you formed up your set with men in one line the ladies in another you were opposite or "contre" to your partners.

What connection was there between country dances, presumably done in fashionable circles, and those done by the villagers at their own local hops and festivals?

There has always been a certain amount of two-way traffic in social dancing up and down the social scale. I think most people would agree that a great many of the earliest-known country dances of the Sellengers Round, Gathering Peascods type were certainly peasant dances possibly of ritual significance. They were very basic and probably somewhat rustic, but then they suddenly became fashionable among the upper crust and that is why they were published by John Playford. The reason they became fashionable was because of their "gay simplicity". They were a pleasant relaxation after the formality of the court dances. Along with these, more and more country dances were invented by the dancing masters.

Some of these doubtlessly slid down the social scale and were danced by the middle classes. They don't seem to have gone further than that, as Hardy points out somewhere (I'm not sure where), in his time there was a distinction in the villages between the dancing of the farm labourers (mostly reels and step dances), and the dances done by the squire and his family and so forth (mostly country dances). Probably the only time in the year when the two met and farm labourers would dance the country dances was the Har-

vest Home when the whole of the community got together and had a celebration.

*Do we know really what the villagers were dancing before say 1800? What were
the real folk dances?*

On the social side I wouldn't like to answer that question in any detail. It
depends what you mean by villagers – in any village there's an upper crust
and a lower crust. Presumably you mean the farm labourers. I think they
were probably dancing reels and step dances and possibly they also danced
some of the country dances of the period that were out of fashion. There
was a sort of time lag between the town and the country. There is a very
interesting letter in the National Library of Wales from a man called Jones
who lived in the village of Llangadfan, Montgomeryshire, writing to a friend
of his and describing the dances that were danced in that village about the
1780s. He gives an interesting technical description of three of the dances,
all three couple sets: there are a large number of heys and figures of eight.
How much of this was Welsh and how much of it came in from England one
doesn't really know, but they were very complicated and you would have
had to be a very good dancer and have a good memory to get through them
without a mistake. He gives the description of these three dances and says
that he would send more if his correspondent were interested. So we do
know that at any rate, in one particular village in Wales the villagers were
dancing something quite complicated.

*When Country Dancing ceased to be fashionable where did it carry on and who
was doing it?*

The decline came somewhere towards the middle of the 19th century and it
was quite a gradual process. Some country dances, like the Dashing White
Sergeant (which is of English and not Scottish origin incidentally), remained
fashionable in the Highland ballroom and fairly fashionable in the English
ballroom all through the last century. But by and large, somewhere in the
19th century, people's main interest went on to other forms of dancing, and
the country dances (usually they were the later dances of the country dance
period) survived only in villages and various parts of the country. The towns
had meanwhile turned to quadrilles and lancers and things like that.

*So that the folk dances that we started collecting at the beginning of this century
were in fact a remnant of the fashionable country dances done in the century before, and this brings us to another question: how "folk" are the dances we do now?*

It's awfully easy to think of dances as being simply collections of figures. If
you compare the dance we know as the "Devon Bonny Breast Knot" with
some of the dances round about the 1790s you will find more or less exactly
the same figures. But the style of dancing that survived among the Devon-
shire villages, where the dance was formed and remembered, was probably
somewhat different to the style of the Assembly Rooms of Jane Austen's
time, which was probably when that particular dance first came in. I think
the actual patterns are probably not very "folk" except that a lot of the

figures used throughout the history of the country dance were very much older than the Country Dance itself and are very basic folk patterns. The style of dancing was probably based originally on what the dancing master taught.

And don't forget you get these itinerant dancing masters, whom Tom Flett mentions in his book on Scottish dancing (and I'm sure this happened in England too), who gave people quite a good dancing style. I think however, that the style was moulded by the village people to some extent, and in this way the style of dancing might be said to be genuine folk. There was this two way influence so that by and large the actual dances that we now consider as folk are not as folk as all that. It really depends on what you mean by "folk".

How did the shape of the longways dance evolve, and how did many of the shapes that we now do evolve?

This is very much a question of speculation and theory. I think probably the chain that you get, either as a closed chain as in the Faroes ballad dances and some of the kolos of Yugoslavia or as the open chain that you get in other kolos in Yugoslavia, the farrandole and various other dances of that sort, were certainly some of the oldest forms. Cecil Sharp I know felt the big round, the Rounds for as Many as Will in the earlier Playford collections, were of extreme antiquity, and where those rounds were progressive, one couple leading out to the next and gradually working round the ring, that type of progressive dance may have developed into a longways. As for the other shapes I suppose there is a limit to the number of shapes you can have. How they evolved, how they originated, I just wouldn't know. I should think somebody, sometime just had bright ideas. The square for four, the square for eight, the longways for six, the longways for eight: I believe that these shapes were known in Italy before they came to England, but I'm not sure on that point.

What is the difference between English and Scottish dancing?

It depends what you mean by Scottish and what you mean by English. To the worlds of most people today what you see of Scottish dancing is dancing in a style created by the Royal Scottish Country Dance Society, and this bears little resemblance to what you find going on to this day in villages in Scotland where the people dance the way they have always danced, without any tuition from the RSCDS. The English style is possibly based a little more on what Cecil Sharp and other people found being done in country districts and we do try, even if we don't always succeed, to get our own steps to be authentic. We do pay a little more attention to the village styles than do the RSCDS, who have deliberately turned their backs on anything traditional. In that line they aim to try and reproduce the style of the ballroom of the mid-19th century; I think they have expressed this as their basic aim. But the main difference, I would say, between Scottish and English dancing, and it's quite a wide one, is simply a difference in outlook between two organisations and nothing basic at all. As regards repertoire, the Scots do an immense number of dances taken from English collections. There is the standing joke about a dance they took from Thompson called The Thatched House, but in order to make it Scottish they changed the name and called it "The Theekit Hoose".

It would be true to say, would it not, that there are no such things as national borders as far as dancing is concerned, and certainly as far as basic shapes, like the four-hand reel or the whole set dance or the threesome, are concerned. Would it be truer to speak of regional differences appearing in the British Isles and also over the whole of Northern Europe?

I wouldn't like to say that there are no such things as national borders, but certainly you get the same dances and similar styles I think both sides of the border between England and Scotland. As to the border between England and Wales, I don't really know because, by and large, dancing died out completely in Wales. Remember too that there is the sea between England and Ireland and this is a much bigger barrier. Although there are similarities, there's a much greater difference between the Irish style of dancing and the Scottish and English. Certainly you get four-hand reels, whole-set dances and three-somes and others all over the place, and there is far more unity than perhaps is generally thought.

Can you describe the affinities between British Folk dancing and that of the rest of Northern Europe?

The folk dances one sees done from Northern Europe are mostly of a later date and more of the quadrille type, and by quadrille I mean square set. The quadrille really came into England from France. I don't know how it came into France but it was based on the square set although they do have some figures in common with country dance figures. There are exceptions in Scandinavia. For instance, in Norway and also in Sweden to some extent, you get one or two primitive types of couple dance where the woman simply trails after her partner and the man does all sorts of exciting leaps; it's a sort of test of virility. But all the various quadrille type dances that you get in Sweden, Denmark and Norway are later in origin than most of the English country dances. Apart from these, you seem to get in Sweden and Denmark both double quadrilles and single quadrilles. You also get some longways dances in Denmark and in some cases the history of a particular dance can be traced back through Germany and France to England, both as regards tune and dance pattern.

The folk dance in America seems to be made up of many influences and comes out as the New England longways, The Western Square, the New England Square, and the Running Set, can you comment on this?

For "Running Set" read "Running Type of Square". Just as the people of America came in from many parts of Europe, so in the various types of folk music in America you get very much the same mixtures. In certain types of New England square you get quite a lot of Scandinavian influence and French quadrille influence, although much of this must have come via England.

A lot of longways dances are British in origin. For instance you get the American version of Petronella which they call Pat Mellor where the figure is exactly the same, except that it represents the dance in a slightly earlier stage, in that, instead of having a swing round the other couple or the poussette as you get in most of that type of dance in England, you get the right and left through. You have probably noticed that in a great many, almost all in fact, of the North country dances you have got the same distinctive figure at the ending of the dance, namely, the lead down the middle and back and what we usually call swing round the other couple. This is basically the same figure as what the Scots call a poussette. But in the New England contras, especially in the earlier collections, you get this lead down the middle and back and cast and a right and left through as the standard ending. Now the Southern Square as it developed in the Appalachian Mountains was based on a pretty ancient form of dance; it wasn't necessarily done in quadrille sets like the New England Square and probably grew out of these progressive rounds that you still find mentioned in the earlier Playford collections (at least, that's one theory). Finally, the Western Square, as the Western part of the country was settled with people coming from various parts and bringing various influences, is a sort of amalgam of the whole lot. For example you get influences from the running set type of dance, especially in the speed which is the fastest speed you get, and also considerable influences in figures from New Zealand, from the Scandinavian countries, from Ireland, and from all sorts of other places.

The rhythms we dance to nowadays, the jig, the reel, the hornpipe, etc., have been pretty fundamental all along, haven't they?

Some of them, a jig for instance, are very basic rhythms, although they may not be called jigs necessarily; you get jig tunes in the early Playford books. Even-time rhythm, as opposed to broken-time rhythm, is again very basic, and although you don't call them reels, what you do to them is more or less the same. The waltz, which we dance to now, of course came in from the Continent, but before the waltz, don't forget, we had the minuet which was a court dance in triple time, although I don't think there were many dances before about 1670 in triple time. We get the triple-time hornpipe, tunes like Mr Isaac's Maggot and Mr Beveridge's Maggot and a lot of the other Maggots which are a slowish three. I don't quite know where this came from (Purcell wrote hornpipes). It's probably a development out of one of the court dances like the Gaillard or something like that and this I have yet to find out.

Exactly how the horn-pipe ceased being a triple time dance and became a slowed down sort of jerky reel that we know now as the broken time horn-pipe, the sailor's horn-pipe type of thing, I don't quite know. Nor do I know when this came about; some time in the 18th century I would say. Strathspeys and Schottisches I have a feeling are a later development. Originally a Strathspey was simply a kind of reel, and the way certain Strathspeys are played today I'm fairly sure was not the way they were played originally. I think formerly it was a much more of an even-time tempo, less jerky altogether, but this is rather surmise than theory.

How old are these figures that we do now: hands across (or star), ladies chain, basket, ballroom hold swing and any others? The grand chain is obviously very old. But when did I first grasp my partner round the waist and give her a swing?

Well, I don't quite know when you first grasped your partner round the waist because I didn't know you at that age. I would say the ballroom hold came into this country with the waltz at the end of the 18th century. Certainly before that you didn't grasp your partner round the waist. The closest contact you had with her was probably in a figure called Allemande which is something without the speed of the swing; it's something like what the Scots call a "Reel o' Tulloch Swing" when you interlace your arms with your partner behind each others' back. That came in round about the 1750s. Let's deal with some of the figures. Hands Across I would say is a very basic figure and I should say it's been in use since time immemorial. Ladies Chain was originally a quadrille figure and was known as the English Chain or as la Chaise Anglaise in France. Basket, I would say is late quadrille period.

The various Figures-of-Eights, Rings, Grand-Chains were all I would say pretty basic figures. Right and Left Through, after all, originated as being simply a grand-chain for four people, and it was done like that until 1760. You get variations of the Right and Left Through developing along different lines in different places after that. What other figures have we got? Back-to-Back and Gipsy, which were probably one and the same thing at one time and is just a walking round your partner, is a fairly basic sort of movement. The Turns-Two and One-Hand I should say are pretty basic and have been in existence for a good time.

Could we say something about steps, for instance, the "Rant Step"? How did that develop? What has been the influence of clog dancing on stepping in a social dance? In the 1760s if I'd been lower crust village would I have done my dancing with a powerful skipping step with virtuoso leaps and bounds flung in, in the choruses?

There's rather a lot to answer there. Let me remind you of what I said earlier that Hardy said that the dances of the farm labourers were not so much the pattern dances, the country dances, but were the reels where you have a basic figure walking a serpentine figure of eight alternating with stepping. Clog dancing is a form of step dancing where clogs are worn. But you get step dancing in ordinary hard shoes in places like Dartmoor and Cumberland. In Westmorland, where they didn't wear clogs so much, you still got step dancing, and in the areas where they had a step dance tradition, they would introduce the clog steps into the social and country dances. This is shown by one or two dances that we don't usually see very much of these days, but have been collected in the Lake District. At the time when country dancing was the accepted thing amongst the upper crust, to have a reasonable ability to step was considered as being one of the signs of being a good dancer. You very often find the term "foot it to your partner" which must have been a "free and easy"; you put in whatever step you felt like doing and it was your chance to show off your dexterity to your partner momentarily. It's pretty clear that the steps of the English were never really formalised and that there was a good deal of liberty to choose whatever fitted in.

Skipping was probably also used, at least Sharp thought so, and there is Feuillet's description, as translated by John Essex, referring to little hops which were then fashionable. Going on to the rant step, which you asked: I personally believe this to be a particular regional development of the basic double step, one-two-three-hop or step-close step-hop, or whatever you like to call it, but the hop has become so delayed that it coincides with the first step. I don't think it's a step that has existed since time immemorial; it has grown up out of the double step in that particular region of England.

Could you say something about what steps would have been done in village dancing?

This I think is pure conjecture. The basic steps must either have been single step-hop, step-hop, step-hop, etc. or double steps for travelling. Where they had step dance traditions, they undoubtedly made use of this form of dancing on the spot. Many of the villagers would ape the upper crust and would probably learn some of the fancy steps they did and learnt those as well. One step I am pretty sure was not done very much, except in specialised dances and then probably by the upper crust only, was the "Walk". I was told once, and I'm not sure what the evidence is, that they deliberately introduced the "Walk" in America into the country dance after the American War of Independence in order to create a style of dance that was not British.

Can I ask you how old some sample dances are, for instance, the Cumberland Square, The Yorkshire Square, Morpeth Rant, Cumberland Reel, Circassian Circle, Wiltshire Six Hand Reel and La Russe?

Cumberland Square and Yorkshire Square are 19th-century quadrille figures. In any case the whole of the Yorkshire Square as we do it now is a bit dicey, I think it's been pieced together from bits and pieces by Leta Douglas. La Russe: Tom Flett said he has traced the origin back to about 1840. Morpeth Rant and Soldiers Joy and those other North Country longways dances; probably a bit earlier, and as they go back to the longways period, early 19th century possibly late 18th.

The Circassian Circle, as the Scots do it, is simply basically the first figure of the quadrilles done in circular formation, and I should think came in probably in the early 19th century. Wiltshire 6 Hand Reel: reel dances are very basic indeed and are very ancient with this idea of walking a certain time figure or dancing a certain time figure and then having some kind of stepping alternating with it. But these things have never been completely static; there has been a continual process of growth. Cumberland reel and that type of dance, which is a whole set dance where the first couple end up at the bottom: I should say these are fairly old.

Just to finish up. Some people seem worried because some of our dances don't seem as "old" as they should be. But wouldn't it be true to say that, even if our material is often of recent origin, nevertheless it is part of a continuous process and is in nearly every case, derived from something else; that probably what has happened is the best thing that could have happened, and that by and large in our material today we have something which is up to date and fits modern man, his physique and his temperament, and yet still has the essential characteristics of folk dancing, that is natural grace, spontaneity, human contact and something indefinable which I would call "elemental"?

Yes, I think that is perfectly true. If you're being terribly purist about it, most of what we dance today is, in origin, not "folk", and let's not pretend otherwise. Does that really matter? If you want to do the oldest dances we have, you drop all the so-called traditional country dances and you concentrate on the very early things like "Gathering Peascods", "Sellenger's Round" and "Maid in the Moon" and others from the very early editions of Playford, some of which have all these elemental qualities. But we don't want to do that. I don't think that origins matter very much. It's what is made of them, the use that is made of them and whether it fits or not. Obviously a lot of these dances have been composed at one time or another, so if the time happens to be the 20th century, why worry? If the thing is accepted and is acceptable and supplies a particular need for the people who dance it, even if it's just maybe for a short time, this is all to the good. I don't think the actual folk origin is of really very much importance.

Just one further question? How do you think things will develop in the future? What will be our future trends?

Well, I'm no prophet. I don't quite know. There may be a swing away from the individual dancing that you get in the pop world today, where it doesn't really matter whether you have a partner or not, back to something which is more of community dance in its nature (I'm thinking right outside the Society just now). Within the Society, I think you will always get people with an intellectual approach who will want more and more difficult dances. Things will go in cycles; this is a natural human process. If you look at the history of any form of dance – it's equally true of ballroom dancing – you always get complexities coming in for their own sake. This is not necessarily a bad thing, but it is a bad thing if it tends to rank uppermost and if it is forced down the throats of people who don't always want more dances or more difficult dances. The danger is in the actual dance quality getting lost in the complexity of the figures. I'm very much against the fact that everything must be easy and should be able to be done perfectly with no practice and no work whatsoever. Dancing was never like this, and if you think of the complexity of the ritual dance and how completely natural a thing that has become when the techniques have been absorbed, I feel the same thing can be applied to the social dance. As regards the Society, one's got to face this too, that there will always be people who want to dance simply as a social pastime, and there will always be other people who want to take dancing seriously for its own sake, really study it, get to grips with it, and learn. Both these attitudes are necessary for the vitality of a Society like ours, and because you get a group of people who are taking a thing seriously, maybe slightly intellectually, it does not exclude the social side of it.

3. A SHORT BIOGRAPHY

Patrick, or Pat as he was later called, was born on 24 December 1917 at Old Vicarage, Stratford-upon-Avon in Warwickshire. However, he always considered himself to be a Londoner as he spent most of his childhood in London where he started folk dancing at the age of six.

Pat was twelve years old when his mother died suddenly at her home in Hampstead on 14 August 1930. Douglas Kennedy recalled that *the bereft and desolate Pat adopted us and for some years he spent summer holidays with our family.*

His father was anxious for Pat to have *something special to occupy and amuse him during the school holidays* and hired Mademoiselle Yvonne de Coppet, a professional violinist from Switzerland, to teach him French and help him with his music. The arrangement worked out well and Yvonne became Pat's stepmother in 1932. Pat adored his stepmother as much as his own mother. Pat's half-brother Christopher was born in 1933 while Pat was still at Harrow. For Chris, Pat became "Uncle Buzz" (his best pronunciation of brother was "buzzer"). For Pat, Christopher was "Baby Buzz".

At the age of twelve, Pat composed his first published dance **Monica's Delight.** Apparently Monica was *a beautiful Edinburgh lass on whom I had a crush at the time.* He continued to write dances and tunes for friends throughout his life. (For list of dances see Appendix 1)

Pat was a conscientious objector which was why he joined the National Fire Service during the Second World War years, first in Birmingham and then Cardiff. Indeed, he was in Wales when his father's house in Hampstead was hit by a German V1 bomb on 28 June 1944 in the London blitz. His father died six days later on 5 July 1944.

A keen student of dance, song and music, Pat became a skilled performer of morris, sword and country dancing and folk songs, an inspired composer and arranger of choral and folk music, a keen and accomplished collector and researcher of dance and song, and played various instruments. He was a delightful and supportive dance partner; his timing and interpretation were impeccable.

From 1942 Pat started to write tunes in his small Manuscript books, the first being **My Boy Willie** for Bernard Willey, a policeman in Birmingham.*

Pat purchased a house at 2 Holly Mount in Hampstead in the mid to late 1940s.

His singing lessons from Edric Conner, the well known West Indian actor and singer helped him to develop his voice. He took up singing professionally in 1946. Pat's folk song repertoire was always vast, his speciality being songs of all nations in their original languages including Macedonian and Zulu. He spent much time collecting tunes and some songs in the Shetland Isles, where he started playing the piano-accordion, his original instrument having been the oboe. He also played the guitar – he learned it to accompany himself when singing. There was hardly an instrument of any sort that he could not pick up and play – including the kalimba from South Africa, an ocarina and indeed an alpenhorn.

In 1946 he went on holiday to the Shetland Isles and thus began his involvement with the people of Shetland (see chapter 8). He went back several times collecting. In April 1947 he recovered a version of "King Orfeo" from John Stickle

---

* A list of tunes in the Mss books can be seen in the Vaughan Williams Memorial Library.

of Baltasound, Unst, the importance of which was expressed by Bronson in his "Traditional Tunes of the Child Ballads", Volume I. He collected the "Papa Stour" sword dance on one of his visits.

To amuse himself he also composed some of his own jigs and reels dedicating them to the friends he made and places he visited in Shetland. One set of three marches in the Shetland style were privately recorded and over 500 copies sold. Few people realised they were his own composition. Pat's gift for friendship and sympathetic interest secured him an invitation to take part in the Viking ceremony of Up Helly Aa, which at that time was little known outside Shetland.

Also in 1946 he recorded some folk songs for Boosey & Hawkes (see Appendix 6) and recorded several editions of Children's Hour for the BBC – including folk songs from Switzerland.

In the 1950s, the Society was asked by the BBC to start a series of country dance programmes on the radio and later television. Pat came into his own as caller, musician, singer and musical arranger. It was not long before he was responsible for these half-hour programmes – not only from the West Country, where they started, but also in the London area, the Midlands and Wales.

In August 1952 he, with Maud Karpeles, who had been Cecil Sharp's "right hand man", collected folk songs in the Forest of Dean – "The Cherry Tree" and "The Holly and the Ivy" that were both different versions from the well known ones.

Throughout the rest of his life Pat was on the staff at various summer schools and courses as well as continuing to visit Shetland and collecting there, and composing many dances and tunes.

Besides his Shetland connections, Pat was involved for over 25 years in Holland with the Nederlands Volksdansstichting, who perform English dances.

In the 1960s Pat also became involved with the Welsh Folk Dance Society, starting by going to a course at Pant-y-Fedwen, Borth. He became a member of their Executive Committee for a number of years and researched Welsh Dances as well as composing seven of his own. (see chapter 10)

At this time, his research interests led him to Feuillet's "Recüeil de Contredances" (1706) and Essex's "Chorography" (1710) and he edited "Six Simple Country Dances" as a result. He also transcribed – although did not publish as a whole – dances from the Thomas Bray 1699 collection.

From 1964 till 1975 Pat presented and produced the Christmas Carol Concert at Cecil Sharp House (see chapter 14). He made this event his own and many memories have made mention of Pat in this context. He also produced the EFDSS's Albert Hall Festival in 1968 and co-produced it in 1970 with Nibs Matthews, Bob Parker and Ron Smedley (see chapter 13).

Pat Shaw's other international connection was with the American dance scene. He visited Pinewoods Folk Camp in 1974 and many of his most well known dances were composed for American friends. (see Chapter 11)

In 1971 Pat was awarded the English Folk Dance and Song Society's highest honour, its Gold Badge, in recognition of his superb service to the Society:

Douglas Kennedy said in his citation that, if you wanted to know anything, 'Ask Pat' –

Born at Stratford-upon-Avon of a mother who willed the creation of Cecil Sharp House, Pat has been through life a singing, dancing, playing, teaching, talking, tumbling exponent of folk art and a high force in the existence of the

Society. Ready at all times to support its cause with his brains, his body and his breath, he has been the constant candidate for all its tasks however laborious and taxing. How often, when it seemed there were none available to fill the bill or shoulder the load, has the answer been 'Ask Pat'.

Although still young in years he is old in the Society's service to which he has brought a wide experience and a musical talent exercised in broadcasting, in composition, and creations of rich invention produced for the notable event and the apt occasion. 'Ask Pat'.

Through the years he has developed a special folk-musical scholarship which has enriched our journals and which will bear more fruit in coming seasons and help to answer the questioning of new generations seeking sources and variants. 'Ask Pat'. The time is clearly ripe to 'Tell Pat' that it is our unanimous wish he be given the Society's form of accolade, and with our gratitude and affection award him its Gold Badge.

Pat's response was typical *Talking was mentioned but there are occasions when I feel I just cannot talk; so I'm going to sing,* (to the tune of "Searching for Lambs")

> *In Stratford-upon-Avon I was born*
> *A long long time ago,*
> *I then moved down to London Town*
> *Where folk was all the go.*
>
> *My mother taught me folk songs galore*
> *From Britain and from France*
> *At the age of six in my little short knicks*
> *I was sent to learn to dance.*
>
> *Galopede and Butterfly I found as easy*
> *As falling out of bed,*
> *But then one day in the Black Nag Hey*
> *I completely lost my head.*
>
> *Then Morris and Sword I did begin*
> *And attended many a session,*
> *And Flowers of Ed and Trunkles, Bled,*
> *Soon rid me of aggression.*
>
> *But then I got the creative urge*
> *And became an awful pest*
> *To try my Maggots my friends I badgered*
> *And gave them all no rest.*
>
> *But members of the EFDSS*
> *Are a very friendly crew*
> *For your help and kindness in my moments of blindness*
> *I must give my thanks to you.*

And now today you have honoured me
All with a Badge of Gold
My mind is reeling with pride and feeling
Just like some hero bold.

It really is quite undeserved
What I've done has been my pleasure
Singing, playing, and dancing are the most entrancing
Ways for me of spending my leisure.

And now to finish up my song
No matter where you be
I thank you all both great and small
For this honour given to me.

In the early 1970s, Pat agreed to undertake the massive task of editing the eight large volumes of the Greig-Duncan collection of manuscripts under the aegis of the School of Scottish Studies. The collection comprises well over 3000 texts and tunes of folk songs from North-East Scotland. He left Hampstead and moved to Edinburgh in early 1972 specifically to start working on the collection. Edinburgh was a particularly useful location for Pat, since he was still interested in researching folk music in the Orkneys and Shetland Islands. While Pat spent much of his time working on the collection he continued to travel around the United Kingdom and abroad.

On 11 November 1977 Pat and Douglas Kennedy organised a lecture/recital in memory of Dr Maud Karpeles. This was the last concert where Pat sang and people have recorded how ill he looked on this occasion. He went to Weymouth in Dorset to participate in and lead a folk music event for schools there. On 16 November 1977, he had a heart attack in his hotel and died, aged 59, within an hour of arrival at Weymouth District Hospital.

Pat died while doing the musical work he loved. He was a very talented musician who was greatly respected world-wide in his specialist musical fields and who will remain internationally well known. Pat was multi-lingual and possessed a wide knowledge on almost any subject. He was generous to a fault, a witty and entertaining man and a marvellous friend. He never said an unkind word about anyone. He is still greatly missed by his many friends.

Christopher Shuldham-Shaw, Pat's half brother, has few early memories of Pat. *From 1940–1966 I was away from home for much of the time thanks to ploughing through prep school, Haileybury, National Service, Cambridge and starting my career based in London and the Midlands. For the whole of that period I have only three solid, specific memories of Pat. First, when he gave my mother an old Marconi radio for her Christmas present – hers having gone wrong. Second, when he gave a solo recital one Saturday evening to virtually the whole school at Haileybury. It was a "sell-out" evening and I was a proud brother. Third, when he gave me a present of a very old despatch rider's motorbike. It was my first ever motorised transport and I used it all over the country until it finally expired.*

For the whole of the above period, Pat was himself in an orbit that did not cross with mine. Aged 25-50, holder of a Queens' College Cambridge music degree, he had seen out the war years and was moving successfully into his own chosen musical career. I hardly met Pat at all during my bachelor years (1958–1966) in London and Warwickshire.

After I got married our meetings were more frequent as he stayed with us for one or more nights on numerous occasions. Being located in Oxfordshire and Warwickshire we were very well placed for his endless journeys up and down the country.

Ursula and I were married in 1968 with Pat bringing my elderly mother down to Devon for the occasion. On the night before the great day he must have noticed my increasingly tense state and promptly advised a large glass of sherry. I accepted of course. Then, becoming aware of some improvement, Pat suggested a second glass. Who was I to refuse? Thus fortified, I settled for a third and the evening continued to progress happily. It goes without saying that the next day, "W Day", passed in a state of totally relaxed euphoria and, from our position at the front of the small village church, Ursula and I could not ignore the quality and volume of sound behind us as Pat single-handedly undertook the roll of an entire choir. What a day: and thanks for ever Buzz!

One of Pat's more interesting hobbies was that of collecting, and enjoying, unusual malt whiskies from all over Scotland and the islands. He seemed to choose those with suspiciously home-made labels, unpronounceable names and varying colours and strengths. I only appreciated the full extent of this hobby after his death when I inherited no less than 72 bottles, some unopened but most well tasted. I have continued to enjoy his hobby and, despite the passage of time, the 71st bottle is only now down to the last wee dram in our dining room. One to go.

Random memories from those times include –

- His endless generosity in always bringing us presents, food and drink
- The extent of his generosity bearing in mind that he was frequently broke
- The fact that when he did have money he would spend it on others or give it away
- His car always appeared to be borrowed and/or on its last legs
- He always did the cooking – and did it very well indeed!
- He almost always had some clothes to put through the washing machine
- He loved his food and was almost always on a diet of some kind, but not very successfully

Pre-war EFDSS HQ team with Pat in the middle. Second couple from the left are Nan Fleming-Williams and Nibs Matthews and the couple on the extreme right are Douglas and Helen Kennedy.

- *He would practise his singing while having a bath: spreading water everywhere and making a tremendous noise in the process*
- *He would talk non-stop while walking all round the house, irrespective of whether Ursula or I, or anyone else, were in the vicinity to listen*
- *He had the ability to discuss almost any subject in depth – even those that would appear to be way outside his sphere of interest. His intelligence and breadth of knowledge were quite extraordinary*
- *When he had a firm view on something, which was frequently, he did not like it to be challenged*
- *His ability to speak fluently in several languages and make himself understood in many others was amazing*
- *He had tremendous charm and was well loved by countless people*
- *He was incredibly well read, particularly in his own spheres of interest*
- *He appeared to have an enormous circle of friends from all nationalities, colours, creeds, professions, and walks of life*
- *He was not good at managing his financial and business affairs.*

Ursula and I will never forget Pat and our memories of him remain indelible. He was indeed: a great musician; a larger than life character; generous to a fault; the bearer of a formidable intellect; an unstoppable talker; a five-star cook; a bon viveur; a wearer of multi-coloured and sometimes extraordinary clothes and hats; a detester of central bureaucracy; a keen supporter of occasional eccentricities; a nerve-testing driver; a collector of strange pipes as well as whiskies; a much loved "Buzz" to myself, Ursula and our son; a much loved friend of countless other people from many countries; and of course a life-long, true and influential member of the EFDSS, as was his mother before him.

In conclusion; for all the right reasons, in his chosen field of music, Pat's name will live on. And rightly so.

4. Reactions Immediately Following his Death

"The Times" published his death notice on 22 November 1977:

Shuldham-Shaw – On November 16, 1977, suddenly and peacefully at Weymouth, Patrick Noel (Pat Shaw to many of his friends), of Ettrick Road, Edinburgh and formerly of Mount Vernon, Hampstead. Private cremation at 2.30 p.m., on November 24th, at Weymouth Crematorium. Flowers to Shepherd and Hedgar (Dorchester) Ltd., 8 Cornhill, Dorchester. Memorial service at St. John's Church, Church Road, Hampstead, London, N.W.3, at 2.30 p.m., on Friday, December 9th.

Pat's ashes were buried with his parents in the churchyard of the Parish Church of St. John at Hampstead in London.

Many tributes were written at the time of his death. Here are highlights from those written by his friends.*

Hamish Henderson *1919-2002 singer, collector and poet* wrote:

Patrick Noel Shuldham-Shaw – an outstanding collector and maker, and "Admirable Crichton" of the post-World War II English Folk Dance and Song Society – died suddenly on 16 November 1977. He was not yet sixty. His loss is a major blow not only to international folk song and folk dance scholarship but also to the still developing and expanding folk revival scene, of which he was a generous and sympathetic if at times shrewdly critical friend.

Hamish continues

Pat's foremost preoccupation at all times, however, was the dissemination – the "ploughing back" – of what he and others had collected. An accomplished dancer himself – morris, sword and "country" – he carried the standard of English folk dance not only through the length and breadth of the mother country but also as far afield as the USA and the Netherlands.

Pat Shaw knew that he had a serious heart condition, but he went full speed ahead to the end, fulfilling and enjoying his manifold self-allotted task. Much love went out to him in many parts of the world. His friends here and elsewhere are bound to grieve for him, but they can be quite sure he would not have wished his death to come in any other way.*

Douglas Kennedy *1893-1988 Director of EFDSS then Vice-President* wrote:

Throughout his life he worked as a free-lance and used that freedom to benefit other musical and national folk societies. Teacher, dancer, singer,

---

* Full texts will be found in the Appendix 2.

composer Pat Shaw seemed able to play any instrument, pick up any language, even Zulu, and to solve any problem or puzzle. Like a poet laureate he was expected to rise to the special occasion and invent an appropriate dance or melody and write verses to suit the needs.

Those of us who worked with Pat acquired the habit of turning to him whenever some problem called for special faculties. A bright light went out of the music world, especially the folk-music world, with his untimely death. * †

Nibs Matthews *1920-2006 Artistic Director of the English Folk Dance and Song Society from 1966, Director 1975-1985* wrote:

I met Pat at the first post-war Stratford Festival in 1947 and my memories of him are vivid and various. He always wrote the wittiest rhymes in the Visitors' Book – he never said an unkind word about anybody – he was an entertainer on and off duty (his Nina Sabrina was unforgettable) He was a raconteur, a connoisseur of food and wine and a first class cook. He read, he remembered, he knew his facts and was generous to a fault as well as lovable. He died suddenly in Dorset three days after staying with Jean and me in London, but he had achieved his own stated aim 'to get folk music appreciated and known at home and abroad and to help my fellow country-men to understand the music of other peoples'.

I am not alone in having lost an unforgettable and irreplaceable friend.†

Mollie Du Cane *Long-time musician for the EFDSS and organiser in the Hertford-shire District, Mollie Du Cane played violin for classes and in bands, participating in festivals such as those at the Royal Albert Hall, Stratford-on-Avon and Sidmouth,* wrote:

My chief remembrances of Pat are those of his great generosity in imparting his wealth of knowledge of music and dance to those of us on the staff of the EFDSS. There have been all too few trained musicians in the Society who have been able to use this training to further their influence in the folk scene. Apart from his playing – oboe, guitar and accordion – his singing was a real joy to listen to.

In his love of inventing country dances, he wrote dances for all his friends, **Four Winds** being my own special dance named after the house in which I have lived for most of my life. At my retirement dinner, Pat came from the farthest table with his guitar and sang a song, to the tune of "Mollie Malone" which he started writing in the train and finished while eating his dinner. The song, which I shall always treasure, contained all the memorable points in my career as a member of staff.

On his death the Society lost one of its most brilliant and artistic members.*

* From the CDS special edition.
† See appendix 2.

Ruth Noyes *Librarian of the Vaughan Williams Memorial Library at Cecil Sharp House, 1961-1969* wrote:

> The sudden death of Patrick Shuldham-Shaw, known to his friends as Pat Shaw, has come as a great shock to all those who knew him and it would be difficult to exaggerate how much he did for the EFDSS.
>
> He had a very great knowledge of all aspects of folk music and dance and he was most generous and took endless patience in imparting what he knew to those interested in these subjects. He was a very able member of the Editorial Board and he contributed many articles to the Society's Journal. He was also a helpful member of the Vaughan Williams Memorial Library Committee. He did a tremendous amount to promote folk music in schools and he represented the Society on the Standing Committee for Music in Schools. He was a gifted singer, an able lecturer and a talented musician and many will remember his exhilarating Carol Concerts at Cecil Sharp House, where he captivated his audiences. He was also a composer of dances and showed great skill in choosing the title to fit the occasion for which the dance was composed. He was a lovable person and most humble in his accomplishments, which were also well known in other European countries and in the USA, but his work did not go unnoticed and he was presented with the Society's highest award, the Gold Badge.
>
> It is very sad that his life was cut short, when he showed so much promise. He had spent years working on the James B. Duncan manuscripts at the School of Scottish Studies in Edinburgh, and these he had hoped to complete so that they could be published.
>
> His loss is irreplaceable, but his gifts will never be forgotten.

Nan Fleming-Williams *from 1935 EFDSS violinist for many years and member of 'The Countryside Players'* wrote:

> There seemed no end to his inspiration. If he wasn't arranging music, singing or playing one of his several instruments, he was lecturing both at home and abroad, or conducting courses in music, dance and song. At home he loved his garden and was an excellent cook. He set himself to research the dances of John Playford and other 18th century dancing masters. Pat himself became a dancing master par excellence and was much in demand all over the country and overseas.
>
> He was a busy and a brilliant man: generous to a fault, never tiring of passing on his knowledge and skills to others. Lucky are those of us who have had the pleasure and great satisfaction of being included in his life. Alongside all these memories, he has left behind him a great mass of tunes, dances and other writings. It is by these we shall all remember him as he takes his place amongst the other great folk musicians of the British Isles.

See further comments from Nan in *Colleagues* chapter 5d.

Miss Isabel Bedlington (*written 8th March, 1978*)

I first met Pat at a summer school at Cambridge in 1925 or 6 when I accompanied his Mother at a recital she gave to the students. Pat used to attend all our rehearsals, showing real appreciation at that early age. Soon after this I began giving him piano lessons during his school holidays and continued doing this until be went to Harrow, and afterwards Cambridge where he read music, and developed his talent in many directions, showing great skill in arranging and singing folk songs. I accompanied him at concerts in London and all over the country, and we made one record together, much treasured by me.

He had a most attractive voice with impeccable diction in many languages and a delightful and intimate way of singing which always captivated his audiences and the critics: as his Mother had done before him.

I enjoyed our work together most enormously and greatly appreciate having a tune named after me, which I often played at his "Another Look at Playford" classes, at Cecil Sharp House, which I shared with Ruby for several years.

Pat had a very great talent, and an equally high standard, and always gave of his best. He will be sadly missed by his many friends, but we must always remember his gaiety and enthusiasm.†

Kathleen Adkins *"Kattles" and her friend Elsie Whiteman were founding members of the Benacre Band. Pat Shaw dedicated his dance "K & E" to them; "K" played orcon flute, "E", concertina.* Kathleen wrote:

It was a great shock to hear of Pat's sudden death in December 1977. This occurred only a few days after he had been singing at Cecil Sharp House, to illustrate a lecture/recital given by Mr Douglas Kennedy in memory of Dr Maud Karpeles. We could all see that Pat was not well and we feared he was sickening for influenza, but no one realised he was seriously ill. It was a tragedy that he should die so young.* †

Denis Smith *member of The Countryside Players – written for ED&S Spring 1978.*

At the time of his death, on 16th November, Pat was on a concert tour of schools in Dorset, having taken time off work on the Grieg and Duncan song manuscripts at the School of Scottish Studies, in Edinburgh. He was, in fact, both a versatile performer and a scholar.

Pat's mother, Winifred Shuldham-Shaw, was herself a fine musician and an important figure in the early years of the Society. So it is not surprising that after prep school, Harrow, and studying music at Cambridge, Pat devoted his career as a free-lance musician to British folk music. As a musician he

---

*   From the CDS special edition.
†   See appendix 2.

was not only a performer but an arranger and composer. As a performer many will remember him best as a singer with that distinctive quality of voice and wide repertoire, but he was also a talented instrumentalist. In addition, he was in great demand as a caller for square dances and as an MC for folk dances and Playford Balls.

Pat was also a gifted arranger of traditional music for various combinations of instruments – for dance band recordings, for the "Jolly Waggoners" band formed for West Country broadcasts in the 1950s, for the Albert Hall Festivals, for the Countryside Players, and for those memorable gatherings of orchestral and folk players for his Christmas Concert at Cecil Sharp House. As a composer, Pat had an enormous output of dance tunes and he was a master of styles ranging from the eighteenth century ballroom through traditional jigs, reels and hornpipes, to that of the Scott Joplin rag. It was in this field, and in that of devising dances to go with his tunes, that Pat fulfilled the function of a Folk Poet Laureate or Keeper of the Queen's Folk Music. Many special events in the lives of his friends have been celebrated by a dance and tune to mark the occasion.

As a scholar, Pat should be gratefully remembered for his collection and transcription of traditional songs and dance tunes from Shetland and many other parts of England, Scotland and Wales. His encyclopaedic knowledge was willingly given to the editorial board of the Folk Music Journal and the Vaughan Williams Memorial Library Committee.

Pat was born into the first revival of folk dance and song and lived to make a distinctive contribution to the second. Throughout the British Isles, Europe and America, folk dance players, singers, dancers and scholars will miss his unique blend of intellect, performing talent, warm personality and generous nature. His enrichment of the folk scene, in giving so freely of his talent, will be remembered with pleasure and gratitude.

Members of the Welsh Folk Dance Society, people from the Netherlands and the USA also wrote of Pat at the time of his death (see under separate chapters).

A memorial service that was held for Pat at St John's Church in Hampstead on 9 December 1977 was packed to overflowing. The service included two memoirs – the first from Douglas Kennedy OBE, Vice-President of the English Folk Dance and Song Society followed by the Co-operation Choir led by Jonathan Cohen singing "Drop, Drop, Slow Tears". The second from J. K. Owens CBE, Chairman, Standing Conference of Amateur Music, followed by Members of "Sing for Pleasure" singing "God be in my Head" and "Christ was born on Christmas Day" (words and music by Pat Shaw).

A musical interlude was introduced by Alice E. Williams, Chairman, Welsh Dance Society with music by Denis Smith (accordion) and Frances Môn Jones (harp).

"Lord of the Dance" was sung. Sydney Carter had put these words to the Shaker hymn "Tis the Gift to be Simple", after hearing it in 1969 when Pat had used the tune for the basis of an item at the Royal Albert Hall Festival 1962 which Sydney Carter had attended.

After the blessing, Pat's arrangement of "Lady Winwood's Maggot" was played. This was one of the most popular of his arrangements for the Countryside Players' programmes.

It was truly a Service of Thanksgiving with many of Pat's dearest friends and Pat himself present through his music.

Jonathan Cohen wrote recently:

I played the organ for this Service and my Choir (The Co-operation) sang "Drop, drop slow tears". The Choir could hardly get through it. He had always said it was his favourite hymn and I remembered that. Someone said you oughtn't to do that, you need to be folky – that wouldn't be Pat. I said 'No, no, that's what he loved' and it was, of course, fantastic.

Pat Shaw

5. THE MEMORIES

Pat had a great physical presence. Mention has been made many times of the fact that he was a big man with a large beard, who was surprisingly light on his feet and who played a big accordion! Conversely, mention is made of the enduring image of a gentle lilting voice, twinkling eyes and a well trimmed beard.

Many memories focus on first meeting Pat through the Society or at Cecil Sharp House. In the early 1940s Pat was just beginning to make a significant appearance on the scene at Cecil Sharp House. It was obvious that he was well known by the Headquarters staff *as they called him by his Christian name which was very unusual in those times.* The impression given at that point was that he was an up-and-coming youngster not long out of school, whom the staff were grooming and encouraging. He apparently looked very young – he was in his early 20s – and had that "little boy lost" look which he never entirely got rid of, despite the beard he sported in later years.

When he moved to the midlands to work as the EFDSS representative in Birmingham he met a wider range of people as his influence spread. Eventually he came to be mentioned in almost reverential tones which, it is felt, would have amused him if he had known.

It was also common to have first met Pat at various summer schools and workshops. Such memories are recorded from the 1940s till the time of his death. First impressions often seemed to have been that of a hard task master but Pat's easy manner quickly dispelled any such thoughts.

The memory of meeting a friendly man with such a wealth of expertise, leading the dancing and singing during workshops is enduring. Whether teaching children or adults the actual dances – both morris and social – and songs he taught have been remembered by many.

§ *I first saw Pat at an EFDS (sic) Easter course in Exeter during the war. A group of us had come down from Liverpool and were accommodated in a hostel some way from the University where the course was held. I remember one occasion when several of us were walking back from classes in line abreast across the road with Pat in the middle singing "Auprès de ma blonde". I did not then know who he was, but it was good fun.*

In the early 1950s Pat was at the Society's Stratford Festivals and he also taught at Attingham Hall, Shrewsbury in 1955 and 1956.

Naturally, Pat was invited as caller for events around the country and so such occasions were often the first contact with him. In the 1950s he regularly called at "Square Club" in the Gloucester area and ran some Saturday nights, confirming the bookings on a brief postcard signed "Pat Sh-Sh".

Young Pat in Stratford

One enduring memory of the first sight of Pat comes from an occasion when he was MC at the Morecambe Ball. Having promised to sing during the evening, he took out of his pocket a little stool with collapsible legs, put it down to rest his foot on, took out his guitar and gave an unforgettable and brilliant performance of folk songs – such that has never been forgotten more than 50 years after the event.

Some people first became aware of Pat through the weekly "Everybody Swing" radio shows which were transmitted nationally from Broadcasting House in Bristol in 1951 and 1952. University students practised the dances which were mainly from the Country Dance Manuals Books 1-3 together with a few easy American Squares. Nibs Matthews called the English dances and Pat called the singing squares as well as singing one or two folksongs. One or two years later a few shows in the same format were shown on black and white television.

The recordings of Pat playing the Shetland tunes he wrote became a first practical contact for some. Good musicians were hard to come by and so these recordings were used by callers and clubs.

A chance really to get to know Pat came to those on the six week tour of South Africa in 1955 and again in 1960. There he was a real asset to the group as he took the trouble to learn Afrikaans and other African languages so that he could explain the dances and, as usual, be quite amusing – to the delight of the audiences. (See Pat on Tour, chapter 12.)

The feeling of not having quite appreciated the man is not rare –

§ *When I first came into contact with Pat Shaw I was not aware of the importance of the man.*

§ *Pat used to call quite a bit round our way in the fifties and we none of us had any idea how important he would prove to be.*

§ *In those days, I knew that Pat was special but not that special. From his approach and manner you would never know that he was by far the top all-rounder of his age, the most talented composer of music and dance, caller, singer, accordionist and raconteur.*

§ *We had no idea of his stature and potential stature.*

Pat Shaw has been described as a mentor and a guru but mainly as a really wonderful friend whose company was enjoyed very much indeed.

§ *I came to London at the beginning of the 1960s to work for the BBC and was told by some of my colleagues about Cecil Sharp House in Camden Town so I went there one Saturday night to a dance to see what it was like. What I met was this large man with a beard calling the dances with great gusto and charisma. I remember the dance was Morpeth Rant. 'Come on, you morris dancers', he shouted, 'Let's see some of that stepping!'*

Many folk don't realise that Pat Shaw was born in Stratford-upon-Avon. When asked *guess who was the first Midland Area Organiser for the EFDSS* the answer is usually Ken or Sybil Clark but it was Pat Shaw! He worked in that capacity from 1939 to 1942.

He is remembered as a very charming, articulate man, who smiled a lot. He was very sociable and held popular parties (some all night) at his house in Hampstead. The house was tastefully decorated and full of antiques. Although one memory recalls Pat coming to CSH one evening very pleased with himself. He had painted his bedroom – either all red or black – the memory fails on this point. But another respondent reports the dining room in black!

His parties are legendary – both at his house in Holly Bush Lane, opposite The Holly Bush pub, in Hampstead – and later whilst lodging in Abernethy House with Daphne Evans. Most of his money he gave away causing his personal circumstances to veer between comparative wealth and poverty. His house had a small garden and he would talk about the various types of clematis he grew. He seems to have been a keen gardener.

Francis Keegan knew Pat in London 50 years ago – when Pat lived in the house in Hampstead belonging to friends of his (presumably Daphne Evans). Pat would travel around Britain from there. He shared an Anglo-Irish background with Pat and, although they were not close friends, Pat gave him a couple of rare books by Irish Authors that are still in his collection. Francis says –

I thought of Pat the other day, and was amazed to see how much legacy he left in folk music circles. He was one of nature's gentlemen, and indeed was connected to the Irish aristocracy – Lord Carew – but he was most unassuming about his well born connection. All I know about his Scottish connection is that one day, when he was away travelling, and whisky had run out in the house and the owner had some guests in, they raided Pat's drinks cupboard and took a bottle of very special whisky which he had collected on his travels. On his return, rather than raise a huge argument, Pat explained that this was a rare whisky, and that any bottle bought at a London bottle shop would only be a mere shadow of the quality of his whisky.

I am pleased to hear that his memory lives on.

He also collected bottles of every type of whisky and perfume – he was interested in the phenomenon of people thinking up concoctions.

Having been a gymnast at school and Cambridge he could handstand on a wooden chair back and sing verse after verse of "Nina, from Argentina". But then he would give a Wigmore Hall recital and bring tears to the eyes of his audience with his beautiful voice.

However he also had a more practical side. § *While talking one time in Burton Manor College, Pat got to listing the merits of owning versus hiring a car. At that time, Pat hired a Mini. He said it was far better for him to hire, as, living in London, when he was at home, and not needing his car, he could return it. That way, he never had to bother about parking. Also, he always had a clean car to go out in and never had to pay for servicing, or to tax it. It made one think, as he often did.*

The consensus seems to be that Pat always seemed a pleasant enough person, always friendly, very talented in the way he could pick up languages, very knowledgeable on English Folk dances, traditions, songs etc., but always rather a loner. He was perhaps an extreme example of someone who as a consummate performer – singer, caller, musician – was completely at ease on a stage or in front of a microphone. He would carry a Spirograph set around with him and he often gave the results to friends.

He was continually looking for suitable gifts for his innumerable friends. Although he often had travelled around the clock, perhaps taught all day, and sang or played all night, never once did he refuse to copy out the extra set of instructions or few bars of music. He gave his knowledge and help unstintingly to young and old, never asking for anything in return.

Pat was a very kind person and by all accounts generous to a fault. Other words used to describe him are light-hearted, amusing, affable, humble, modest, quietly humorous, gentle and rather shy. He was a vibrant person, overflowing with music and the joy of music making.

As summed up by one correspondent *Pat was a most generous person, giving time, ideas and hospitality in abundance. His generously sized body fitted into the Mini, and with his expert map-reading skills and sense of adventure, drove around the country on so many of the mountain tracks, suitable for tractors, to instruct and participate in folk dance and song events across the British Isles. Using an OS map, he would follow the white tracks in preference to all others.*

§ *His energy and kindness were amazing and will never be forgotten.*

Eileen Phelan – *Pat was so kind to us. I met him at my first staff conference, a summer week in a Sussex college with Douglas Kennedy and Helen. One evening, the door opened into the room where Douglas was lecturing and Pat and Kenneth Loveless stood there: two black-bearded men in flowing cloaks and large black hats. Pat with accordion and guitar, Kenneth with concertina and Douglas said 'Ah, Elsie and Doris Waters!'*

At these conferences, Pat would put us in his latest amazing car and drive speedily around the beauty spots and historic places and buy us wonderful cream teas. He would give us huge bunches of gladioli to take home to our mothers.

Alongside this universal admiration of Pat's numerous talents is the memory of how funny he was; even the youngest, shyest people who met him comment on his great capacity for humour – his sense of fun.

Examples of this are quoted in other sections but here are some more personal anecdotes:

Ada Hollands – *When he found that I'm a Salvationist he would tease me with a song about the Salvation Army and a chorus that contained the words '...rum by gum...' One year I couldn't go to Summer School but was taken to the last night's concert by my young sister. We were talked into staying the night as there were spare beds at the school. When Pat saw me he was very pleased and we stood in the middle of the common room with our arms around each other and I discovered that kissing a chap with a beard isn't prickly. My rather staid young sister was horrified and I had to explain that Pat's cardinal rule was that he only ever kissed a woman in company.*

Judy Parry – *At the beginning of 1969 I remember being at Aunt Kit and Marjorie's (Fennessy) house in Gloucester Crescent after a Whirligigs meeting with a few other members including Pat Shaw. Richard and I were getting married that July and we could not decide on the folk tunes as music for our wedding. Over tea, certain folk tunes were suggested. After some considerable time, Pat suddenly said: 'You could always have this one!' and started to tinkle on the piano "Here comes the bride", much to the great amusement of all.*

Jill Jefferson – *He had my kind of humour and often regaled me with funny little stories. This joke occurred one Burton Manor week. Pat arrived in his Mini with a full sized Alpine horn strapped to the roof. Even though it could be split in two, it was far too enormous to go inside. He came rushing down to the terrace to tell me he was going to get up early the next morning to blow the horn as a reveille call to wake everybody up! Believe me, at 7 a.m. it would certainly cause a great deal of chaos, as few at Burton found rising early one of their favourite things! Going to bed late was the rule with most people in those early days. It worked beautifully. The horn was enormous, it stretched down a flight of steps: Pat at the top blowing with vigour and the end down at the bottom emitting the most enormous noise – it certainly woke everybody up! The memory I really cherished of that episode was the impish expression on Pat's face. He really was enjoying the whole event. I so adored Pat's sense of fun.*

Donald Ashton also tells this story though he adds – *the reaction of the local cows had to be seen to be believed. Being rather large, Pat got out of the car a bit at a time. He usually had a habit of travelling with all his music and unloading what seemed like a dozen bags from the Mini on his arrival.*

A final story about the alpine horn came from **Elvina Trinder –** *A leading conductor of A Coeur Joie (Sing for Pleasure), Marcel Conneloup, who had written instructions to singers on voice production, how to breathe etc., asked Pat to let him* *try the horn. Pat agreed but Marcel found, to his great amazement, that he was unable to produce a good sound!**

Before the horn episode, he would sometimes arise early and go for a two mile run before breakfast

Peter Oakley – *Another time we got talking about funny or unusual things that happened to one. He never went into great detail, but told us of a time he took a fully made-up Alpine Horn on the Underground, and the fun he had getting it in and out of the tube train doors, and getting people to help the "foreigner" into and out of the carriage. Also he said he had great fun on the escalators, with the station staff not quite knowing what to do with him. I will leave it to you to imagine what fun he must have had, as he left it to us.*

Kate Riley – *I remember him at another war-time course at Reading University. As was customary on such occasions the staff put on an entertainment for us one evening. Among the performers was Pat, on leave from his service with the Fire Brigade, giving a very spirited mock morris jig based on the gymnastics of his training.*

Peter Boyce – *Also on the staff at a course in Jersey was Pat Shaw. On the way over to the island the sea was unpleasantly up and down, whipped up by a strong wind. Some of our party spent much of the journey hanging over the side feeding the fishes; the rest felt very queasy, when along came the portly figure of Pat Shaw, rosy cheeked and as fresh as if the sea were a mill-pond. 'What's the matter?' he said 'You should go and have a good meal in the restaurant like me'. He then told us in some detail what he had been eating, at which point the remainder of our party joined those hanging over the side. Pat thought that was a good joke.*

Mary Isaacs (Clark) – *In 1958 an EFDSS team went to Portugal, taking a hobby-horse made of basket-work to save weight. On arrival, it was discovered that some of the bells had become detached from the skirt of the horse. The next morning several of the girls settled down to sew the bells on again and whilst we were busy, Pat came along to us, plus guitar. We chatted and laughed and Pat started to play and sing. It was an old song, "Oh, No John". I soon realised that it was not the usual version – not very different, just a little. The questions were put differently. It was very funny and we had a good laugh. Then he picked up his guitar, gave us a wicked smile, and left us, still laughing.*

Ian Porter – *The EFDSS organised three public dances each year at the University of Birmingham in the late 1950s to mid 1960s. These were held in the Union building and it was traditional to decorate the main hall for each occasion. It must have been in 1959 or 1960 when Pat agreed to call a University dance. The Committee decided that the theme of the dance would be "Heaven and Hell" so we set about making decorations for the hall based on this theme. The centre point was a huge picture of the devil, pitchfork in hand, which we mounted over the entrance into the hall. In due course, Pat arrived in good time for the dance, walked into the hall and had a good look around. His gaze lingered on the picture over the door, and it was only then that we realised that it bore a striking resemblance to Pat himself! He never said a word.*

Pat was a lover of risqué double-entendres, and **Brian Willcocks** treasures three limericks which Pat told him:

---

*   See also piece from Frances Môn Jones in the Welsh section, chapter 10.

Young loves who frequent picture-palaces
Don't hold with this psycho-analysis.
    And although Doctor Freud
    Gets distinctly annoyed,
Still they cling to their long-standing fallacies.

Brian felt that the other two were perhaps not for this publication.

Pat seems to have had a love of eccentric clothes or of being different from the crowd. He was always well dressed in a slightly casual way though one occasion remembered well was when, at – probably a Christmas Dance at CSH – everyone came attired in evening dress with just Pat, as MC and the person remembering – **Ray Mortlock** – were the only two in smoking jackets.

Isabel Bedlington said in her piece written when he died that *he often appeared for singing engagements in a red-lined black cloak and a large black hat – the effect being like a Sandeman's Port advertisement. It was a little embarrassing if one had to walk some distance from the car, but I think Pat enjoyed every moment of it.*

Ada Hollands also recalls – *Pat wanted a top hat and had no idea where to obtain one. I offered to make one using his precious, extremely battered, straw hat. All those who had badgered him to get a new sun hat were very pleased when he was seen sporting a smart new one. The black card top hat was a success and he used it on other occasions.*

When in 1950 the fashion industries started using fluorescent colours, this gave rise to a good Pat Shaw story:

Paul Bradley wrote – *Pat came across a selection of ankle socks in luminous lime green, offensive pink, violent yellow, yucky blue etc, and wore them with great relish as a "statement", so to speak. At his daily workshops, not too many people were exposed to this spectacle (helped by wearing dark glasses). However, on one afternoon later in the week, Pat gave a solo performance of the morris, Queens Jig.*

A large man, probably six foot in height, probably fifteen or sixteen stone in weight, he was no lightweight, and yet he graced the floor as a ballerina, to see him float upwards two feet off the floor, arms outstretched with such grace and poise was absolute Magic.

The **socks** *however were now at eye level and apparent to everyone! Whispers of 'Oh no', giggles, sniggers, echoed around the room. However, when the dance came to an end there was instant applause, much cheering and clapping indicating general approval by one and all. I repeat, ABSOLUTE MAGIC.*

Marjorie Fennessy can recall that he used to wear fluorescent shirts with matching socks, which **Jonathan Cohen** can also remember as being hideous and saying to Pat 'This isn't good. What are you trying to do here?'

Pat had a great appetite and *his enthusiasm for food – as well as for strange musical instruments – was legendary* recalls **Jan Willcocks**. She has a memory of being on a dance trip to Skopje when, whilst exploring the city, Pat disappeared into the Turkish Quarter and emerged clutching arms – and pockets – full of strange Turkish sweetmeats and snacks which were generously handed around to all the company.

Another foreign foodie memory came from during the tour of South Africa. This involved Biltong which is dried meat. Pat liked ostrich biltong and would share it with all his cronies on the back seat. It came in strips which had to be chewed for ages like chewing gum.

When he was taking the Dutch Christmas Course he insisted in taking the band out to supper on the last evening before the Ball. This was usually to an Indonesian restaurant.

Pat himself was a very good and inventive cook as was discovered by various people with whom he stayed when on his journeys around the country. One killer "starter" he devised was haggis omelette. Cooking for him was therefore a challenge. He appreciated a meal prepared for him by **Barbara Graham** from an Elizabeth Craig recipe book "Escalopes de Veau Medicisti" and enthused about a "Trimaladeti" made from grapefruit, orange and lemon.

He owned many cookbooks from all over the world. He loved to cook and serve elaborate meals for his friends, shopping for weeks to get the correct ingredients. Yet **Marjorie Fennessy** recalls how her mother found it was difficult to feed him – sometimes he would eat almost everything and another time he was on a strict diet! **John Stapledon's** family remembers an occasion when Pat joined them for a meal insisting that he was on a strict diet to reduce weight, then proceeding to pile on about eight potatoes with his meal and devouring the whole lot in record time!

Keith and Maggie Uttley sent in a piece recalling *how he would often come for a meal and then stay for two or three days with us. He had some funny foibles like washing up but refusing to use any washing up liquid!*

An easy guest who was very generous with his time especially when we were organising Concerts in the Theatre in Livingston for Charity. His music and singing enhanced these events and the audience loved his contributions.

An evening we will never forget was when Pat wanted to repay the hospitality of Rosemary (Redpath) and Hugh Gentleman and ourselves by inviting us to a meal. Pat loved cooking and experimenting with recipes. The banquet could have fed at least ten people. Every course was delicious, unusual, tasty, but by the end of the meal we were so full we could hardly stand up. He was a wonderful host, but we did wish there were at least six more people to help us eat the fantastic spread he created!

When travelling around he made use of the opportunities which presented themselves for buying local food and presenting them as presents to his hosts. A memory of this sort is of a huge round of cheese he bought from a farm on top of the Mendips. Another family's memory of Pat is triggered whenever the household has Cotherstone cheese as this was introduced to them by Pat who got his supply from the post-office in the village whenever he passed through on his way through the borders.

Donald Ashton told of another memory of an occasion in Aberdeen. *Pat took my wife and myself to a party at one of his friends. There were two long tables, one with every possible variety of malt whisky and the other with numerous types of haggis. Even so, my memory is of a friend of Pat's, a tanker captain, who sat quietly in a corner making the most wonderful music on an accordion that he took with him all over the world.*

He also had a fascination with MacDonald's. He created a dance called **Hamburger Special** to the traditional tune "McDonald's Reel". This is a very fast dance and at one point three people make a double arch – the M sign for MacDonald's.

Some respondents were fortunate enough to have Pat *and his gigantic appetite* visit or stay with them whilst in different parts of the country. On such occasions, it frequently seemed that the householder had to be ready for anything:

§ *I told my father to leave Pat to do as he wished during the day. When I got home my father said to me 'I don't understand your "chap". He has spent all his time alternatively walking up and down the hall and then suddenly rushing into your room to go to the piano.'* I explained to my father that was nothing to worry about and I was not at all surprised at Pat's behaviour.

§ Then – I think in the sixties – Pat came down to Devon to introduce local secondary schools to folk song and music. So Pat came to stay with us at our house – Longways (for as many as will) – and performed, amongst others, at Redworth Secondary School, Totnes, which was just across the road. I remember that Pat was having some trouble with the tendons in his wrists which was aggravated by him playing the guitar, and each night, before he settled down to sleep, he would lay both forearms in casts and I would bind them with crepe bandages so that he couldn't move them during the night.

§ I was at home in Newquay, bathing the children (probably in 1964) when the door bell rang. To my surprise it was Pat Shaw, who was giving a concert in the area and had a couple of hours to while away. He was most friendly and at ease.

§ We lived at St. Margaret's-at-Cliffe, near Dover then (in the late nineteen sixties) and for some reason he stayed with us for a day or two. I think he may have been teaching at an adult education course nearby. He was most entertaining company and insisted one night on taking over my kitchen and cooking us a special meal to say "Thank you" for our hospitality. We didn't realise the preparation would take several hours and we were all starving by the time we sat down to eat it!

§ Pat was staying with us when our son and new wife came to visit. Pat handed over a well wrapped parcel which she thought was very nice of him. She opened it expecting a wedding present only to find his dirty washing.

Norma Battle – *By far the greatest thrill was when he came to stay with us. What a lovely, gentle man he was, who at that time was trying to lose some weight! I still feel honoured that I could call him a friend and only wish I'd kept a visitors' book at home all those years ago.*

One very happy memory from childhood arose from when Pat stayed with a family when giving a concert in the area. Pat needed quiet for a couple of hours before the event to allow him to prepare for the evening. The writer had to go into the room to get something and stopped to listen. Pat said to sit down, so she sat on a stool near him and he started to play and sing to her. Her mother came in and told her to leave but Pat said she was being perfectly quiet and well behaved and so he was happy to have her there. So she stayed as he rehearsed singing his programme – her own private concert.

Daphne Baker wrote – *One afternoon he got in rather later than we had expected. Apparently he'd spotted a group of young Dutch tourists in the village pub and got "rather involved". At the time I didn't know about his great affection for their country or about the ease with which he seemed to be able to communicate in almost any language.*

Another time he inadvertently let out our little black dog, Sooty, who disappeared rapidly, very happy to have some unexpected freedom. He came back eventually and Pat made up a little poem about him. Unfortunately I didn't write it down and now can only remember that it finished with '...into it his sooty foot he put!'

Joy and Lionel Parkhouse said – *He was always very generous to his hosts when he came to spend the night, bringing the most expensive food and wine although he himself was always on a new diet to lose weight. He also charged very little for coming to take dances or workshops. As a result he was always broke, so he sold us his old valve amplifier together with some microphone stands and an assortment of microphones and lots of leads in a large suitcase. We still use the* *stands and suitcase as part of our band equipment, and are proud to tell people where they came from.*

Rosemary Lant told how just after the war – *Pat turned up on one of his visits to the prefab (where her parents were living) in the depths of winter wearing an enormous, ankle length astrakhan coat with matching hat and, of course, a very full beard. The neighbours were convinced that he must be a relative of my mother (who was Austrian) on a visit from darkest Austria and harboured suspicions, as my mother later discovered, that he might even be a spy.*

Pat's visits throughout my childhood were always joyous and somewhat noisy occasions. He never gave a second thought to arriving very late at night and getting out his accordion to play for us, despite the fact that the neighbours had long since been sound asleep.

Other memories of Pat staying with people came from Wales, America and Holland (see separate chapters) as well as Bath – when adjudicating at a Wiltshire Folk Dance Festival, Exeter and Harrow.

Not all memories are happy ones. There were a few critical thoughts sent in which serve to make the man more human!

§ *Pat did an enormous amount of research, he being lucky enough to have the time to do so. I have always, however, tended to see him as responsible for starting the unfortunate competition for writing dances with silly difficult bits to catch out "those who don't know". This hastened the obsession with "clever" dancing and brought about the destructive polarisation between Barn Dancing and Playford (type) dancing, seeing off the good, balanced General Dance.*

Trouble was that so many people who came into the dance movement via these "clever" groups scorn anything less academic to the point of denying the relevance of traditional material. I sadly saw it all happen and suffered the consequences as the prospect of a good, varied evening of playing became reduced to a rather tedious requirement for relatively few specific (often poor) tunes.

§ *Pat once asked me if I could arrange a week of work for him, visiting Infant and Junior schools to sing to the children. This I did but I'm afraid things didn't work out well as he had no idea of how to hold the interest of children. The leaflet he gave me to advertise the events had a photograph of himself with some children being very attentive, but I think it must have been a studio photograph. Sad really for more than once I witnessed him holding a huge audience of adults absolutely spellbound but somehow it didn't work with children.*

§ *On another occasion Pat Shaw announced a dance and several dancers stated that we all knew it. The music started but about half way through Pat Shaw stopped the dance telling us that we were wrong. He insisted on coming onto the floor and showing us how it was done in the area where the dance had been collected. The dance was then resumed but we continued to dance as we always did. He was furious. Most of us were aware of the great work Pat Shaw was doing in research. We felt this was not the time for a lesson. When the dance was over and we were clearing up he came up to me and complained that we were very difficult people and he may not come again. I replied that he may not be asked. Sad situation. I was, like many people, so sad when he died so young. Perhaps he was feeling unwell during the period I have mentioned.*

§ *In the early 1950s the SIFD decided to hold a folk show at the Royal Albert Hall. They booked various teams from abroad and some groups of foreign dancers who were living in England. I remember particularly the Russians and a group of Polish displaced persons living in London. For the chorus they would use the club* members. They asked Pat Shaw to give us some tuition in English folk dancing. We met him in a hall near Baker Street. He soon proved to be very grumpy with us and we took this badly. When I think of it now he has all my sympathy. We knew very few English dances, Morpeth Rant, La Russe and Cumberland Square Eight. In the latter we galloped across the room as far as we could and back just in time. In the basket the main aim was to make all the women fly off the ground. Pat would have been used to Sunday Club and Whirligigs. What could he do with us in one easy lesson? Poor man. No wonder he was grumpy.

§ Pat came to Burnham on Crouch to call a Saturday dance, and there we saw his other side for he really lost his temper during the evening, to the astonishment of those present.

This anecdote was related by two different contacts – an incident at Pendley Manor where Pat was running a weekend. *It was the custom to have a break at half time when everyone went downstairs into the cellar where the bar was situated. Now the bar was an opening in the wall about two feet wide and a little bit taller. There was barely room for one person to communicate with the barman, one of Dorian Williams' jockeys who, to say the least, had a very relaxed way of serving. Before the interval one of the Bucks Committee members went down to the bar and ordered Pat's drink. Then the dancers arrived at the hole in the wall and a queue quickly formed across the room and half way up the stairs. At the end of the interval very few of the dancers had been served and there was a distinct lack of dancers in the hall. Pat waited for quite a while then said 'Well if you don't want to dance I'm going to bed'. And he did just that! The incident was chuckled about for some time afterwards and Nibs Matthews's remark was that Pat was known to sometimes "have a touch of the old dog".*

§ I first met Pat at Lilleshall Hall in Shropshire, at the Sports Centre. He was running a weekend course and, whilst I enjoyed his teaching of dances, mainly Shetland I think, I hated his singing sessions, for he was like a bear with a sore head! We did our best but nothing pleased him. This must have been in the early 1950s I believe. Possibly a year or two later I went to Bangor, N Wales, and Pat was on the staff there, and was a completely different man and I really enjoyed his teaching.

§ He was generally kind and patient but he wasn't a saint. This was especially noticeable at the first workshop on the third day of the course when the after-effects of the parties were taking their toll. He would shout at those lazy, stupid dancers and we were as quiet as mice! I shall never forget the suffering endured in the Red House of Cardiff on one of those mornings.

§ My chief memories are of a week at Halsway in early September 1976. It's going back over 30 years, so I don't guarantee that all the details are accurate. He was being a bit awkward, refusing to do much teaching. He didn't arrive until the Sunday afternoon, and Gerry Phelps, standing in for Ruth, asked someone else to run dances and workshops on Saturday night and Sunday morning. Pat kept sighing tiredly and saying that it was his holiday too. However, my mother told him how she had learned some morris dancing in part of the pre-war folk dance revival, in Sunderland, about 1912-13, I think. Pat wouldn't be pressurised into doing anything, but he went off into the library and did some research on things that my mother and other people were interested in.

§ At one of the dances at Twickenham we had invited the Mayor of the Borough – a very lovely lady named Mrs Owen. When she had finished her speech she turned to Pat Shaw and said 'I have heard you singing on the radio so often, will *you please sing a couple of songs for us now?' Pat Shaw replied 'No, I only sing when I have been booked to do so'. Mrs Owen tried to persuade him, and I went up on the stage to ask him, but was dismissed. So he did not like to be taken for granted.*

§ *I remember hearing him sing on many occasions and for some reason feeling embarrassed by his high and rather thin voice.*

But the main overall impression is of a man with a most pleasant personality, a great dancer, singer and musician. He was light hearted, amusing, affable, humble, modest and quietly humorous, making puns in words and music. **Jonathan Cohen** thinks of him as having an extraordinary "anagram" mind – see the titles of some of his dances – **"Quite carr-ied away"** or **"Joan Transported"** for Joan Carr for example.

Pat was a 20th century dancing master whose legacy will endure long into the 21st century – and that could be an understatement. He was something of a genius and his music and dances have given a lot of people great pleasure, and will continue to do so for a long time to come. He was in a class of his own and a huge influence on the folk music of his time – all feel privileged to have known him and enjoyed his talent. Although nobody is indispensable, certainly, as far as Pat is concerned, it seems agreed that nobody else comes close to matching his many abilities. He made a big impression on everyone, with many memories of him centering around the idea that he was certainly something special, that he certainly stood out from the crowd and that he is still greatly missed.

Often people had no idea of his stature and potential stature when they first met him and only later was it realised how greatly honoured and fortunate they had been to have met him. Though many – particularly the young – were in awe of him.

Anne Andrews – *We were spending a few days at the only hotel in Encamp where a large youngish, though older and distinctly more sophisticated than us, bearded Englishman engaged us in conversation. He told us that he liked to visit fiestas in the various small villages round about and join in with the local bands playing his accordion. He asked how was our Catalan. Non existent of course. We were too shy to ask how was his? He drove a red Citroen Traction, a common enough car in France at the time, though usually black, but distinctly unusual in England. He told us his name was Patrick Shuldham-Shaw. This meant nothing to us at the time. I had been dancing with The Round at Cambridge for less than a year, but when I mentioned it to friends on our return they seemed distinctly impressed.*

§ *The dances he researched and the music and dances he composed are a wonderful legacy from a great Dancing Master.*

§ *Nationally and Internationally Pat was revered for his gifts*
  of playing and singing
  for his true upholding of the English tradition on trips abroad
  for his capability of singing a song in the host country's language
  for his mastery of the accordion & playing in bands
  for his wonderful singing voice
  for the records he made both of songs and square dances
  for his dance compositions
  for his humour.

§ *Two of his memorable sayings about dancing –*
Dancing is singing with your body.
Dancing is a public demonstration of a private desire.

§ *I have never forgotten his lessons and can picture him quite easily.*

§ *His passing was indeed a great loss to the Society and the folk dance world.*

§ *When I was living in London and able to attend events at Cecil Sharp House, I really got to know and appreciate him for his many gifts. I owe him much.*

§ *His sudden passing away was a tragedy for all of us, whether dancers or singers. In our area I think I am about the only person dancing who remembers him.*

§ *He didn't take care of himself and later on had problems with his health, but he stayed on duty till the end. When I received the message that he had died I thought I would never dance again. Luckily for me I didn't keep that promise.*

§ *I count myself fortunate that my first few years of "folk" overlapped with his last few years and that I did actually learn some of his own dances from the master himself. My favourite dance of his was, and still is,* **Miss Avril's Delight**.

§ *We miss him terribly as do so many others who were touched by his magic.*

§ *My last memory is of a Phoenix dance called by Nibs Matthews. He told us all that Pat had died that day and that he had spent the morning with Pat's brother. Nobody felt like dancing.*

§ *While we continue to dance his dances and play his tunes Pat will always be with us. A fitting memorial to a truly remarkable man.*

§ *Many, many thanks to that remarkable man: PATRICK SHULDHAM-SHAW.*

5a. REMEMBERING PAT THROUGH MUSIC

Marjorie Fennessy reminds us that Pat was surrounded by folk music and music generally from birth. *His mother, Winifred "Holly" (Holloway) Shuldham-Shaw was a fully trained professional singer. She was Secretary of the Cecil Sharp House Fund to build it after Sharp's death in 1924. She gave a lot of recitals – the proceeds going to the Fund.*

Pat was an oboist originally and was classically trained. He learnt the accordion when he went to the Shetland Isles in the late 1940s, so that in the all-night sessions he would have an entrée. Later he learnt the guitar to accompany himself singing folk songs. He also learnt to play an alpenhorn, kalimba, ocarina, etc.

Pat composed many tunes during his time in the Fire Service during the War and in his time in Shetland. Pat used to turn up at the home of my mother (Aunt Kit, as she was known to everyone) and myself, sit down at the piano and play some of his own tunes from his small manuscript books and comment whether he thought it was a good or not so good tune.

Aunt Kit

Jonathan Cohen also recalled how Pat championed a lot of "newish" music. *He absolutely loved Nielsen, a Scandinavian composer, he was absolutely mad about him. Pat wasn't a fuddy-duddy musically or in any way.*

I played Hamilton Harty's version of My Lagan Love (Irish folksong) for Pat. Harty arranged it in semi-classical style. Wonderful piano accompaniment. Wonderful Irish tune. Pat sang absolutely beautifully.

Pat went to see "Wait a Minim" (South African music and dances) at the Fortune Theatre, London. I remember Pat handing us all kalimbas and we had to play them. Pat sang over the top of them – all pentatonic notes.

Musicianship

§ *His playing had great zest, energy, danceability, and creativity.*

§ *At the Society Training Course at Westminster Methodist Central Hall in the 70s Pat was the tutor for the musicians' group while I was a student in the dancing group. I do remember one incident while I was watching the musicians practising a selection of tunes. Pat was leading this group play-ing his accordion when someone approached him*

and began a conversation with him. Pat continued playing, and turning his head towards the visitor and without looking at his music began to answer the visitor's questions. To me, who has no knowledge of music making, this was remarkable. Many musicians reading this may say 'I do that all the time'. But that picture of Pat is something I can clearly remember.

§ *One day I asked Pat to put the tune* **Levi Jackson Rag** *on to a tape for me as I needed to practise it. He said he had not played it for some time and I must admit I enjoyed hearing him have trouble with one bar of it!*

§ *He was a pianist, guitarist, exceptional oboe player, and accordionist – indeed he could draw music out of anything from an African kalimba to an alphorn!*

§ He would turn up with different instruments. On one occasion he had different-sized kalimbas.

§ He was always very kind and helpful to budding musicians when he played with them in music workshops.

§ Pat and music just could not be separated.

§ Pat was also well-known in music circles in Holland, Belgium and France, to name but a few countries.

§ His own compositions for dancing are lovely and rather complicated. I remember going to sleep to the sounds of "Up Jumped the Devil" and **Levi Jackson Rag** being practised on the violin by Elvina.

Pat with jig doll

Naomi Alexander – *About 1976, when Mixolydians were pretty new we were booked to play for an evening dance at Derby, with Pat Shaw calling. We were somewhat apprehensive, as we had had no warning of his programme. I was alone in the hall (the men of the band away changing) when Pat breezed in, swept off his fur hat, and said 'Can your band sight-read?' I replied that our leader, David Bradley, was very good and we would do our best. 'Good. I've just written an excruciatingly difficult dance, with an excruciatingly difficult tune'. This turned out to be the **Levi Jackson Rag**, and although I murmured that he would be best to leave it till the second half, he put it into the first half; David did brilliantly, but I was pretty lost! He also introduced **Long Pond** to us, without warning.*

*On another occasion Pat was calling at a Halsway Manor weekend, and I took my accordion thinking there might be a beginnerish play-in at some time. I was greeted at the door with 'Ah, Naomi; have you brought your accordion with you?' He had brought his new dance **Round Pond**, and needed me to play the third part with Brian Willcocks and himself playing the other two! I was pretty terrified, but practised hard in the bedroom. When during the performance I lost my place for a bar or two, Pat noticed, filled it in while also playing his part, until I recovered. What a man!*

Fred Grimshaw – *In those days I played with the Thamesiders Country Dance Band, and I can remember us playing for Pat at a dance at a London University College in Regent's Park. Pat was calling but once he was happy the dancers did not need further instruction he would sidle over to me and play for a while on the upper part of my accordion keyboard. We were thus performing a three handed accordion arrangement invented by him on the spur of the moment. My bellowing arm had to work twice as hard that evening but it was great fun.*

Peter Boyce – *One of the best times was with Pat and me playing as a duo.*

Vic Godrich – *Many of his tunes I learned from Nan Fleming-Williams who ran the musicians' classes at that time. Pat played in a number of bands with her and was responsible for a lot of the music which was played in the EFDSS annual Royal Albert Hall Festival by the big band organised by Nan for the event. Both he and Nan were great lovers of Shetland and brought back tunes from their visits there such as "Villafiord" and "The Shetland Fiddler" which they used for dancing and taught to us. 'You really should go there, it is such a wonderful place', they said.*

Pat with dulcimer

Dennis Owen – *At a Cymdeithas Dawns Werin (Welsh Folk Dance Society) Easter workshop at Borth near Aberystwyth in the early 60s, I recall seeing Pat teaching a group of young musicians how to achieve the "lift" when playing for dancers. He demonstrated the technique on his accordion and asked the band to try it. After several attempts, the band, led by Pat, achieved the elusive "lift". The musicians were very animated and pleased with themselves and of course with Pat.*

Ian Porter – *A memory which can probably be repeated by many. I was occasionally asked to augment a folk dance band from Leeds University. I cannot remember the year, but the band had been invited to play at a dance in the old Spa building in Whitby. As far as I can remember, this was a dance which was put on at the end of the Whitby competitive Folk Dance Festival, so it would be in March. It was a drive of about an hour and a half to Whitby, so there was a certain amount of apprehension about getting there in time. This we achieved and set up chairs, music stands and amplification. As a band which never rehearsed altogether, we had a fairly limited, but standard repertoire of tunes mostly in G, D and A with an occasional foray into F, B flat and even A minor and E minor. Pat arrived, gave us a brief outline of his programme, and distributed copies of the tunes he wanted us to use for some of the dances. Our hearts sank a little as we looked at tunes with, to me at any rate, inaccessible key-signatures, which would require me to explore bits of the keyboard rarely encountered before. Pat was a lovely man, but he seemed to have, on this occasion, little idea that very few amateur accordionists were as gifted as he was. He still thanked us at the end, although we had had one or two hard looks during the dance.*

Daphne Baker – *He was very encouraging to me, then an enthusiastic but very inexperienced musician, still feeling my way with playing the piano for dancing. Hearing me play one of his own tunes, he made my day by saying 'How fascinating! That's just exactly how I would have played it!'*

Tricia Hamilton. *Although famed far and wide for his talent in the folk dance world, my enduring memory of Pat Shaw was at a dance weekend in Kent, when he produced and played a small hand-held African musical instrument called a kalimba. The one he played was very crudely made by one of the natives from scrap materials. Although it was described as a fairly new instrument, it has a long history! After he had finished playing it, he called for volunteers from his captive audience and I found myself being pushed forward, but very soon, with Pat's patience, I was able to play an extremely simple tune, and soon became quite hooked. Needless to say, I bought a rather modern wooden version from him, which I still have today.*

Alan Robertson. *This concerned the consequences for Pat when, with no warning, he dropped the music for his then newly contrived* **Levi Jackson Rag** *on the Chiltern Ramblers' music stand at an Amersham dinner dance at which Pat was guest of honour. If we were going to fall out it would have happened then but he was honest enough to see my point of view after I seized the initiative. It was all very funny.*

§ *For me, the best and most vivid memory of Pat is from that amazing last night party at the EFDSS training course in 1975. Towards the end of the evening when it seemed as if the festivities had reached a peak and could go no higher, out came Pat, Denis Smith and Nan FW to put it over the top. Pat, according to my diary, "sang like one possessed". We will miss him greatly.*

§ *Sometimes at Bucks weekends at Halsway Manor he would join in playing with the Chiltern Ramblers on one of his many kalimbas.*

The Countryside Players – Music of the Countryside

In 1949, Pat and Nan Fleming-Williams (whom he had met in 1936 at the Christmas School in Chelsea, London) formed "The Countryside Players" to raise money for the new Lerwick lifeboat in Shetland. The success of this concert (which is recorded by Nan in her piece in Colleagues, as is a comment about this event – chapter 5d) led to the devising of a concert called "Music of the Countryside" which included songs, solo instrumental music and dance music for listening.

The original line-up of Nan and Brian Fleming-Williams, Jean Matthews and Pat Shaw continued to play "Music of the Countryside" recitals all over the country, including CSH and Fenton House in Hampstead, where they made a recording. The first evening such a concert was given was on 9th March 1952 in the Village Hall, Bryantspuddle with these four original members of the Players. Later on Denis Patrick Smith joined The Players and, in the Recital List set out as Appendix 3, such musicians as Willie Hunter, Alan Humberstone and Cyril Tawney are listed as joining them on occasions. This list was kindly supplied by Denis Smith.

The programme of a concert by The Countryside Players at Cecil Sharp House on Wednesday, 15th December 1971 consisted of:

1. Field Town Processional
2. Gems from the Telly
3. Manx Melodies
4. Songs
5. Accordion solos
6. Fiddle Tunes

7.   London Calling
8.   INTERVAL
9.   Shetlandia
10.   A Feast of Maggotts
11.   More Songs
12.   More Fiddle Tunes
13.   Simple Gifts – variations on a theme
14.   Whisky Galore

entry was 50p, members 40p. On that occasion the players were Nan Fleming-Williams (violin), Pat Shaw (accordion, songs, guitar) and Denis Smith (accordion).

Recordings

Pat, Nan and Brian Fleming-Williams, with Geoffrey Ginn from Bedford made a private recording "Shetland Isles" – in fact the three marches are Pat's own. One track has a beautiful drum roll by Geoffrey. (**Marjorie Fennessy** – *Pat threw my copy of this record to me – to my horror – across the floor of the Hall at the back of the Stratford-on-Avon Theatre where we danced then. It was one of the first unbreakable records!*)

The Countryside Players made a 45 rpm record in 1967 –

"Playford Dances" (arranged Pat Shaw) – played by Pat (guitar), Nan Fleming-Williams (violin) and Denis Smith (accordion) – Holborn March, Greensleeves and Yellow Lace (Les Manches Vertes), Nonesuch and Mr Beveridge's Maggot (revised version), including its notation. PR-EP 318 costing 16/- only for EFDSS Members and Associates

Jonathan Cohen recalls making a recording in Fenton House, Hampstead which was organised by Pat. At Fenton House there is a collection of old instruments, including those which belonged to Winifred, Pat's mother. Jonathan was playing on her Handel harpsichord which is there. They recorded four dances –

"Dances from the Apted Book" PR-EP 317 recorded at Fenton House, Hampstead, by kind permission of The National Trust in 1966. Nan Fleming-Williams (violin), Monica Dewey (recorder), Susan Sheppard (cello) and Jonathan Cohen (harpsichord). Arrangements by Pat Shaw. Bath Carnival, Touchstone, The Comical Fellow and The Freemason. Cost 16/- for EFDSS Members and Associates only.

Composer

Pat composed four hymn tunes* (**Mount Vernon, Holly Mount, Mount Square** and **Christchurch Choir** for "Onward Christian Soldiers" – this was also the alternative tune for his **Pride of Newcastle** dance.) He used to sing in the Choir of Christ Church, Hampstead, when Ian Graham was organist.

There are arrangements by Pat of four tunes, for the Fleming-Williams family. The tunes themselves are **David in the Sandpit**, **Nan goes Shopping**, **Brwyno** (their cottage in Wales) and **Brian's (car) Breakdown**, published in the Pat Shaw Collection Books 4 and 5.

In the Forewords to The Pat Shaw Collection, Books 4 and 5 – Dance Melodies, **Nan Fleming-Williams** wrote –

This is an interesting collection of tunes in that they represent many facets of a man's life. Pat Shaw, the composer, is well known to everyone con-

---

*   Three of these are reproduced at the end of this chapter.

nected with the folk world as he travelled widely during his lifetime fulfilling his role as singer, musician, teacher of song and dance and so generously passing on to others his great knowledge and skills.

Wherever he went both at home and abroad he made friends and was never forgotten as he frequently left behind melodies where others would write thank-you letters. In this way he immortalises his friends and happenings perhaps too personally to be recognised by any but those for whom he wrote.

These tunes, some quite brilliant, some ordinary, must be thought of as the inspirations of a well-loved man as he played and sang his way through life. These tunes were not necessarily conceived as dance tunes, although most are excellent used in this way.

Lucky are those who having known Pat, can use this selection of his tunes in his memory.

Pat with The Countryside Players (Jean Forsyth, Nan and Brian Fleming-Williams) communicating through music.

Pat Shaw 1917 – 1977

HOLLY MOUNT

Pat Shaw

MOUNT VERNON

Pat Shaw

MOUNT SQUARE

Pat Shaw

5b. REMEMBERING PAT THROUGH DANCE

Pat Shuldham-Shaw as Composer/Choreographer of Dances

Christine Helwig in the CDS Magazine of April 1986 (see Acknowledgements) gives an analysis of Pat's choreography – albeit to only two of his collections.

In his introduction to **New Wine in Old Bottles***, Pat wrote "Style and tempo should come from the music" and there should be "plenty of flow... no creeping diffidently about". One outstanding characteristic of Pat's choreography is the flow of figures with the music even when the "embroidered or extended" figures are complex. One of the most interesting examples of the interweaving of figures and musical form is in **Round Pond**, which is a round for three couples. The B music for this dance is written as a round and the dance designed so that each of the couples identify with a particular part of the music – ideally with a particular instrument of the band – and move with it throughout the B figures. This is reminiscent of **John Tallis's Canon** which requires two instrumental voices to which, respectively, the first and second corners move in the dance. **Round Pond** is not for inexperienced dancers or musicians!

It would be interesting to have Pat's ratings for this collection (**Pat Shaw's Pinewoods**). In *New Wine*, he rated the dances according to their difficulty, noting "In no case did I deliberately attempt to be difficult". He continues "Many of the dances were composed in bed at night which may account for a certain nightmare quality about some of them!" His stated intention is to "keep everyone moving" while "retaining a responsible balance between what is fun to do and what is nice to look at: the dances in *New Wine* are essentially connoisseurs' dances ... not intended for ordinary social hops".

Fortunately that is not true of **Pat Shaw's Pinewoods**. While some of the dances in the Pinewoods collections are challenging – and some of the music as well – there is something to please everyone. There are simple, zesty dances that are suitable for a one-night stand as well as cleverly patterned figures to challenge experienced and sophisticated dancers. To understand Pat's intention for a given dance, it is instructive to read his comments. For example, he notes that **Pinewoods Square Eight** "should be done with an American square dance walking step, New England rather than Western in tempo and style" – this in a dance that contains a figure "similar to, but not identical with, that occurring in the last figure of *Oranges and Lemons*": it is such unusual combinations of idioms that make the dances intriguing to do.

Another example is in the **Shy Mer-chant**: Pat notes that the "names of the figures are those used for the figures of a series of dances ... derived from a manuscript in the National Library of Wales in Aberystwyth".† This dance "should be very lyrical in character and not too fast" and the movements are

---

*   New Wine in Old Bottles is a collection of 54 dances composed to music of old Dutch songs and country dances, published in 1971 and dedicated by Pat Shaw "to all my friends of the NVS"

†   Mellor, Hugh. "An Early Traditional Country Dance" Journal of English Folk Dance and Song Society, 1 (1932) pp. 60-64.

familiar from 17th and 18th century dance books. For "The Tracings" in the second figure Pat specifies "side-by-side" as described by William Jones, who wrote that, in High Arcol, Shropshire, in 1686, siding is "to go forward to one another and fall back two or three steps always facing but veering to your left or right".* The formation is a four couple set, but there is a difference – two couples side-by-side face two couples side-by-side as in a set for *Portland Fancy* and Pat could not resist another anachronism, a Texas Star at the end; certainly "fun to do and nice to look at" if a bit unorthodox!

Many of Pat's notes relate to the music he composed – which ranged from "the character of a minuet" for **Quite Carr-ied Away** to out and out ragtime for **Long Pond** and **Levi Jackson Rag**. There are reels and jigs, and a dance, **The Martial Baron** in 5/2 time which "should be steady and dignified" and there is **Helwiggery** for which the A music is seven bars and the B nine bars. Unfortunately, we do not have comments on the dances and music in **Among the Pines**, except, in some cases, where Pat had written "not good enough" and started over!

Some of the dances in the Pinewoods collections have already become popular. Single sheets for **Buzzard's Bay**, **American Husband**, **K & E** and a few others have been available. But most of the dances have not been put together in an easy-to-use and legible format. Now that **Pat Shaw's Pinewoods** is available, his other dances should add to the repertoire that we now enjoy. In his Foreword to **Between Two Ponds**, Pat wrote "Then I thought of various other friends I had made while in the US and the list of dances for people I met grew and grew and so I decided to split my effort into two collections, possibly more if I don't run out of ideas".

Pat Shaw never ran out of ideas. To our great loss, he ran out of time in 1977 and was never able to finish all of the dances that he planned to write for his Pinewoods friends. His enthusiasm, his wit, his vast knowledge and his generosity in sharing his many gifts endeared him to us all. **Pat Shaw's Pinewoods** is not only a feast of dance and music, but a treasured reminder of a great Dancing Master and a good friend.

Working on the project it is clear that Pat is thought of as the Twentieth Century Dancing Master – as time goes by his dances are the ones which remain popular. Other dances and composers may be "top of the pops" in the dance world for a short time but it is Pat's dances which have stood the test of time. How many people can remember the first occasion they danced something as timeless as **Levi Jackson Rag** and have subsequently watched the same stimulating effect on other newer or younger dancers when they meet it. It is a dance which combines enjoyment, fun and exercise as well as a sense of achievement.

As a dance composer Pat often showed a wonderful combination of innovation and logical balance. His dances range from the simple – such as **Hamburger Special** to the tune "McDonalds Reel" to the more complicated **The Rose of Tankerton** and from slow and stately **Waters of Holland** to **Salop Galop**!

---

*   Mellor, Hugh. "An Early Traditional Country Dance"; Journal of English Folk Dance and Song Society, 1 (1932) pp. 60-64.

For some, it is the dances that exercise "the old grey matter" that are their favourites whilst for others it is the symbiotic relationship between the music and the figures which make particular dances so special. Pat has given us plenty of each.

Pat's first published dance **Monica's Delight** was composed when he was aged thirteen. Pat said, *Monica was a beautiful Edinburgh lass on whom I had a crush at the time.*

His first dance composition after the War was **Freda's Fancy (Hope for South Africa)** in 1949. This was for Freda Pash, who went out for the EFDSS to South Africa as the EFDSS representative in place of Mrs Barney Heffer, who had returned to this country.

Many people think **Margaret's Waltz** is traditional. Aly Bain, a famous Scottish fiddler told Pat that he had come across a wonderful tune. Pat said 'That's mine!' (see Pat in Shetland for Aly's story about this incident). The Scots think it was composed for someone in Scotland. Actually it was composed for the retirement of Margaret Grant (EFDSS Devon Organiser) with a second tune **Farewell to Devon** played alternately for the dance.

Clarance House/Whit Monday. Pat took a Whitsun Course at the Essex Residential Youth Centre, Thaxted in 1953 and composed this dance as a farewell gift to the Matron who was Mrs Jones, wife of the first warden.

Pat wrote many dances for friends and anniversaries of significant dates for friends. His love of language led him often to play with words when he looked for titles of the dances and music he composed. For example, when Fried de Metz asked Pat to write a dance as a birthday gift for her husband Al Herman, he called it the **American Husband or Her Man**. When he wrote a dance for Joan Carr, he called it **Quite Carr-ied Away or Joan Transported**. Similarly, a dance for Jim Morrison, the expert American teacher of English dance, was entitled **The Jim Morris-On**.

In 1963, he composed the dance and tune **Walpole Cottage** for the farewell to the EFDSS party for Grace Meikle and Leonie Morris of Walpole Cottage in Chipstead, Surrey. He wrote on the copy he presented to them "N.B. This should be danced with the vigour of the 'morris' and always, naturally, with 'Grace'." He devised and composed a dance called **Mrs Foxley's Fancy** for a lady of the same name. She founded the Twickenham Group and he also devised **Twickenham Ferry** for her group.

Very often he would make up a dance for someone when he was on the train going to a dance he was taking. **The Pride of Newcastle** (Newcastle-upon-Tyne) was written in the train on his way to take a dance at Alnwick Castle in 1963. Pat told Stanley Hutchinson that he had composed this dance/music for him.

Pat composed a dance for his accompanist, Miss Isabel Bedlington – **Miss Bedlington's Fancy**. This was published in a booklet called **Quartet** in 1964 together with **Miss de Jersey's Memorial** (For Everal de Jersey – pianist), **Mr Ganiford's Maggot** (For William Ganiford – violinist) and **Miss Avril's Delight** (For Elsie "Ruby" Avril – violinist).*

---

* In the Introduction to the Quartet Booklet, Pat wrote –
> These are dances for connoisseurs rather than for Saturday night rompers, but I hope that does not mean that the only pleasure in them is intellectual.
> There was a time when it was said that any dance that was difficult was therefore a bad dance. With this I cannot agree. The merits of a dance have nothing to do with its difficulty and it is only when the difficulties have been mastered that we can really judge its quality. There is ☞

§ *Pat became very friendly with Joe and Gladys Muschamp when Gladys was the chairman of Lancashire District of the EFDSS and he stayed with them when he was in the area or travelling to or from Scotland. Gladys and Joe ran a hardware shop in the village of Bare in Cheshire, and, it is thought by some, that Pat suggested they called it Bare Necessities, an idea that they readily accepted. He certainly wrote a dance with the same name. He wrote four dances* **Gladys's Galop (or Gladsome Gladys)**, **Joseph's Jig (or Jovial Joe)**, **Muschamp's Maggot** *and* **Bare Necessities** *which were published in a small booklet –* **Muschamp's Mushrooms.**

When Nibs and Jean Matthews were leaving for America in 1964, Pat composed a dance called **Nibs Goes West** with two tunes, one with the same title and the other called **Jean's on the Fiddle**. Mollie Du Cane was an inspiring and accurate teacher. Her home was at the top of the hill in Townsend Drive in St Albans where she lived with her mother. It was named "Four Winds" and **Four Winds** became the title of a dance written by Pat.

Miss Fennessy Smiles. Marjorie felt very honoured to have a dance named after her. It got its name because there is a Scottish tune "Miss Nancy Frowns" and Pat wanted this to be the opposite.

John Tallis, long serving member of the Manchester District Committee, wrote to say how one year, at their annual Weekend School *on the Saturday evening Pat Shaw introduced a new dance which he said he had composed only the previous evening. I had told him in passing that Thomas Tallis, the Elizabethan composer, was almost certainly an ancestor of mine, though there were a few gaps in the family tree. Anyway, Tallis' Canon, with which Pat was familiar, must have triggered ideas with him and* **John Tallis's Canon** *was the result.*

Pat Wilkinson – *When Pat went to the Morecambe Group in 1972 for the second time he presented them with the dance* **Morecambe Bay**. *They were all very thrilled. The Group held their Annual Ball at Warton Grange just outside Morecambe and had to use the Grange's musicians which were organ and drums. Pat was quite taken aback but soon realised the organist was a fine musician who had seen the music for the programme in advance and had been playing for their Annual Ball for a few years.*

A complete list of the dances that Pat wrote and for whom they were written can be found as Appendix 1.

Trying Out his Dances

Pat would try out his new dance compositions at various places around the country and groups were obviously pleased to have this experience.

"The Whirligigs", run by Marjorie Fennessy, was one of these groups. When he was in London, Pat went to most of the Whirligigs' fortnightly meetings at CSH. The Whirligigs often had the honour to be the first to learn a new dance of Pat's and it gave all the members a great deal of pleasure to be Pat's guinea pigs.

Other groups also suggested to Pat that they would be very willing for him to use them as a visual aid whilst interpreting the dance notation. In the late 60s he made regular visits to the Reading University Country Dance Group to try out

---

a certain satisfaction, intellectual perhaps but none the less genuine, in getting to grips with the problems and overcoming them; and this satisfaction becomes total when the dance is so well known that it can be performed as effortlessly as the simplest party dance. Providing the end product justifies the hard work involved and providing the social atmosphere in the learning stages is good, the toil and effort can actually contribute to the pleasure and not become mere drudgery.

some of his newly composed dances and the Reading University Playford team worked with Pat in this way.

When at dance courses at Halsway Manor, Pat would use the dancers there as guinea pigs to walk through some of the new dances before he published them. Much to their delight!

Burton Manor College, on the Wirral, was visited many times by Pat and there he would try out many of his new dances and even ask the opinion of the dancers on the preferred tune for a particular dance as he often wrote more than one tune for some of his dances. Although when someone once suggested that one of his dances might be done differently he replied very nicely that he liked the idea – but not enough to change it in the next edition.

Another contributor particularly remembers trying out **The Rose of Tankerton** and **Four Winds** which was a wonderful dance training experience although they initially *doubted whether they would ever be able to master them.*

It seems that often, when Pat was teaching one of his newly composed dances, people would write out the instructions as soon as they could. **Cyril Jones** apparently still calls **The American Husband** from a prompt card marked "Unnamed Dance" – Pat called it at the Sunday Afternoon Albert Hall Festival "At Home" at Cecil Sharp House on 21st February 1971 and Cyril noted it down.

"Another Look at Playford"

These classes ran from 1959 to 1972 in CSH and were on the first Monday of the month.

As well as looking at the three volumes of dances of 17th and 18th century published by Playford, Pat looked at many other composers/publishers, such as Thomas Bray 1699, which no one had come across then and also some of his own compositions.

The "Members' News" October 1965 said "Pat Shaw has made an intensive study of dances of this period, and presents them with a new look". Members' admission was 2/6d, Double 4/–.

Marjorie Fennessy hopes to present a book of some of the dances which Pat had "Another Look" at in 2010.

The Square Dance Craze

Nan Fleming-Williams recorded in her piece in *Colleagues* (chapter 5d) how Pat was in his element when square dancing became the latest "in" thing to do following a visit to Canada in 1951 by the then Princess Elizabeth and The Duke of Edinburgh. Pat loved the fast music and the dressing up. In 1956 he, with Marjorie as his partner, attended a Square Dance Callers Workshop and Dance at the United States Air Force Service Club at the RAF Station, West Drayton, Middlesex. There was an hour lecture on square dance calling followed by two and a half hours of dancing. He obviously wanted to be as proficient in this style as he was in dances of the 17th century.

He composed some excellent singing squares such as **Little Gipsy Girls**, **The Coronet** and **The Streets of Loredo**.

A memory from this time from **Mary Purdie** is of *a course being run by Patrick Shuldham-Shaw at Ruislip. Quite a gang of us attended and I can recall Pat, accordion strapped on, beard pointing prominently forward, teaching us all the moves and seem to remember that he wrote "Dip and Dive" at one of the weekends we spent with him (hence I could always sing along if his record was played) – we had caught the* *bug by then and would attend all the courses he ran. In photos of him at that time he would be seen dressed in dark coloured trousers and waistcoat with a white shirt. Words sung or said by him that always stick in my mind are 'four hands, four hands' but I can't think of the actual connection – I can hear him even as I type this!*

Radio and TV

During the fifties there were a number of broadcasts on the BBC Home Service with various folk connections, such as the "Dancing English". Pat was often heard on the BBC West of England programme "Country Dancing", both as caller and singer. When broadcast from the Midlands it was often fronted by the local Area Organiser, Ken Clark.

Ralph Harrison – *I do remember one short series which was linked with other countries and when a few of those were based in Birmingham, Pat came up to front the British end because of his linguistic abilities. I do remember one particular programme when Pat was so fascinated with the technical side that he popped out of the studio into the control room – and I think also to talk to others in the broadcast with the technical links to other people involved. He was so engrossed that the return back to our part of the broadcast was due and I can still see him sprinting back and just making it before he was due to join in.*

Keith Uttley also remembers dancing in a 1951 TV presentation with Pat calling "Dip & Dive".

I recollect his involvement in one of the West Country radio folk broadcasts which Nibs used to call. I believe it was the occasion of the Jolly Waggoners tenth anniversary, so Nan and Pat were both playing.

Margaret's Waltz was first performed at a Country Dance Party Broadcast from Clyst St George on 25 March 1959.

Contributors' Memories of Pat as a teacher of dance and caller are, in many cases, surprisingly fresh. Those with dates embedded are quoted roughly in chronological order.

Ian Holland – *In 1948 or 1949 I cycled from my home in Hertfordshire to attend a Whitsun weekend of folk dance and song at Clarance House, the Essex County Council residential youth centre in Thaxted in Essex. Pat later composed the dance* **Clarance House**, *named after this centre. I was already involved in folk dancing and was keen to attend that event as the tutor for the weekend was Mr Patrick Shuldham-Shaw, as he was more formally known at that time, and what a memorable weekend we had! As a course leader and tutor Pat Shaw was an inspiration and whether we were learning complicated dances, or songs out in the sunshine in the garden, his innate skill as a teacher made it all seem so easy. His friendly manner and empathy with us youngsters made everyone feel that they were in the company of a personal friend rather than a teacher.*

This was my first meeting with Pat Shaw whom I met at many folk events over subsequent years and his manner was such that he always made you feel you were in the company of a close personal friend.

Ellis Rogers recalls – *In about 1950 I attended a weekend course for Youth Club Leaders in Acton, West London. As light relief from lectures on Committee Procedure and Club Finances we had a session on introducing folk dancing into youth clubs. This session was taken by Pat Shaw who, among other dances, taught "La Russe". At some point he was asked to demonstrate the "Pivot" swing. Leaping from the stage and with his accordion still strapped in front of him he grabbed the nearest* *young girl and taking her in a waltz hold proceeded with his demonstration. Unfortunately during the swing the "Air Release" button was activated and as the accordion closed-up the young lady's breasts were caught and crushed in the pleats of the bellows. I can still hear her anguished screams.*

§ *Our memories of PS are that he was always there in our early days of dancing at CSH (1950s) and his dances had a special appeal for us. One memory we have is walking through a square dance prior to an evening's dance which Pat had composed to the tune "Sugar Bush". The song being popular at the time was sung by Dame Shirley Bassey.*

§ *One special evening – 10 March 1951 – we travelled to Hammersmith to a dance evening where Pat was the MC. There he sang folk songs, as we often heard him on the radio and called all the dances. My fate was sealed when a young man asked me to dance the Cumberland Square Eight ... Two years later we were married and now after 54 years are still together and dancing. Our thanks to the wonderful Pat Shaw!*

§ *We got to know Pat better when in the late 50s we invited him to call at Square Club in the Gloucester area to which we had moved, and also to run some Saturday night "square dances". he would confirm the bookings on a very brief postcard signed "Pat Sh-Sh".*

Beryl Jukes – From a letter written in August 1959 by Phil Jukes to his future wife, Beryl Vivian, referring to Pat Shaw – *I had quite a long talk with Pat Shaw on* **Margaret's Waltz** – *he said that the back to back was included because so many dancers are bad waltzers. I said that back-to-back in waltz rhythm is much harder – anyhow, we ended up by dancing it in the library – me being Pat's partner! Very gay! Pat is coming to call a dance at Cardiff on 9 Sept – that's an evening out for me.*

Les Barclay – *My last main recollection of Pat is at the EFDSS NEC/staff conferences in the 1960s. These weekends were most productive in terms of forging links between the National Executive Committee and the staff (more numerous in those days) and in discussing policy issues. But the weekends also included practical dance sessions and I particularly remember Pat teaching us the Papa Stour sword dance.*

Ian Porter – *After moving to Yorkshire in 1965, our dancing was a bit curtailed because of our lack of transport, but I remember an occasion when we were offered a lift to a dance in York at which Pat was calling. I remember very little about it, except that it was held in a school hall. One thing that does stand out, however, is Pat's remarkable memory for people. I had met him a few times while in Birmingham, through EFDSS events and through Jockey Morris, but I could hardly say that he was a close friend. We walked in the door of the dance, paid for our tickets and within a few seconds Pat was there, saying 'Hello, Ian; glad to see you,' then, in a quieter voice, 'We never get many men at these dances, so you are very welcome'. Sure enough, a quick survey showed that ladies outnumbered men about fifteen to one. (I am glad to say that the proportions are much better these days in Yorkshire: much closer to equality.)*

Dave Stephens – *In the late 1960s and early 70s, when I knew Pat, he was already being hailed as a modern day Dancing Master. At that time Pat usually joined the staff of the country dance weekends held at the Glenwood Hotel in Cliftonville, Margate. For a young dancer, it was an inspiration to witness a character of Pat's stature displaying his ability as an MC and musician.*

Even more entrancing were the closed soirees when the youngsters from local clubs invited Pat to a room where he would entertain us by playing his accordion and guitar and singing. You can imagine the star-struck youth of East Kent sitting at the feet of this giant of folk absorbing every last drop of Pat's personality.

Brian Jones – *Pat became an Honorary Vice-President of Reading University Union Folk Dance Society (RUUFDS) in the late 1960s. He was the caller for the 2nd, 3rd and 5th Playford Balls (1968, 1969 and 1971). For details of the dances he called see the "Playford Ball and Playford Team" page on www.ruufds.org.uk. The Inter Varsity Folk Dance Festival (IVFDF) in 1970 was held at Reading. The RUUFDS Playford Team performed* **Mr Shaw's Apologies** *and Pat was a guest of honour. Pat also ran two or three (perhaps more) workshops for RUUFDS. As well as his own dances, he also taught us the Papa Stour sword dance.*

His voice, both as a caller and as a singer, had the same light but purposeful elegance. When I published "A Berkshire Bundle" in 1986 I wrote in the introduction – "Trips to Pat Shaw's workshops at Cecil Sharp House, and to have him come to the University to run sessions specially for us, had quite an influence on me and the club as a whole. It was his dances that encouraged me to compose dances myself."

Peter Bridgman – *I did not have a lot of contact with Pat Shaw, but there was an occasion that I was involved with which shows the kind of person he was. In the early 1970s our small Gloucestershire club booked the Countryside Players, comprising Nan Fleming-Williams, Denis Smith and of course, Pat Shaw. In our publicity for the dance we were putting on, we highlighted Pat's name on our posters. On his arrival, Pat immediately came up to me and severely berated me for doing this, saying 'we play together as equals and my name should not be given prominence over the others.' They went on and played superbly for the evening, but I learned a lesson that I shall never forget!*

Eileen Sutherland – *It was years later that I came in contact again, though I'd heard lots about his dance research and choreography. I'd dropped into Cecil Sharp House on the way home from a lecture, and Pat was teaching "Joy after Sorrow" for the first time, it was a real hit with everybody. Later, we heard from Bernard Bentley, who had also researched the dance, how generous Pat had been in ceding to him the right to publish.*

Mary Bazley – *It was a super week, (Jersey Folk Festival,1954) we flew from Northolt – my first flight – and we stayed in St Helier, meeting in various venues throughout the week for workshops, dances etc. as well as having time to see the Island. Pat conducted workshops. He taught us "Shepherd's Hey" and other morris dances and singing/dancing sessions where we learned "The Gypsy Girl "and other songs as well as dancing to singing rather than instrumental music. He started off with "Belfast Duck" to a ditty which would not be considered "politically correct" these days. It went like this –*

Run nigger run
The paterole (patrol) will catch you Run nigger run
For it's almost day (this repeated while the hands four circles take place.)
Over the fence and through the pasture
The white man runs but the nigger a little faster (this also sung twice for the arches and progressing.)

Pat was full of fun and very talented as his many dances indicate. He had a beautiful singing voice and played many instruments. The song above he had brought back when he'd been to Pinewoods, I think not long before this week.

§ It must be forty years ago when I was doing the bookings for Guildford dances, we had Pat Shaw a lot in those days and the one thing that comes to mind is when booking him to MC a dance I always sent a letter of confirmation and he asked for a stamped addressed postcard for him to sign and return by way of con-

firmation – I never did get a postcard.

Trijn Nijdam – *At a weekend or a festival whenever there is a session of Pat Shaw dances it is very special to me. It reminds me of the way he taught us to dance and what he told us.*

'Lift yourself up
Start a figure and finish it properly
Look at your partner and the dancers around you
First your head and shoulders and your feet will follow your body
Dancing is singing with your body
Dancing is a public demonstration of a private desire.'

He also inspired the musicians and always played with the band when it was possible.

Alison Messer – *I remember going to a party and Pat was there. He played for a group of us to dance "Dorset Four Hand Reel" as the others at the event were much older and wanted to do civilised things. I think he suggested it as something lively and trad we could do to let our hair down a bit. This means that I have a very positive memory of him wanting to do something trad and inclusive, even in a crowd who loved his creative and clever stuff.*

Hilary Herbert recalls – *He was a good teacher, and I benefited from this at Liverpool and Manchester workshops and at Burton Manor summer schools, although he could get a bit irascible if we weren't trying our best. I particularly remember him teaching us the Papa Stour sword dance out on the terrace at Burton in lovely summer weather.*

Mavis Roberts (Williams) – *My first meeting with Pat was at Rhoose in South Wales. It was a bitterly cold winter weekend and I had left my young baby daughter for the first time to enable me to attend. I learned such a lot that day. Pat was using a simple dance, "The Cumberland Square" to teach some basic points of dance which have served me well always.*

Points such as:
- *being ready to dance right on the first beat of the bar*
- *leading from the upper body*
- *pushing off the back foot as you move forward*
- *acknowledging your fellow dancers.*

Cyril Jones – *My personal admiration of Pat is for the way he introduced so many good original new dances together with the music he composed for them. At some time or other I have called and taught nearly every one of his dances at weekly dance classes, club dances, country dance holidays both in the UK and the USA. Pat's dances have become my most called dances.*

§ We have had much joy in dancing and calling Pat's dances over the years. Two dance occasions stand out. These were both anniversary dances of the Phoenix Club held at South Mimms and called by Pat Shaw. For the first he wrote **Phoenix Rejuvenated**. *What a great caller and such a delightful person he was.*

§ And what fun we had when Pat Shaw was the caller, his deep, powerful voice musically warning us at the right moment of the next change in the dance.

§ My first thought is that it was always a disappointment to find that he was not the MC or band leader on the odd occasions that I turned up and he was not at CSH, Thaxted or wherever I had expected him.

§ Pat Shaw had been calling a barn dance and ended by saying 'That's all and kiss the caller'. Two ladies advanced on him and kissed him, much to his and the company's delight.

§ *For me he was an inspirational teacher of dance and it was an unforgettable pleasure to experience at first hand the results of his researches into old dances and creation of new ones.*

§ *Pat sang, played, arranged, composed and certainly I've seen him dance sword, morris and country.*

§ *A dancing master I regarded with awe as a near-genius and still do.*

§ *My main memory of him is of him asking me (a seventeen year old beginner) to be his partner to demonstrate "Pins and Needles" which I'd never danced before. He got me through it all right but afterwards my boy friend informed me I was the only one doing a kick balance and it was about time I learnt to set properly.*

§ *We have very fond memories of our dancing weekends at Pendley Manor, Herts, and Halsway Manor, Somerset, when Pat Shaw was the tutor.*

§ *Dances and melodies flowed from him and he was always very generous in passing on his knowledge far and wide.*

§ *I remember him as the adjudicator at The Aylesbury Festival of the Arts when together with several other teams we competed for The Holland Cup.*

§ *He really was (had) a talent and so free with his knowledge. They say nobody is indispensable but certainly, as far as Pat was concerned, I've never found anybody who comes close to matching his abilities.*

Pat and Morris

§ *Whilst Pat was at Harrow he excelled in gymnastics – which led to him doing back somersaults in the capers of a Bledington Morris Jig.*

§ *Within the morris world there were a number of tales, mainly apocryphal, which I found too tall to believe but I remember him fondly as larger than life and also at times too clever by half for ordinary mortals like me!*

§ *Pat Shaw taught morris and folk singing at morning workshops and I still sing one or two "taught at his knee" even today. Three members of the Grenoside Sword Dance team were there and helped to spread the art of various sword dances among us.*

§ *I encountered Pat occasionally at Cecil Sharp House. One of my most vivid memories of Pat at the House (he may have been taking a class for Sinner – Miss Sinclair) is of him demonstrating a morris jig and covering an amazing amount of floor space with his capers.*

§ *Pat had remarkable energy and when he did a morris workshop with his accordion strapped on, his capers were higher than ours and we were quite unencumbered. He was an elegant and purposeful dancer, particularly light on his feet.*

§ *Eric Langford, a teacher at the Blue Coat Senior School in Walsall (where I was a pupil) had organised a week long folk dance camp at the school's permanent camp in Sutton Park at Streetly. Eric asked Pat to come and teach morris and sword dancing to the 24 boys and 24 girls (12 – 15 year olds) which he did with enthusiasm.*

§ *Pat said of morris dances 'Fast ones keep you cool as the air rushes through your hair!'*

Pat teaching and dancing in 1958

Publicity photo of the Whirligigs taken in the garden of CSH. Marjorie Fennessy is on the extreme right.

Whirligigs

Marjorie Fennessy – *When the square dance craze in this country started, I formed the Whirligigs, as I would not send any dancers to a "show-and-drag-in" unless I knew their standard of dancing was sufficiently good.*

Pat was an enormous help in advising on dances and dance sequences. When he started to compose more dances with their own tunes and to research 17th and 18th century dances, he often dropped in at our meetings to try something out. He would bring tiny bits of paper with the tune on it, either his own or one he had researched, and put it in front of Jonathan Cohen and say 'Play this.' He would then try out the dance with the dancers. He enjoyed having a dance group on whom he could experiment and we enjoyed having him.

It was Pat's idea to join several dances together for demonstrations, rather than do single dances and this he introduced to the Whirligigs. In 1961, at the Royal Albert Hall Festival, we did a sequence called "House Party" which was choreographed in this way. It consisted of three dances "Bartlett House" (Bray 1699), "Whimbleton House" (Playford 1721) and **Clarance House** *(Shaw 1953). The Whirligigs had previously danced, in 1955, a Running Set routine at the Royal Albert Hall choreographed by Pat, based on the dance Whirligig, finishing in a "W".*

When the Whirligigs had their "Final Fling" on 15 March 1973 (The Club was too successful matrimonially!), Pat wrote **The Whirligigs Last Bow** *for us. It was a* *very great pity he could not be with us that evening.*

In 1962 Pat Shaw was to give a talk illustrated by The Whirligigs and Jimmy Coleman. The Whirligigs did several groups of dances, though actually Pat was ill and his talk was read on the occasion. One group finished with "Nonesuch". At a rehearsal I told Pat that I felt this was too quiet an end. His reply was 'Well, there's "A la Mode de France" which is the same tune in the major key'. Nowadays everybody changes from minor to major in the middle of the dance as a matter of course!

The Whirligigs danced in the Easter Parades at Battersea Park, London three times – in 1961, 1962 & 1964. The Parade was 3000 yards at three miles per hour, which was quite a feat considering no dance goes straight forward all the time! Pat composed **Battersea Processional** *for us in 1961. Pat and Vi Le Maistre played for us and had to walk playing their accordions for the first two Parades. In 1964 they travelled in style on a Tuborg Lager lorry/float decorated with panels of dancers drawn by Lila Fraser.*

The band for Whirligigs at Bagneux (Paris) 12th and 13th September 1964. The only time Jonathan Cohen ever played an accordion.

In September 1964 Whirligigs went to dance at the Festival in Bagneux (Paris). Our musicians were Nan Fleming-Williams, Vi Le Maistre, Pat and Jonathan, the first and only time Jonathan played an accordion.

Whirligigs were very fortunate in that they often had Nan Fleming-Williams and Pat as musicians in the early days. Eventually **Vic Godrich** was asked to play by Marjorie Fennessy – *Marjorie asked if I would play for her demonstration group. Pat used to come to Whirligigs meetings bringing the new dances that he had devised so that they could be tried out and used for demonstrations. I remember him presenting me with a tune and asking 'Will that go alright on a fiddle?' I looked at it and it was far too difficult for me to play at the time but I think I told him that it would fit on the fiddle. I hope that whoever got it to play thought the same!*

The Whirligigs were invited to a 21st birthday party in Hampton Court Palace on 30 June 1961 and Pat came as the musician. *In dancing* **Clarance House** *we made a mistake at the beginning of it by not inter-twining the forward and back movements for the heads and sides at the beginning of the dance. Pat, of course, came to our rescue and played the necessary additional music.*

One of the Whirligigs recalls one of the most memorable of those times with Pat in the 1960s. *Pat had been asked to supply a dance team to learn some Welsh dances for a BBC Wales TV programme, "Twmpath Dawns" (barn dances). In his usual clear, no-nonsense way, and together with Marjorie Fennessy, he taught the dances which were charming, enjoyable and different. We all went to Cardiff for a couple of days and it was most successful.*

5c. PAT THE SINGER

Pat had a very distinctive and powerful tenor singing voice: for the most part it was beautifully melodious and he delighted in encouraging people to sing folk songs. Many choirs and folk bands have cause to thank him for the courses and workshops that he ran. Even those not fortunate enough to have attended such events themselves have been influenced by them through their own teachers who had.

His fine voice was a "natural" for folk songs although one person who heard him sing on many occasions felt that his voice was rather high and thin. For some, he came to prominence as a singer first – especially after Douglas Kennedy left for service in the RAF during the war.

It is remembered how easy it was to learn a song under his tuition. He would sing a line and get the group to repeat it, doing it again and again, adding new lines as the first were learnt to his satisfaction. His song sessions are reported as always being excellent – not just the wide range of songs and his playing of many different instruments but the way in which he involved everybody. One memory tells of him bringing several unusual small musical instruments to a workshop and teaching an ostinato (a short repeated pattern of notes) which was then played whilst the others sang. Pat, of course could do both at once whilst the participants had to concentrate on playing the right notes.

By his late twenties, Pat was well established as a collector and singer of folk songs. He travelled to remote parts of the world where he would sing for his supper, learn the language and collect tunes and songs. After he had been to South Africa he brought back various instruments and singing rounds. When organising singing rounds, he gave each group different calls and chants and "strange instruments" to play and the overall result is recalled as being really marvellous. Even non-singers and those who did not usually enjoy singing rounds found themselves joining in the fun.

There are memories of Pat teaching singing at Barford, Burton Manor, Cliftonville, CSH, Merseyside, Sidmouth and Weston. Songs and rounds particularly mentioned are:

- two unusual songs at an Easter day of dance at the House. One was "This joyful Easter-tide"; the other was the Caribbean calypso-style "Lord's Prayer". He was very insistent on the correct rhythm for the latter
- various street calls from London and a haunting one from Wales
- two of his own rounds **I sat next to the Duchess at Tea** and **To Stop the Train**
- The Four Maries
- The Ploughman
- Everybody Loves Saturday Night – in 48 languages
- Foggy Dew – different versions from around the world
- Blow the Wind Southerly

- Oes Gafr Eto (Calling the Goats) This is a traditional Welsh song and Pat spoke Welsh fluently. He would hold the first word "Oes" on the first note "Oooooooooooooooooes" for several seconds as if he were calling the goats*
- My Boy Billie – in Afrikaans when in Africa
- Old Joe Clark
- She Moved Through the Fair
- a scurrilous version of "The Spaniard who Blighted My Life"
- The Sally Gardens
- Venezuela
- Stanley and Dora
- Have Ye Seen Owt o' My Bonny Lad
- The Seeds of Love.

This last song was remembered – by **Geoff Rye** (his memories were sent in by his daughter, **Esther Parker**) as being sung at the unveiling of a plaque at Hambridge Vicarage to commemorate Cecil Sharp hearing the song that started him off collecting folk songs. Bill Rutter had raised enough money for the plaque and Maud Karpeles performed the unveiling. Unfortunately, the church clock struck whilst Pat was singing and despite all attempts the clock could not be erased from the recording so Pat had to sing the whole song again.

A Barford weekend, under the direction of Patrick Shuldham-Shaw was held 13-15 January 1950. The report of this folk song weekend records that Pat was in charge and had prepared a syllabus of lectures which led participants by easy stages through a chain of ideas. He taught many songs in varied languages by rote, carefully repeating phrases until the students had mastered them.

Pat also included singing squares at his dances so the lucky participants would have the joy of Pat as both MC and singer. If there were a special occasion for an evening he would include verses about the birthday or wedding or whatever.

One highlight of the Society's year was the annual Christmas Carol Concert at CSH that Pat was involved with in various capacities but always singing (see chapter 14). Then the audience would all sing Christmas carols together with him and with lots of choruses.

Ralph Harrison – *A specific memory I have is there was an event put on by Nibs Matthews in Cheltenham Town Hall, again in the early 50s. Jockey Morris had been invited to do a spot. It was a mid-week event and we had to travel down on a dark, wet, foggy night with one of our more erratic drivers, Bill Astley. It was with relief that we arrived and were glad to relax in a dressing room near the hall and stage. We found we were sharing with Pat. I think he realised that some of us were a little fraught after the journey and so under the guise of rehearsing, treated us to a short session. I gather it was typical of Pat in every way and lifted our spirits even though some of the songs were of dubious content. I still remember it as one of the greatest times of folk experience and so exquisitely sung.*

Hilary Herbert – can recall a teachers' Easter vacation PE course in Blackpool, where Pat was teaching on the folk-dancing course. *He took a couple of sessions on singing games and the memory is of a big, bearded, mature man skipping blithely round singing 'When I was a school girl, a schoolgirl, a schoolgirl'. I thought he was great.*

Trijn Nijdam recalled that during the intervals at some of the socials (during the Dutch Christmas Course) – *he would take a chair, his guitar and his little foot-*

---

*   See Appendix 5 for this song.

stool and we would take our chairs and gather round him. He would sing his beau-tiful ballads, his South African songs and his songs from Wales. Then we would all sing Christmas carols together with lots of choruses.

Marjorie Fennessy's memories of Pat singing include –

- *In his early days, before he did much calling, he had a lovely tenor voice. He used to sing at recitals, including one at the Wigmore Hall on 12 July 1948 – accompanist Isabel Bedlington and another "British Music" on 6 June 1951 again accompanied by Isabel Bedlington on the piano. Pat was large and Isabel small – they must have looked wonderful going on the stage!*
- *Pat also sang madrigals at Cambridge and at Vaughan Williams' home (See The Purcell Singers, conducted by Imogen Holst, a record of folk songs and music & songs Pat sang) ***
- *Pat's last recital was with Douglas Kennedy in memory of Maud Karpeles on Friday, 11 November 1977, in Trefusis, Cecil Sharp House, London, just a few days before his death.*

Marjorie was hoping to get some of Pat's private recordings of his singing and playing onto a CD. There is a record where Pat was accompanied by Gerald Moore.

Pat made two special records for David Fleming-Williams (Nan and Brian's son). David believes one was made in a recording booth at Boosey and Hawkes in (Upper) Regent Street and the other at the Festival of Britain site. One of them starts with Pat speaking.

On 18th March, 1970, the EFDSS presented "In an English Country Garden" – an informal evening of Folk music collected and arranged by Percy Grainger with

Pat Shaw, singer and compere

Shirley Collins, folk singer

The Prospero Symphonic Wind Ensemble

The Co-operation (The London Co-operative choir conducted by Jonathan Cohen)

The Westminster Morris Men

The Kavanagh Irish Dancers

The EFDSS Orchestra

The evening was held at the St Pancras Assembly Rooms and Percy Grainger's widow attended. Jonathan accompanied Pat in "Six Dukes went a-fishing", "Died for Love" and "The Sprig of Thyme". The Choir sang "Ye Banks and Braes", "There Was a Pig Went Out to Dig", "Brigg Fair", "I'm Seventeen come Sunday" and

Pat the troubadour

---

*   A list of songs and music Pat recorded is in Appendix 6.

"Shallow Brown" for male voice chorus with Pat singing the solo part.

The words of two – perhaps not quite the usual – folk songs that Pat collected, but he loved to sing:

Stanley and Dora

Stanley and Dora were lovers.
Lived in the Charing Cross Road.
Met every night at the Mecca
Where the strawberry milk shakes flow;
She loved her man – a Lonnie Donegan fan.

Dora worked at the Dominion.
Best usherette in the flicks.
She showed Stan a seat for 4/9,
It was really worth 6/6.
He left his cosh in his mackintosh.

Dora was quickly promoted
To the circle she rose in a dream,
When who should she see but her Stanley
With a girl who sold ice-cream.

But fate took a hand for young Dora.
Stan and his Walls ice-cream
Were killed in the rush for the exit
When they played "God Save the Queen".

The Boss of the Big Rag Store

1. I was christened Michael Flynn, when in this world I entered;
   My parents had no son but me, and me their only son:
   They filled my head with learning until it could hold no more,
   Then they gave me a high position as the boss of the big rag store.

CHORUS: Then hurry up my darling, and come along with me
                     And I'll give you whisky in galore
                     If you ask for Michael Flynn you'll be sure to find him in
                     For he holds a high position, he's boss of the big rag store.

2. Pickpockin' is like any other trade, it's sometimes very slack
   When an old man came toddling in with a pack upon his back:
   And the thing that puzzles me to know, they are so ragged men,
   Is whether the man is carrying the rags or the rags is carrying them.

CHORUS

3. You should see me on a Saturday, behind the scales I stand;
   With a couple of Franks all on my arm don't I look mighty grand!
   And as I weigh out the rags by pounds it's 2 and 3 make 4.
   That shows the mighty learning of the boss of the big rag store.

CHORUS

4. Dear friends I bid you all adieu, I must be going home,
   For I've got dear old friends to see, way down in John Malone's
   And if I sing you another song, I hope it's still "encore"
   And I'll remain "Yours truly, the Boss of the Big Rag Store."

CHORUS

Pat published his own thoughts on "How to Sing a Folk Song" – published in two parts in EDS Vol. XXIV Nos 4 and 5 (see Appendix 7.)

5d. COLLEAGUES

Nan Fleming-Williams (1912 – 1991)

Nan Fleming-Williams for many years was violinist for the EFDSS. She played with Pat Shaw and Brian Fleming-Williams as "The Countryside Players" and recorded a number of Playford dances, which were arranged by Pat Shaw. This was written for the CDS magazine April 1986.

Pat Shaw was eighteen when I first met him at the 1936 Christmas School in Chelsea, London. He was a fine athletic young man, given to doing back somersaults in the capers of a Bledington morris jig. He also enchanted everybody with his singing and was a smash hit at midnight parties with his impersonations of "Diva Serina the Prime Ballerina". Those were the days!

The next time I met him, he was playing the oboe and cor anglais in the Marlborough College performance of Bach's *St John Passion*. I was also helping to swell the school orchestra, and was captivated not only by the ravishing tone he drew from his instruments, but also by his complete musicianship.

After this he disappeared for some years, busy with the studies for his Cambridge degree. But he appeared now and again at Cecil Sharp House, sometimes leading a group of fellow students in a programme of madrigals and his own arrangements of folk songs. He had grown a luxuriant walrus moustache at this stage and was very intense, as were they all.

When the war came, Pat joined the Fire Service and did his bit toward saving the cities of Coventry, Birmingham and Cardiff, but in between times he was busy at his musical pursuits and amused himself in the Fire Station Jazz Band and other concert-party activities. If he had leave he would come down to Cecil Sharp House and join in whatever was going on at the time. And when his own home in London was destroyed by a buzz-bomb, his friends were only too delighted if he chose to knock on one of their doors. Our attic became a dumping ground for his stacks of music and gramophone records, not forgetting the alphorn, which he chose to play standing in the house with the horn in the garden. Our son David grew up to the sounds of his songs and latest compositions.

Exhausted after the war, he began to collect islands, and in 1946 found himself in Shetland. These friendly islands, way out in the Atlantic above Scotland, became his northernmost home and again he disappeared. That winter he phoned from Lerwick to demonstrate to us his latest toy. He had come by an accordion and was already very good. He could rattle off the reels and jigs like any Shetlander. He told us also that he had grown a beard and that it was not red.

Whilst in Shetland he set himself to collect the rich folk-music tradition and culture of these islands. The BBC finally commissioned him to undertake this mammoth task. My husband, Brian, and I were lucky enough to be able to go with him on several occasions for the Mid-Winter Festival of Up-

Helly-Aa, when after the burning of the Viking long boat on the football pitch, there is dancing until dawn in every available hall in Lerwick. Pat, speaking the dialect like a veteran, was round the halls with the squads, but he always finished up where he'd settled us with one of the resident bands. I very quickly learned to play "The De'il among the Tailors" without missing a note whilst a whisky bottle was tipped down my throat.

On a state visit to Canada after the war, the Queen, who was still Princess Elizabeth, with Prince Phillip as her partner, was photographed square dancing and at once, overnight, this became the "in" thing to do. The Society was stretched to its limits trying to cope with a crazy situation, but this gave Pat his chance. He was in his element, not only amid the furious musical activities, but he set himself to become a top-grade caller. Dressed in his checked shirt, boots and Stetson he really hit the high spots and travelled from one end of the country to the other, so great was his popularity.

At this time, Douglas Kennedy was asked by the BBC if he would start a series of country dance programmes on the radio – and later on television also. Pat came into his own as a musician, singer and musical arranger, and it was not long before he was responsible for these half-hour programmes – not only from the West Country, where they started – but also in the London area, the Midlands and Wales.

During one visit to Shetland, Pat had pressed a group of us up there with him into giving a concert of folk music and song in aid of the Lerwick life boat.[*] We thought he was mad, but he persisted and the result was a riot. The audience shouted and whistled, clapped and stamped until the floor almost gave way. This success led to the foundation of The Countryside Players, a group originally consisting of Pat, playing accordion or guitar while he sang; Brian, also on guitar; and Jean Matthews and myself on violins. Denis Smith, another accordion player, joined us later when pressure of work caused Brian and Jean to retire. This kind of entertainment was quite novel in those days. You danced to such a band as ours but it was quite new to sit in rows listening.

This idea took off in a big way, especially as sometimes Pat would emcee a dance afterwards which we played for. There seemed no end to his inspiration. If he wasn't arranging music, singing or playing one of his several instruments, he was lecturing both at home and abroad, or conducting courses in music, dance and song. At home he loved his garden and was an excellent cook. He set himself to research the dances of John Playford and other 18th century dancing masters. Pat himself became a dancing master par excellence and was much in demand all over the country and overseas.

He was a busy and a brilliant man: generous to a fault, never tiring of passing on his knowledge and skills to others. Lucky are those of us who have

---

[*] We tried hard to find a date for this concert for the lifeboat but did not find reference to it either in the Shetland Archives, The Shetland Times newspaper from 1946 where we found the reviews which are in the Shetland section, or the RNLI archives. BG

had the pleasure and great satisfaction of being included in his life. Along-side all these memories, he has left behind him a great mass of tunes, dances and other writings. It is by these we shall all remember him as he takes his place amongst the other great folk musicians of the British Isles.

Douglas Kennedy
Director and then Vice-President of the EFDSS
Letter to Marjorie Fennessy dated 26/1/86 on receiving a copy of Pat Shaw's Pinewoods book –

We are very grateful for this kind gift for we (have) only too little memorabilia of Pat who seems to have ascended directly to Mount Olympus or some other dizzy height far from mundane UK. We miss him terribly as do so many oth-ers who were touched by his magic. For me, now nearing the century, the early scenes do not seem distant for I knew his mother when she was a girl pupil of my father's and I followed her marriage to Shuldham-Shaw and Pat's birth in 1917 in Stratford-upon-Avon with some anxiety as there was such a difference in age.

I was more like a father.

Hugh Rippon
Hugh was a member of the EFDSS staff for a number of years
I have many happy memories of Pat Shaw when I was working at CSH in the sixties. Two things in particular stand out, namely –

1. When Tony (Wales) and I were editing the magazine and we needed help on finding a dance or tune to print he was always ready and willing to help out with material, advice and information. When editing a magazine and with tight sched-ules to keep it is such a help to know that you have someone like that to fall back on and he was always unstinting in what he provided, never demanded money or copyright fees for example.

2. He was one of the few people "on high" who, like me, had a shared interest in the historical background of our dance tradition. Many in the Society simply did not want to know. Pat and I had great fun (some of it in the Spread Eagle in Parkway, Camden Town) putting together a series of interviews on the history of English Country Dancing which we published in the magazine. (See Chapter 2.)

Hugh is also quoted in the Carol Concert section, chapter 14.

John Barber
member of The Ranchers Band
I remember –

The first time he asked me to play in his Carol Concert (possibly 1966) and, although the part was beyond me, Pat was full of encouragement.

The time he gave The Ranchers a piece of music called **Rant Gone Wrong** *and when Ken Hillier – the leader of the Southerners – came to play it (for an Albert Hall do) Ken phoned me up and played it over the phone asking 'are you sure I've got the music the right way up'. Typical Pat.*

The time The Ranchers played for Pat at an anniversary dance in the West Country. Pat had composed a special dance for this group (can't remember who they were). Unfortunately it was beyond the dancers and Pat threw a wobbly. We thought it very funny!

The time he and I went for a curry in Chalk Farm and the parties at "his" house. I think he was a lodger having given most of his money away. He was by all ac-counts generous to a fault.

I remember the tremendous respect I had for him as a person and for his music. In those days I was pretty inexperienced having been playing only for a few years when we first met and to have known and played his music was a wonderful experience. Genius is a word overused but Pat had that touch of genius that as far as I can see, no one in the folk scene has today.

The last time I saw him was at Cecil Sharp House a few days before he died. He looked pretty awful, pale and sweating. I asked how he was and he said he felt dreadful. I can't remember the rest of our chat, if there was any. Of course he must have had the problem then. He died on 16 November 1977.

I'm sorry if all this is disjointed but, as I say, it's a long time ago and one is left with an impression of a man who was so clever and great fun to be with, his puns in words and music.

Brian Willcocks

Founder of The Ranchers with Norman Ellacott in 1953 and leader of the band after Norman's death.

Test Driving

In the Ranchers, we encountered periodically a challenge from Pat to cope with material which was a bit "outside the envelope". Maybe something fast and difficult (Beaumont Rag), maybe gentle, subtle and fragile **(The Waters of Holland)** *or just downright kinky* **(Rant Gone Wrong).** *Whatever the scenario, he was careful not to place us in jeopardy of embarrassment... he just gave short enough notice for the item to be piquant rather than intimidating. And maybe he relished someone else playing the stuff vicariously. His own tunes were sympathetic to a box player such as myself because they were composed via a keyboard, not strings (usually). But his hands were stubby and strong but not greatly athletic, so when I asked him how he coped with Beaumont Rag he responded along the lines of 'I usually leave such things to others'. Wise man. I often wonder whether we or the music were being tested.*

Taking Steps

When composing his dances, Pat paid close attention to the marriage of movements to avoid awkward changes of balance or direction. His dances – once grasped – flow with clarity and ease of movement. But he sometimes overestimated the dancers' ability to synchronise with his own formidable brain, and could occasionally 'lose it' as his own analytical approach became eroded by frustration.

That Brain

Pat's facility for music and language marked an interesting combination; it is not usual for a musician to cope well with language, even if – as with Pat – he was able to take on board just enough to "get by" convincingly, without becoming fluent to the natives. One would more reasonably expect a musician to display an aptitude for maths. (Ref. British Psychological Society). Well, I don't know how Pat got on with maths, but he certainly had technical attributes way beyond the manipulation of multiple salt- and pepper-pots. Long before the advent of today's computer applications like Coda Finale and Sibelius, Pat was hammering out his works on an IBM golfball music typewriter.* About as easy as juggling jelly standing up in a canoe ... many of his Shetland-collected tunes were published thus, and **New Wine in Old Bottles**. *View them in awe and reflect on the Tip-Ex bill. No-one's perfect.*

Brian is also quoted in the chapters 9 and 14.

---

* see reference to this machine in chapter 15.

Peter Boyce
musician and band leader

In about 1970 I ran a week for dancers and musicians at Halsway Manor as I sometimes did in those days. At the end of the week who should turn up but Pat Shaw who I already knew as a colleague musician. He said he had a problem for the following week. He was to take a week of dancing but he had no musician, did I know of anyone who might be free? I was able to tell him that there was someone at my school who would do very nicely on accordion and piano. This was, of course, Chris Carpenter, then Collings. I gave Chris a ring and she became Pat's musician for the week. Chris feels so pleased now as she thinks that she was probably the first musician to play for some of Pat's dances that he later published. She now realises what an honour and pivotal occasion it was. How could the 18-year-old Chris not take up playing for country dancing having been exposed to the influence of a week playing for such a giant in the folk world? Accompanying Pat was Madeline (Smith). That was another bonus.

I had known Pat from my days at Weston-Super-Mare. I led the Weston band that included such people as Lynda and Barbara Wood (Lynda is the wife of Denis Smith and Barbara is the sister-in-law of Jim Coleman), and John Brock on piano. In spite of the quality of these musicians, at one public dance that we played for at Weston Pat had to stand in front, face the band and conduct! As I was leading it was a case of mea culpa I fear.

Also in the late 50s at Weston, Geoff Rye, by then a recruited dancer, head librarian of the local library, had booked Pat for an evening of song at his library. That evening was unforgettable. Pat was in tremendous form. I remember particularly the Four Maries and some miles-out-of-character raucous Highland song. My word, he had a powerful voice but for the most part it was beautifully melodious. When calling, he always included his singing calls: The Head Two Ladies Cross Over, with the extra chorus, Billy Boy, Redwing etc.

Another incident from the early 50s I shall never forget. It concerned one of the superb courses that the Society used to run. This one was in Jersey. The cream of the Society staff were there: Nan Fleming-Williams, Douglas and Helen Kennedy, Ron Smedley, Nibs Matthews, Margaret Grant, Eileen Gunnell and, most of all, Ethyl Anderson from Liverpool, a fabulous teacher of Playford. We spent a whole week learning to dance Confess; these days we knock it off in ten minutes and think that's it. Of course, also on the staff was Pat Shaw.

When I moved to Chingford, Pat played in my band several times. On one occasion at my school, Mervyn Clayton was taking a barn dance. In the middle of quite a brisk dance a string broke on my fiddle so I withdrew to replace the string, returning just in time to catch the last chord. 'Oh', says Pat, 'That was interesting. I didn't know those tunes.' Pat was a lovely man; always friendly, uncomplaining and charming to all. What he should have said was 'Thank you Peter. Where did you get this rubbish from? I could hardly read your scribble.' Anything of that sort would have been right out of character.

In those days, I knew that Pat was special but not that special. From his approach and manner you would never know that he was by far the top all-rounder of his age, the most talented composer of music and dance, caller, singer, accordionist and raconteur. One of the best times was with Pat and me playing as a duo.

Chris says that he had a detailed knowledge of the dances he called i.e. he knew where everyone was and should be all the time. He knew how he wanted the dance to go. He was light hearted, amusing, affable, humble, modest, quietly hu-

morous (all Chris's words). She had no idea of his stature and potential stature when she played for him. She has felt, and feels now, greatly honoured to have been lucky enough to have had the opportunity.

John Stapledon
West Kirby Band

Some years later Pat was invited, again by Ethyl, to MC a big dance at Wallasey Town Hall in the Wirral at which our early West Kirby Band was also booked to play.

I can't remember what the occasion was but on looking through my files I came across a letter from Pat concerning his proposed programme for the dance. I thought you might be interested in this so I've made a copy of it for you. A pity it's not dated, but I would guess it may have been in the 70s. I was rather amused by his P.S. – I can't imagine him getting away with that nowadays! (See Letters section, chapter 15.)

I am not sure whether it was on that same occasion or at some similar event where Pat was the caller and the Mersey Morris Men gave a very relaxed performance of morris during the interval. In thanking the morris men, Pat came out with his remark – 'and now we know what Shakespeare really meant when he wrote – the Quality of Mersey is not strained'.

So far as I remember, Pat's other link with this part of the country was through the Summer School held each year at Burton Manor College in the Wirral. Again organised by Ethyl Anderson, this was a very popular residential event which took place every summer for a number of years, in which Pat was sometimes invited to share the teaching duties with Ethyl.

Jan Willcocks
An EFDSS teacher, learning to teach from Marjorie Sinclair, Thora Watkins, Nibs Matthews and Jack Hamilton. She taught the Thursday class with Hugh Rippon at CSH.

I was aware of the presence of Pat the minute I became a full member of the EFDSS in November 1955 with one of my first pay cheques.

May 6th 1960 was Princess Margaret's wedding day. That evening we danced Princess Margaret's Fancy *and Pat sang* Mairie's Wedding. *One of those "wow" moments that were possible with Pat. (Princess Margaret was then President of the EFDSS.)*

At Sunday Club we learned dances from the Isle of Man with Pat, including one (Peter O'Tavey) *to test the sobriety of guests at a wedding. Never mind a wedding... it called for intense concentration on balance, and complete sobriety! And* Mona's Delight *which included some apparently rough ankle-banging – and hurt if you got it wrong! For me the sight of Pat side-stepping nimbly across the floor with his arms aloft has stuck in my memory; Pat was no light-weight!*

Also at Sunday Club we all enjoyed the tunes and dances of the Welsh waltzes, dripping with sentiment. We learned both his own compositions and adaptations!

Pat's instructions to his crowd (at a dance) were dependent upon those he taught having an intimate knowledge of the dance. I remember him getting very cross with a roomful of West Country dancers, and they getting increasingly frustrated with him.

In 1964, Nan Fleming-Williams, Brian (Willcocks), my friend Patricia and I spent a week on a course with Pat at Bangor University. At the end of the week we were to make our way home via Llanrhaeadr-ym-Mochnant with Nan, Brian and Pat running a barn dance for Welsh farmers. It was not a happy evening... at least they enjoyed it! But those of us who were cannoned into or squashed found it tiring but very funny. In a circular dance where one faced one's partner across the circle at times, it was as if the Red Sea had parted and the centre of the room became empty! We had a delicious picnic before the event, supplied by Pat who had wildly over-catered. There was enough left for the four of us on the way home next day. We stayed with Frances Môn Jones in her lovely wavy-floored, highly polished farmhouse.

Marshfield, Gloucestershire, the home of the "Paper Boys", was one of our neighbouring villages and each year we went to watch their Christmastide perform-ance. We got chatting to Felicity Blake, who lived in the High Street with her mother and probably took us home to warm up! Pat was a frequent visitor: 'He came for quiet', Felicity told me, 'and liked to write upstairs in his room'. I gathered his stays were quite extensive. When we moved from Bath to Box, Pat reckoned we had moved from 'a flat in the bath to a house in a box'. He was right. He couldn't re-member our new address and a letter arrived addressed to: Brian Willcocks, Oppo-site a Pub, Box, Wiltshire.

Felicity went to pottery classes and gave me an ocarina in the shape of a small bird; I'm sure this was Pat's influence. It actually works quite well.

Pat could be infuriating, but we were all very fond of him. Shortly after we moved here (Newbury) in 1977 we learned that Pat had died. Mutual friends told us that Pat had told them he didn't feel well and yet could not bring himself to drop out of judging – I think it was a schools' competition – and disappoint the entrants. He was advised not to go. Poor Pat... we grieved for him.

Jan also has memories in the Royal Albert Hall and Tours sections.

Nicolas Broadbridge
musician, teacher, caller, composer of dances, publisher

The first time Nic ever saw Pat Shaw was at a Christmas Dance at CSH when he was wearing a green velvet dinner jacket which he wore a lot. Pat was not the caller at this event; it was Douglas Kennedy calling on the platform. Douglas and Helen Kennedy were in the set to show "Newcastle" – which was done in a beauti-ful Playford style even though this was pre-1962, at a time when Playford was banned at CSH, although it was still done in the Provinces. Douglas had decreed 'let the people dance' and so Playford was "out". Nicolas can still see Pat in green, dancing, he thinks, with Nan Fleming-Williams. Both she and Denis Smith were dancing that evening.

Nic's connection with Whirligigs began in 1966 when he was recruited for a country dance wedding suite at the first Broadstairs Folk Week. He had a lovely week with Whirligigs so wrote to Marjorie Fennessy to ask if he could join the group permanently. Whirligigs evenings were a lot of fun. Nic recalls how Pat used to appear saying 'I've got this little thing I've been working on'. Marjorie would say 'this isn't right let's sort it out' or that she just had 'one or two suggestions' and it was marvellous that Pat could accept them.

Nic talked with Pat when he went to a couple of Pat's "Another look at Playford" evenings at CSH in May/Jun and June/July 1969, immediately before Nic's wed-ding. He can remember doing some of the Kynaston dances that Pat had re-searched. Apparently, Pat only looked at a limited number of Kynaston Books – 1710 in particular. But he looked at so much else – Bray, Essex, Thompson, Wil-son – all that Cecil Sharp had looked at and more.

Nic knows how Pat could turn on the charm and sweep all the women before him – which was how Pat changed the face of English country dancing in America more quickly than it changed over here.

At Nic and Nell's wedding, in 1969, they wanted to do appropriate dances – *Wives Victory, Bonny Nell, We'll Wed and We'll Bed* – (which Bernard Bentley published under the title *Dublin Bay*). Nic wanted to do the latter from the original manuscript so Marjorie suggested he asked Pat to look at them. (Pat apparently was not always entirely happy with Bernard Bentley's scholarship). Pat didn't get around to looking at the dance but Marjorie did – although Nic still has the photocopy of the original that Pat did for him. He also asked Pat to arrange an Appalachian folk song that he wanted performed during the wedding – When "Adam was Created". * Pat was not able to be at the wedding, but the day before the wedding, a brown envelope was delivered and inside were lots of copies of a four-part arrangement of the song and copies of an "Amen" that Pat had based on "Searching for Lambs". The Amen was later published but not the song.

Pat's dance **The Rose of Tankerton** was new in 1969 and very popular so Whirligigs performed it at the wedding.

Whilst Nic did not go to any of Pat's famous parties in Hampstead, he remembers the gatherings at Marjorie's house with "Aunt Kit" † after Whirligigs' meetings – Pat sitting in the corner scribbling and making odd remarks whilst everyone else would be eating sausages on sticks.

One memory of Pat dancing – again in the green dinner jacket – was when he was demonstrating **Margaret's Waltz**. Nic cannot recall with whom he was dancing – but feels he knows exactly the right tempo for playing the tune. It all depends on the diagonal chassés and Nic can still see Pat going out diagonally to the right and then to the left; then turning right into the star not still holding his partners hand but turning back singly – 'it looks mucky if you keep holding on'.

Pat came to stay with Nic and Nell in Crarae, Scotland, only once – seemingly for no particular reason than he wanted to investigate the Kintyre peninsula. He was driving his mini and would always go on circular routes. Nic recalls he was a "white road man" – he liked to follow the small, sometimes unsurfaced roads. He wrote in their visitors' book "Home par excellence of shaggy dog stories – gorgeous". They have always bred Bearded Collies – very shaggy dogs.

Nicolas bought Pat's Gallanti accordion. This with other of his effects was left to John and Kathy Mitchell when he died. After Kathy died, Nic discovered that Pat's things were to be auctioned and so he attended the sale – sometime in 1990 he thinks. After a rather adventurous journey, he managed to buy "this very fine machine" as the auctioneer described it. The next lot was described as "a box of miscellaneous musical instruments". Again Nic was successful in his bidding (even though he did not know what was in the lot) and became the proud possessor of an Appalachian lap dulcimer, an African finger piano and an eight string table harp, all of which must have been Pat's.

Apparently, Pat persuaded both Vi le Maistre and Lynda Smith (both fine accordionists) to buy Gallanti accordions, another indication of his influence and enthusiasm.

When Nic was planning his CDs of Pat's tunes to mark the 25th anniversary of his death he wanted to include some of those from Books 4 and 5 of the Pat Shaw collection – tunes which do not have dances attached. Denis Smith and Nan Fleming-Williams had edited these for Marjorie Fennessy to publish. These tunes were hardly used but some are very lovely – in particular **Rosemary Brown** and

---

* See the following pages.
† Everyone called Marjorie Fennessy's mother "Aunt Kit".

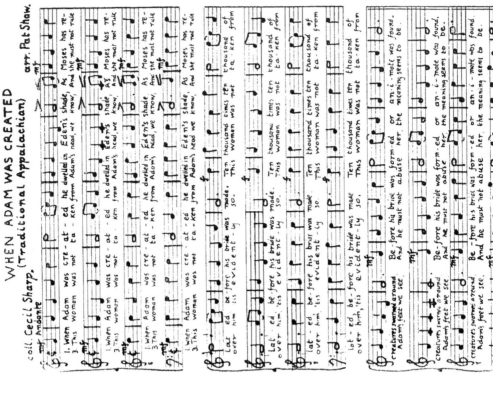

A present for

NICOLAS BROADBRIDGE

on the occasion of his wedding

from

Pat Shaw

1. A threefold AMEN based on an English folk song

2. WHEN ADAM WAS CREATED - Appalachian folk song

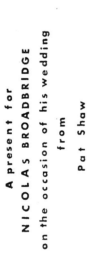

Peter Waterson's Farewell to the Holly Bush. Nic worked on tracing some of the people for whom the tunes were written. Rosemary Brown's story is written up in the Shetland section, chapter 8.

Like many, Nic wishes he had spoken more with Pat but, at the time was in awe of this great man.

Madeleine Smith
teacher, dancer and composer of dances

The first time I saw Pat Shaw, he was teaching at Burton Manor summer school, and we were dancing on the lawn. He strode purposefully up and down and be-rated us for "creeping diffidently about" – one of his favourite expressions. Of course, trying to dance with grace and verve on damp grass is not easy, but we managed it. He actually turned out not to be at all terrifying, but a witty and charm-ing person, and an excellent teacher, hoping to bring out the best in everyone.

He was modest about his own dances, and generous to a fault in giving them away. I treasure a photocopy of the hand-written instructions for **The Rose of Tankerton***. In those days, we danced mainly standard CDM and Sharp-Playford repertoire in the evenings at summer school, and he did not push his own dances. 'That was a good Dorset Four Hand Reel', he would say. He would also explain his dance interpretations and describe the research he did. As he produced more and more wonderful dances, he was persuaded to take some specific classes to teach them.*

We were at Burton when he introduced **Levi Jackson Rag***. We danced it that week at every available opportunity, and it swept the country like wildfire, causing some mayhem when callers expected bands to sight-read the tune. He was sur-prised at its popularity.*

In those days, we had a song session every day, and morris and sword classes, so we had the benefit of Pat's expertise in these fields too. Pat was steeped in the whole folk tradition, and this shows in his dances and music. Some of his dances are technically demanding, which could be why they are not done as often nowa-days. He certainly liked a variety of steps in a dance, and always hoped for good dance technique from everyone.

In the seventies, there was a national PE teachers' training week annually in Blackpool. Folk dancing was one of the options, led by Ethyl Anderson, the EFDSS North-West area representative. Pat Shaw was sometimes the musician (accordion), and he also added useful comments about calling, teaching and dancing and taught singing games. One year he spent most of the tea breaks playing and honing **Another Nancy's Fancy***. That was the year I remember the students learning the Oxo reel to the* **Levi Jackson Rag** *tune! I don't think the students realised how privileged they were! There was a huge barn dance (we did not call them ceilidhs then) for all the students one evening in the magnificent Winter Gardens Ballroom, with Pat as caller with the Bs Band. He was a wonderful barn dance caller, and did some singing squares as well. I learned more about calling and teaching on these courses than on some national ones aimed at experienced dancers and call-ers!*

Another memory is playing **Round Pond** *with Pat and Chris Carpenter at a Halsway Manor week. Chris and I were on recorders, Pat on whistle, or possibly recorder.*

June Wilson-Lay
dance teacher for the ISTD and the EFDSS (notes from the NVS album pre-sented to Pat by the NVS to mark his 25 years in Holland)

I was a teacher of many branches of dancing. It was whilst at the Ballroom studio during the square-dance craze that I was asked to get in touch with Mr Shuldham-Shaw at Cecil Sharp House. He was not an easy person to find, letters went unanswered, he seemed quite elusive. However, we did meet at a special course for Ballroom teachers.

Even now, I smile when I remember the questions that were asked and the evasive answers, but not by Pat. Most of the teachers there realised that there was money to be made in their "Happy Hoe Downs" to keep the public happy. I realised that there was more to it than that and with Pat's gentle guidance found myself at a Playford evening.

Another thing that sticks was his love and knowledge of music. Too many dance teachers lacked any musical appreciation and this, to me, was impossible to understand.

Thinking back over the years, several little incidents flash through my mind. Pat, in his 10-gallon hat and full regalia driving Harriet (his tiny car) after a square dance party; Pat in Yugoslav costume taking a group of friends to see the Yugoslav dancers then performing at a London theatre and afterwards to a Yugoslav restaurant, all drinking Slivovitz.

Pat, hand-standing in our garden at home and father timing him. Pat performing the tango with great dexterity. Pat speaking Portuguese fluently at the Festival in Oporto. I could go on endlessly.

Hugh and Rosemary Gentleman

Excerpts from a letter to Marjorie Fennessy 30.6.2008. Rosemary, then Rosemary Redpath, worked as a secretary for Sibyl Clark in the Midlands EFDSS Office. The office was in a building owned by the CAB whose Director was E. J. Nicol, a great supporter of the EFDSS.

Sibyl met me in 1954 and I worked there from 1956 until 1965. The office used to arrange adult and youth weekend courses: dance, song, musicians, MC training and large festivals at Stratford-on-Avon and at the Central Hall in Birmingham. I got to know Pat when he ran folk song weekends at Barford, was soloist at some of our Festivals and also appeared with Nan and Denis as the Countryside Players etc.

In 1957 I won the unaccompanied folk song solo at the first of the EFDSS Folk Music Festivals at CSH with Sydney Northcote and Michael Bell as adjudicators. A boost for an outsider from Birmingham! I see looking back at the programme that Pat was listed on the organising festival committee. The competitive nature of the Festival was at odds with what was happening to song around the country, so the following year it was just a shop window for singers and musicians. In 1958, wanting a local singer, Pat asked me to illustrate a talk he was giving, on the BBC Third Programme, about Herefordshire Carols collected by Lavender Jones – though he had to come up to the Midlands in order to teach them to me.

At a Barford folk weekend in the spring of 1963 Pat introduced those attending to a few songs he had collected from refugees from Tristan da Cunha. The only one I have words for is The Rich Merchant's Daughter as sung by Mary Repetto. Presumably they exist in the Library somewhere. In 1960 the British had "rescued" the residents after a volcanic eruption threatened to devastate the island and the opportunity to record their songs and tales appealed to Pat. However, most of them *returned home within two years, not liking the UK and its climate!*

When Pat came to Birmingham for such things as festivals or rehearsals he would come and dine with us – always a challenge as Pat was such a good and inventive cook himself, as we discovered when he came to live with us. I will never forget a killer "starter" he devised – haggis omelette.

We moved to Liverpool and Ethyl Anderson sometimes invited Pat to MC a special occasion, or to adjudicate music festivals in Liverpool, so we did keep in touch there, though not with such regularity.

In 1968 a move again, to Edinburgh. Hugh to a job in the Scottish Office and me to the History Department at the University. Hugh was part of the Research Staff (i.e. in-house research into social policy issues) covering various planning, housing, social surveys etc. One of the early odd-ball jobs he was given in 1969 was to go out and count Scotland's Travelling People: Gypsies/travellers is currently the "politically correct" term. Up here our active folk involvement dwindled as the Scots didn't particularly want to listen to English music at that time. Nor could we pretend to sing Scots, though interest in the School of Scottish Studies remained, both through Hugh's Traveller interests and then Pat's.

Pat would occasionally stay overnight or for a weekend on his way to Aberdeen where the Greig/Duncan manuscripts were kept under lock and key, while discussion raged about access and finance, and in the spring of 1972 (we don't have exact dates I'm afraid) Pat said that he would be spending more time in Aberdeen and Edinburgh – he was to edit the Greig/Duncan material. When the original records were eventually transferred to Edinburgh he also announced he would be coming to live with us on a more regular basis.

We then lived at 29, Great King Street, in half of a Georgian terrace house. You will know that he taught himself Pitman's Shorthand in order to transcribe the songs before linking them to the music, and many a slightly tipsy evening we had working out obscure shorthand outlines. He was not with us full time, since he had commitments with local authorities down south, on-going involvement with his choirs, dances, festivals, Playford evenings and the full gamut of Pat's interests, at home as well as in Holland. He had decided to tutor himself in the art of fine single-malt whisky while in Edinburgh and a cheque for expenses from a local authority rapidly meant a new and possibly obscure bottle appearing on his mantelpiece. It was not quaffed. Small thimbles-full were discreetly poured for Pat and Hugh to savour and identify. I do not enjoy the taste. The game was the thing, not the drinking! While here he also devised a "puzzle" for his friends, and colleagues in the School of Scottish Studies. The prize, I recall, was £1 out of Pat's own pocket. I enclose a copy "Pat-turn of Islands" – I don't think we ever had the fully completed result, though someone in SSS did win the £1. (See appendix 4.)

Pat was always anxious to break down musical barriers and in December1975 he arranged a seasonal concert for the Edinburgh University Chamber Music Club: he collected a choir from various members of staff to perform a programme of his own international compositions and arrangements, and slipped us in to sing a medley of folk carols. Things rarely heard in that august company!

He was a friendly and interested person, collecting odd – and sometimes strange – people from Edinburgh's musical and academic circles. On many occasions we would come home from work ready to flop to find that Pat had offered our large drawing room as rehearsal space to the Edinburgh Quartet and Leonard Friedman, or as a meeting place for a discussion session which started off at the University Staff Club and then drifted down the hill to our house! He also liked entertaining.

Sometimes we were included in one of his excellent surprise dinner parties – at our own dining table! We had just one bathroom then, and Pat's need to talk and reminisce, usually late at night, often caught one or other of us on the way to or from the bathroom while he expounded on some recently remembered verse, or problem: him resplendent in an old but colourful dressing-gown (complete with a long loosely tied hairnet) while relentlessly pursuing us as we edged our way backward towards our room or the toilet.

You will know all about his involvement with the School of Scottish Studies, just across George Square from where I worked. Emily Lyle has been magnificent in that regard – and meticulous in giving Pat full recognition for all the work he did. We have been invited to many of the publication launches as the volumes came out and also to the final roundup launch and reception, where there was a lovely photograph of Pat on an easel, and some warm and tender comments about his life and contributions to the folk life of the country.

When my parents were to come and live with us, we started looking for a larger property, so it was clear that Pat would have to look for other digs when he needed to be in attendance in Edinburgh, until all was settled. That was when he moved to 11 Ettrick Road, into a self-contained flat, which suited him rather better. Sadly I cannot recall the name of the nice family who owned the flat and a check through old address books does not help. Hugh thinks Pat actually lived with us for only 6-8 months, though we were in touch with him regularly the whole of the time he was here and exchanged gourmet meals and outings and he and I met regularly for lunch at the University Staff Club.

We did eventually find ourselves a three-storey Georgian house, with garden, one street up the hill from Great King Street. It was in an unloved and derelict state and uninhabitable. We had to rent a flat ourselves while major structural and other work was done. It wasn't resolved whether Pat could rejoin us when Northumberland Street was eventually finished and it was during the latter months of upheaval that Pat died down south – still in harness. Indeed, it was Lynda Smith who phoned to tell us the news. We did come to the memorial service in London, but there were so many attending it was not possible to catch up with everyone.

So I am afraid, we do not have much to add. We feel privileged to have known him and enjoyed his talent. We have regular reminders of him, e.g. whenever we have Cotherstone cheese we are reminded that Pat introduced it to our household, getting his supplies from the post-office in the village whenever he passed on his way through the Borders.

We got to know his step-brother Chris and kept in touch for a while after he returned Emily Lyle's car to Edinburgh (Pat had been lent the VW during her absence in Australia and had it with him in the south when he died.) He also claimed Pat's records, books and whisky. He intended to donate the records etc. to CSH which I hope he did, since it was a unique collection which we had sometimes looked after for Pat, who introduced us to (or reawakened an interest in) Bartok and Neilsen which has continued. He really did influence everyone with whom he came in contact. I am staggered to realise 2007 was the 90th anniversary of his birth.

Bert Cleaver
Morrisman – ex Squire of the Morris Ring

Bert's school in London started a folk dance club and they went to CSH which was still a wreck after the bombing (he recalls that as you danced clouds of dust rose up) and then to the premises in Albany Street whilst the rebuilding of CSH was being done. So he first came across Pat Shaw as a square dance Caller and particularly liked his singing calls,

Bert joined Greensleeves Morris Men in 1953 and they went to the Thaxted meeting one year but not a whole team could go. So a scratch side with Ron Smedley and Bob Parker and Pat was got up. After the feast they were dancing in Town Street which has quite a slope. They were dancing *Leapfrog* and Bert had to go over Pat uphill – which Bert still recalls as quite a feat.

Later Bert got to know him better at the EFDSS Stratford-on-Avon summer schools. In 1955, when Bert was in the army doing National Service, he just went to visit the Summer School in Stratford and got greeted with great delight and asked by Ken Clark could he stay and teach the morris class for the week. So he did and Pat was his musician.

The next year Bert spent six weeks at Mons Officer Cadet School, Aldershot. Kathleen Bliss and Elsie Whiteman (the Benacre Band) invited him to lunch one Sunday and arranged for Pat to pick Bert up. Pat arrived in a new black Citroen car (these were the French Police cars at the time). 'These cars are front wheel drive and so you don't have to slow down at roundabouts', said Pat – and proceeded not to do so!

Then Bert was recruited into Pat's square dance programmes on radio and TV. The programmes had a scratch morris team dancing during them – again, scratch being Ron Smedley, Bob Parker, Nibs Matthews and such like!

In 1957/58 Bert was living in Gloucester and Nibs and Jean (Matthews) were in Cheltenham as Nibs was the EFDSS representative for the region. Pat would insist on cooking. Jean was a very tidy cook and always kept her kitchen clear, but Pat was very messy and left the entire area in a terrible state.

Whilst at Cheltenham, with Nibs and Jean, Pat got hold of a Basque three-hole pipe. These are tuned totally differently from ours which are tone-tone-semitone whilst a Basque pipe is tone-semitone-tone. Bert saw Pat three months later and asked how he was getting on with it and he said he could now play the *Winster Processional*. As Pat could "play any instrument", Bert thought this showed how difficult the Basque three-hole pipe must be.

During his teaching for the RAH Festivals and TV, Pat found that "carol" originally meant a dance as well as a song. So he taught a dance and Bert played the pipe and tabor. Bert was often roped in by Pat for various events.

Pat was a great character, a wonderful musician and a crisp accordion player – he could play well for the rapper on the accordion. He was great company, a wonderful dancer and teacher and very light on his feet considering he was a big man. He never seemed to have a stable financial position, he was always either rolling in money or stony broke.

Pat said to Bert that he had had another look at the Lichfield morris hey – which is a sixteen-bar hey instead of the usual eight-bar. Pat thought it should be the normal length but never did get back to Bert, and so he never did find out more about this thought.

Ivor Allsop
Swordsman – ex Squire of the Morris Ring

I first came across the membered body, as opposed to the dismembered body, of Pat in the Autumn of 1952. We, Joyce and myself, had been members of the Sheffield Teachers' Folk Dance Club and three weeks after our wedding I left Joyce to go and work as a display man at the Swindon Co-operative Society and so looking for something to do during the week I joined the Swindon Folk Dance Club. They were in the middle of rehearsals for the EFDSS Wiltshire Area Folk Dance Festival and Competition. I filled in on an "as and when" basis at practices. The judge at this competition and MC for the evening dance was to be Pat Shaw. The competition was for country, sword and morris dances. There were several teams of country dancers and boys' sword teams but only one morris club, White Horse Morris Men, and they had chosen to perform a Fieldtown dance. During his summation Pat told them that their galleys needed working on and with great suppleness he demonstrated what he meant, doing a galley on the right and then on the left leg in such a charming and nice way as not to cause any offence. This manifested itself again when he made points of style to the country dances.

Years later when I was researching the Papa Stour Sword Dance I wrote to Alan Bruford at the School for Scottish Studies and he passed on my letter to Pat who eventually wrote to me several times about the dance (see Academic section chapter 6 and letters section chapter 15). I also had several phone calls from him during which we discussed various aspects of the dance such as the step and how the main beat kept changing from one foot to another, did they change feet to accommodate this change of emphasis or not ("not" in this case). He did say 'that Yorkshire sword dancers could not really perform the step as they were too genteel, the step was a very heavy tramp, not the neat step of all the Yorkshire sword dances'. This was also Tom Flett's view when he came to a couple of Barnsley practices when we were learning the dance. When I asked how many times the team would go through a particular figure when they were dancing out he said as often as the captain wanted. When I pushed him on this he said 'As long as the whisky lasts'. He then told the story about when he had been watching them perform, a bottle of malt was produced and this was passed round the team and they continued to dance and then another and another. They only stopped dancing when the whisky stopped flowing. I am sure that this is an apocryphal story or an urban myth.

Pat mentioned that the person to contact was George Peterson, who was the school muster at Brae and I'm sure that George and Pat would have got on well together as George had taught the dance to numerous boys at the school. Among the papers Pat sent me was a copy of an annotated notation for the dance which he had from N. O. M. Cameron. This rang a bell as I had already been sent a copy of

The Papa Stour Sword Dance at the Albert Hall Festival.

this by Geoff Trewinnard, who was then the Greensleeves Squire. Cameron was the founder (in 1926) and first Squire of Greensleeves Morris Men; again the story goes that in 1929 he had to return home to Bressay to take over the lairdship but whether the previous laird was a relation I have been unable to find out. He was also the first editor of the EFDS News, founded in 1921 and the forerunner of English Dance & Song, which he also gave up on his return to Shetland. Presumably Cameron and George Peterson would have been acquainted but this is not an absolute, what is certain is that Pat and George Peterson were known to each other.

Jonathan Cohen
musician, choirmaster

Jonathan is a professional musician, being an accompanist, a composer and a conductor. His choir, The Co-operation, sang frequently at the annual Carol Concerts that Pat was involved in presenting at CSH. Jonathan and Marjorie Fennessy recorded their reminiscences together. Jonathan recalls that –

Pat was extraordinarily versatile – a real Renaissance Man. It's hard to compartmentalise him (like Percy Grainger in the music field). Pat was so good at so many different things. He could create dances, play instruments, sing in every language under the sun and he made very complex musical arrangements.

He was avant-garde using extraordinary dissonances – very experimental – trying everything. Some of his experimental ones don't quite work because he was trying to be too clever. He did experiment very early on with computer music. Pat was very witty with his arranging. He'd get quotes in from other composers. He'd do something very clever – very Oxford/Cambridge. Pat was just a very, very, very good musician – he must have been an inspiration for so many people. He was one of those creative people.

I couldn't quite marry up the academic, intellectual side of Pat Shaw. I was terribly impressed by this side of Pat, because I assumed he was the folk dancing end of things. It was fun – being between amateur and professional – things would go hideously wrong, but nobody really cared. That sort of wonderful feeling like you were making music in your own room, which is quite interesting for me, having come from somewhere that was so disciplined (i.e. the Royal Academy of Music). Things used to go wrong a lot – but it was the atmosphere at the Christmas Carol Concerts that made them so popular. Everything was on scraps of paper. When the final version came, the choir would say 'Oh thank God, we can read it at last!'

Pat was pretty exotic in a way. He always used to seem so slightly apart from everybody. Even at CSH he seemed to be apart, so, when he came in, it was as if he thought 'Oh, it's an event'. I used to think that, but maybe that's because that's the way I perceived it, or him. He had huge charisma – all I can remember is that his eyes would be very set back – sort of half closed – and his beard jutting out. He would go off into his own world and not listen to you. He was in his own time zone. He didn't take much notice of what real time was. Perhaps that's why he was a terrible driver. He was very scary, because he'd just lose concentration. What on earth was going on in that brain?

I think Pat had a pretty good life really, thinking about it – certainly a very full life. Though, I think all the time worrying about money. He survived with difficulty – I think people "bailed him out" a lot, that's why he started writing dances for people. Without a permanent job he'd have had nothing to live on. But he gave himself – like a wandering minstrel – singing for his supper.

Like a cuckoo – he appeared in people's nests every so often – sort of took up residence. He was a comfortable person to be with so it wasn't difficult or awk-

ward. *He seemed to turn up at people's houses with his washing. But he was looked after, people made sure he had a meal and a place to sleep. He was very thoughtful though – he would always turn up with something as a present.*

I remember going round one day to a party – sometimes some of us would go to his home in Abernethy House, Mount Vernon, Hampstead. Pat was very good at cooking. He loved gardening, particularly Clematis and collected miniature malt whiskies.

Pat said to me 'You probably won't know, there's this wonderful concert pianist staying here called John Lill'. He wasn't very well known then. He said 'right he's going to play something'. I said 'Can you play Chopin's Ballades, you know the one in G?' He said 'Oh, which one?'

Pat knew all the great musicians of his time like Vaughan Williams and singers like Alan Lomax and Jack Langstaff. Pat's dance **Another Nancy's Fancy** *or* **The Lang Staff** *was composed for Jack's wife.*

It would have been interesting if Novello or one of the big publishing companies had published some of Pat's stuff, because I think then it would have got to a much wider audience. I don't think he sent his works out for publishing. He probably could have done rather well on all the choral stuff. He did fantastic arrangements for The Choir such as The Apple Tree Wassail.

Pat was childlike in his love of puns. (Pat said he inherited that form of humour from his Victorian father.) He did this "Pat-turn of Islands". You had to spot the 101 Islands in his piece of prose. Every now and again there was a gap and you filled in an island. (See Appendix 4.)

He was an intense man, a one-off

Marjorie Fennessy

friend, collaborator, teacher of dance, leader of The Whirligigs dance team

Marjorie recorded her memories on a tape with Jonathan Cohen. Various pieces from this recording have been used throughout this project, some are attributed, and here are the rest of her recollections:

In the early days Pat was having quite a battle with the establishment. Because Sharp had written it down, he was 101% correct. Pat always recognised that Sharp had done a wonderful job, but Sharp really had no one to exchange views with. Nothing had changed in the Society during the twenty years since Sharp's death.

He was a very comfortable dancer to dance with. The first time I remember dancing with him as my partner was at a demonstration by the EFDSS HQ team at the Grosvenor House Hotel, Park Lane, London, on 22 July 1947. Helen Kennedy could not go and I went in her place, sewn into her skirt! The last time I danced with Pat was to show **Silver for the Matthews** *for Nibs and Jean at their Silver Wedding Party at the Rembrandt Hotel, Kensington on 18 April 1975, where Pat was MC and The Ranchers provided the music.*

He was remarkably agile on his feet. He was very athletic as a young man – a good morris dancer. In later years he had heart trouble and could not dance.

One of the many things Pat taught me was to think about a dance. If something is not comfortable to do, what could make it so. This is why most of Pat's dances flow so well – always facing in the right direction for the next movement.

If he was thinking up a dance he would be viewing the ceiling and wandering around.

I think he was worried, of course, about money every now and then. But, on the other hand, he would always come to visit with something, even if he hadn't money to buy anything. He would always bring you a present. He was always very kind.

He seldom had his own car – he usually hired one when needed – usually a mini. As you know, he was a big man, so to see him with all his worldly goods piled into it was quite a sight, especially if he had the alpenhorn as well!

He certainly had a presence and a much wider view of everything.

Pat Shaw and Miss Marjorie Sinclair (1890-1971). "Sinner" taught the EFDSS advanced country and morris class which Pat attended.

6. PAT THE ACADEMIC

Pat's academic talents were expressed in his various roles as collector, linguist, researcher and editor as well as in his articles in the Folk Music Journal and his work for the EFDSS and other committees.

The section on the Shetland Isles shows how Pat methodically went about collecting traditional tunes that had not been written down before. **Hamish Henderson** wrote in his obituary for Pat:

His greatest *coup* in the Northern Isles was, however, his recovery of a version of "King Orfeo" (Child 19) from John Stickle of Baltasound, Unst, in April 1947 (Scottish Studies 20: 124). Bronson expressed the importance of the discovery very well when he wrote (in Traditional Tunes of the Child Ballads vol. I, p. 275): "That a tune should in the midst of the twentieth century be recovered for this whisper from the Middle Ages was as little to be expected as that we should hear *The horns of Elfland faintly blowing*." Pat's recording of this rarest of ballads can be heard on Topic LP I2T 160 (Child Ballads, No. 1)

Pat wrote an article in the EFDSS Folk Music Journal of 1947 concerning this find which is different in style from that in the Child text and fills in some of the gaps in that text. It is also different in that it has little trace of the Shetland dialect.*

He also "collected" the Papa Stour Sword dance and took it to a wider audience – he taught it to many teams, including to the Reading University Group. Pat wrote a four page letter to Ivor Allsop in May 1976† which contains his thoughts on the dance and the people he had met whilst notating it. The Shetland Archives have the recording Pat made of the dance in 1951 – complete with the hiss of a Tilly Lamp (Pat had hung the microphone on the same hook as the lamp).

He went on a collecting tour with Maud Karpeles, Secretary to Cecil Sharp and later Secretary of the International Folk Music Council, into the Forest of Dean, in August 1952 where they found new and interesting versions of "The Cherry Tree Carol" and "The Holly and the Ivy". "The Cherry Tree Carol" appeared on the front of ED&S for the November/December 1956 edition (Vol. XXI No. 2) and on BBC recording BBC 18618. "The Holly and the Ivy" appeared in ED&S Winter/Christmas edition 1969 (Vol. XXI No. 4) and on BBC archive record BBC 18619 and Caedmon TC 1224/Topic 12T197 Folk Songs of Britain and Ireland Series (Songs of Ceremony) BBC 18620.

Pat also collected some dances in Herefordshire – Figure Eights from Peterchurch (ED&S Winter 1966) and from Weobley and Madley.

Pat also recorded Mrs Cecilia Costello of Birmingham, the recordings appearing on Leader LEE 4054. He recorded extensively in Shetland in 1952, some recordings appearing on BBC discs 18621-18624 and 18646-18652. The Shetland Archive also has recordings of Pat singing and talking.

---

* Notes for an article about the finding of King Orfeo – see Appendix 8.
† See Appendix 9.

Tales of his linguistic abilities abound – **Hamish Henderson** again:

Pat was a marvellous linguist and he was capable of picking up not only new languages but also dialects and *patois* with seemingly effortless ease. (When the cast of *Umabatha*, the Zulu "Macbeth", visited the School of Scottish Studies recently, he was heard speaking to them in their native tongue.)

Joy and Lionel Parkhouse remembered – *He frequently spent the night with us, and we were amused to learn that his interest in languages had led him to compose a notebook with "I love you" in over fifty foreign tongues. It was therefore not surprising that he always referred to us not as the Parkhouses but as the Parkhice.*

His services as a reviewer and a writer of obituaries were frequently called upon. He wrote an article on the Ashover Book, a review of "The Scottish Folksinger" by Norman Buchan and Peter Hall in 1973, Tom Flett's obituary in 1976 to name a few. Plus numerous articles in both of the EFDSS publications – ED&S and the Folk Music Journal – on many subjects.*

Article by Pat Shaw on the Ashover Book

In view of the recent reissue of the so-called "Ashover Book" a few remarks about the dances might be appropriate. The book bears the date 1775 but the majority of dances contained in it are probably rather earlier; indeed the Russian Dance is dated 1764. It seems probable that the dances contained in David Wall's Ms book were popular in Ashover in his time, but that they were not part of a local tradition is shown by the fact that many of them appear in printed collections of the period, particularly in Johnson's collections of Country Dances, which were published mostly during the 1750s. When the Sheffield Branch of the EFDSS originally published a selection of five of these dances in 1927, they wisely included photostat copies of the originals so that anybody could try out his own interpretation. It is a pity that these have been omitted in republishing. One statement in the introduction to the 1927 edition, which calls for comment is concerning the use of the symbols referring to the musical phrases. The editors claim they are inaccurate. I am quite convinced they are perfectly accurate as the dances in which they occur are all copied from printed sources. I must also confess that I believe that the editors in the main are quite mistaken in their interpretation of these dances. The versions that I give of the four republished dances at the end of this article are based on descriptions in Nicolas Dukes "Concise and Easy Method of learning the Figuring part of country Dances by way of characters" 1752 and comparison with many published collections of country dances of this period.

I do not for one moment suggest that these have greater artistic merit than the Sheffield branch versions. Black Boy, for instance, is originally a dull dance for all except the leading couples; but in dancing the Sheffield interpretations let us be honest and realise we are taking part in dances entirely 20th century in origin and don't let us pretend that, apart from the tunes, they have much connection with what was danced by David Wall in Ashover in the eighteenth

---

* See Appendix 10 Publications.

century. In considering the versions given below, let us remember that every longways dance was danced until all had returned to their places, so that every couple had their turn at leading the dance. For practical purposes to-day the practice of the Royal Scottish Country Dance Society of using four-couple sets, so that each couple leads the figure twice, had much to recommend it

As regards the whole question of step, the position is far from clear, and is beyond the scope of this article. Now let us consider each of the four dances in detail.

Pat was a thorough researcher of Playford, 17th and 18th century and traditional dances. Cecil Sharp was one of the first to research Playford and at the time was virtually alone in the field. Whilst Pat always acknowledged Cecil Sharp's work in this field, he did not always agree with his original findings. Indeed Cecil Sharp himself, in his introduction to Book 6 of the Country Dance Books, admitted he could be wrong in his interpretation of siding and that it should be done in the way now known as "Pat's siding"; but Cecil Sharp felt it was not the time for him to change his interpretation. For this Pat researched and rediscovered many dances of the 17th and 18th centuries from the original books in the Vaughan Williams Memorial Library and developed his new interpretations of figures and movements. Pat's dances and music were based on the early dances but were unmistakably stamped with his own personality. His researches into the Playford manuscripts led to his "Another Look at Playford" monthly dance series on Monday evenings in CSH.*

In August 1959 a letter from **Phil Jukes** written to **Beryl Jukes** states: *I am in the library at Cecil Sharp House. Pat Shaw is here, typing away – he is cataloguing the Gilchrist collection – every so often I hear strange mutterings from his table and he then gets up and searches madly through various volumes of reference. He told me over lunch that he has traced the origins of "When I first came to this land" to a Danish singing game – this information he gleaned from the collection he is working on.*

But he is most remembered, academically, for the Gavin Greig and Reverend James B. Duncan collection of Aberdeenshire folk song which he worked on for the last five years of his life. This collection, *The Greig-Duncan Folk Song Collection* was published in eight volumes between the years 1981 and 2002. Pat was uniquely fitted for this work as he had already, years before, probably in the 1960s, looked through the collection at the University of Aberdeen and spent a long time making a card index of all the songs.

Apparently Paul Duncan, the Rev. Duncan's grandson realised that Aberdeen University did not actually own the manuscripts and that the family had some rights to them. As Paul was based in England, he took two of them to the EFDSS and asked if they would be of interest to them. Presumably he went to the Library at Cecil Sharp House and so Pat Shaw probably saw them there.

The first move towards publication came from the EFDSS, according to the Introduction to Volume 8 of the work, when a letter from Ruth Noyes, the librarian at CSH from 1961-69, came to the School of Scottish Studies (SSS) in Edinburgh in July 1967. She suggested an integrated approach between the EFDSS, Aberdeen University and the SSS with a selection of perhaps 80 – 100 songs. The SSS held a meeting as the result of this letter and, by 1968, were stating *the desirability of a scheme which would ensure the full publication of all the material over a period of years.*

---

*   See Chapter 5b.

It was decided that the whole collection should be published because the inclusion of all versions of a song is its strength. The EFDSS suggested Patrick Shuldham-Shaw as editor – perhaps their suggestion of the joint approach came with him in mind. Certainly, it has been recalled that Pat himself, as a secondary consideration, had had health problems and wanted to stop travelling around the country so much. He had been advised that he needed to have a less hectic life style than he was currently having in the dancing and singing world. Perhaps he thought that editorial life would be quieter. (If so, **Dr Emily Lyle**, of the SSS, thinks he may have over-estimated this!)

Dr Lyle first met Pat at the preliminary meetings about this great collection held in Aberdeen University library. *Everyone knew about it* but she wonders if anyone else would have taken it on – *perhaps Pat Shaw was a catalyst and maybe he was being a bit unrealistic.* Professor John McQueen – the Director of the SSS from 1970 – obtained grants for the project when he first took up his post, about the same time as Emily joined the School in 1970. Some big grants were obtained but were quickly expended on preparation so the School had to keep re-applying for further funding to keep up the momentum of the work in progress.

Pat Shaw moved to Edinburgh in 1972 to begin his work on the collection. Although the manuscripts were held at Aberdeen University, they were sent to Edinburgh for Pat to work on – they made up a bulky van load. It is apparently very unusual for such a thing to happen. Pat had obviously impressed them at the University of Aberdeen when he went there earlier.

He worked in the basement of the main library where the Special Collections Department was housed. Now the Department is on the top floor. **Pat Robertson** met Pat whilst he was still in the basement and recalls:

I had heard a radio programme about Pat's work for the School of Scottish Studies on the massively ambitious Greig-Duncan Folksong Collection. Having been involved in the folk song of the north east world when in Aberdeen, and having time on my hands while my children were small (probably around 1974-ish), I asked whether I could offer any voluntary help. I met Pat with Emily Lyle to discuss what I might do. I remember him as a strong presence, dark-bearded and hospitable. He was very welcoming, and gave me the interesting task of transcribing some manuscript letters received by the Rev. James Duncan.

A substantial amount of the material written out by Duncan was in shorthand. When Emily began to work with Pat Shaw, she learned shorthand in order to be able to read the folk songs as she did most of the transcriptions. Pat himself already knew shorthand. The Reverend Duncan had given a lecture to the Aberdeen Wagner Society about folk song collecting, the notes for which were written in shorthand so Pat and Emily also transcribed them.

Dr Lyle recalls that – *He was very thorough and had an insightful and sensitive approach to the material. The two things that excited him most were working with the music and thinking of the people who had sung the songs – the words were not a major problem, he thought of them as more of a secretarial task.* She thinks he would have liked to follow up the families – to find and involve them and to write about individual singers. Indeed, he did meet a few of the Aberdeen folk families.

Pat worked a great deal on his own whilst Emily transcribed the shorthand texts. In connection with funding applications people would ask him questions about how many of different kinds of songs there were in the collection and he would start over counting them again. He would always be willing to answer specific queries.

It was Pat Shaw who worked out how the final publication should be presented – the general headings and the number of sub-groups for each of the eight volumes and how they should look. He had wanted to print out all the music on a machine he had got from America – he was always very keen on the "state of the art" and wanted to be up to the minute with technology.* He had another machine for printing the words.

Pat had prepared a mock up with a few songs of how he thought it would look but, reprinting all the music, would have involved masses of preliminary work. When he died, as the actual publishing of the work had not started, one of the first major decisions was whether to reprint the music or to reproduce photographically the originals that Greig and Duncan had produced. The latter course was adopted.

Emily feels that Pat was very happy working in Edinburgh. The department had a system of morning and afternoon teas, which would have been very popular with him. His friends at the School of Scottish Studies recall that there was never a more popular adopted member of the School staff which gave good reason for their deep and poignant sense of loss at his death. Shortly before his death it had been decided that he should become an Honorary Fellow of the University.

As Pat had laid the foundation for the final look of the edition, it was only necessary to *pour in the songs* to his framework.

Volume 1 was published in 1981, Volume 2 in 1983, Volume 3 in 1987, Volume 4 in 1990, Volume 5 in 1995, Volume 6 in 1995, Volume 7 in 1997 and the final, eighth volume of this collection was published in 2002. So the mammoth task took fifteen years after his death to complete. Dr Emily Lyle worked with Pat almost from the beginning and took on the general editing of the collection whilst fully acknowledging that she was building on the foundations laid by Patrick Shuldham-Shaw.

In 1973 when he was engaged in making the importance of the collection known, he wrote an article on the collection. The bulk of the article appears in the Introduction to Volume 1 and shows how he devoted such energy and enthusiasm to the project. The Introduction by the General Editor, Dr Emily Lyle, states in the Introduction to each volume how

> the original Editor, Patrick Shuldham-Shaw cast the whole collection into eight volumes and, since his work laid the foundation for the entire collection his name appears on the title page together with the names of the subsequent editors.

> If Patrick Shuldham-Shaw had not been enthusiastic about the prospect of being editor, it is very likely that the scheme would not have got off the ground when it did.

Emily was in America when Pat died but she had seen him shortly before she left and thought he seemed tired. She wonders if he would have worked so hard if he did not need the financial security the task provided. Indeed, it is thought by others that the worry over whether more grant funding would become available contributed to his death. Emily recalled how *he was very aware of his mother's*

---

* See also mention of this machine in sections on Pat in America (chapter 11) and Pat through his Letters (chapter 15).

mantle and how he became very alive when on stage. He lived in two different worlds and so could be both an introvert and an extrovert. After an evening at the Saltire Society, he told Emily that *he liked Scottish audiences as he could draw them in to singing a song with him.*

It has been said that *Emily Lyle has been magnificent and meticulous in giving Pat full recognition for all the work he did. At the final roundup launch and reception, there was a lovely photograph of Pat on an easel, and some warm and tender comments about his life and contributions to the folk life of the country.*

RESEARCH AND PUBLICATIONS GROUP OF THE TRADITIONAL MUSIC AND SONG ASSOCIATION OF SCOTLAND

Pat was a member of this group – other members included Dr Alan Bruford, Peter Cooke, Hamish Henderson, John Macinnes, Miss Morag McLeod, Mrs Ailie Munro, Fred Macauley and Peter Shepheard (the secretary).

In late January 1974 Pat wrote to his fellow members about his concerns that only himself, the secretary and Fred Macauley turned up for a scheduled meeting and so it had to be considered an unofficial meeting. Included with this letter was a questionnaire asking if people wished to remain an active member of the committee. Obviously, Pat took his membership of such groups very seriously.

EFDSS COMMITTEES

Pat was a member of the Editorial Board of the Folk Music Journal from 1948 till his death and a member of the Vaughan Williams Memorial Library Committee until his death.

7. SING FOR PLEASURE (SfP AND SCAM)

Sing for Pleasure was first introduced into England in 1964 by A Coeur Joie's founder, Cesar Geoffray. Avril Dankworth, sister of jazz musician Johnny, made a significant contribution to SfP in its early days and introduced Pat to the movement. He became a pioneer of SfP. In his job as a roving folk singer, he took SfP's songs and philosophy wherever he went – in schools, folk clubs and on teachers' courses. He composed many songs, rounds and jingles for them, and also arranged songs and conducted.

He is remembered as being – *big and played a big accordion. He introduced folksy English songs such as "All Round my Hat"*. He also introduced Hebrew dances and songs such as "Simi Jadech" and "Hevenou". On one foreign tour he had the choir doing "Cries of London" and it is recalled that they had to dress in 19th-20th century costermonger style and shout out their wares – the memory is of being a fishwife.

Another memory of Pat in this movement from **Ken Law**: *I joined Sing for Pleasure in the early 70s and he was one of the tutors on the very first course I went on – I think it was either at Malvern or Wakefield (probably the former). I remember him as a giant of a man and he was very extrovert (something like Brian Blessed the actor). He certainly inspired me and many with his obvious love of folk music and his witty rounds. As you know Sing for Pleasure was an English version of "A Coeur Joie", founded to inspire singing as a basis for all music – a lot of it being taught by rote, to enable all to participate.*

Jim Wild and John Coates were two of the original staff – both based in and around Leeds – so it was always stronger in the North of England than the South – although weekends and training days were also held in the South of England, not to mention the annual Summer week, held for a decade at Ellerslie School, Malvern.

I think they must have used Pat as a roving ambassador, because on one occasion he came to the school in Sidmouth where I was headmaster, and took the junior children for a singing extravaganza which they thoroughly enjoyed and were talking about for weeks afterwards. This was his special magic – to hold people's attention and inspire them to open their mouths and sing – both serious songs and silly ditties (which of course appealed to the children!). My personal contact with him was no more than this – a couple of training weeks/days plus the school visit – but I for one will never forget him and adopted his methods of helping folks sing.

In 1992, SfP published a collection of his music *Simi Jadech*. At the launch of the book **James Wild**, Chairman of Sing for Pleasure, paid tribute to Pat –

PAT SHAW REMEMBERED
Folk singers and dancers of the English Folk Dance and Song Society, members of London choirs and many of us from SfP assembled in Hampstead Parish Church in 1977 to pay tribute to Patrick Shuldham-Shaw, our Vice-Chairman.

The Bretton Hall students who had driven with me from the North of England that morning had insisted on coming along to the memorial service even though they had only known Pat since the previous summer school. That was the sort of impact he had on people and if you were to talk to singers and dancers in the many countries where he had worked, I am sure they would agree.

For those of you in SfP who never knew him, it may seem irritating to hear old timers talking so affectionately about this distant ghost, but the truth is that his larger-than-life personality was so very memorable. To each individual at the Hampstead Service he had meant something special and when the service ended with a rousing performance of "Lord of the Dance" there wasn't a dry eye in the place!

Pat was a big man! Not only had he a large physique but he had the personality to match and he was one of those rare people who could fill a room just by being there. His intellect was sharp, he was extremely well-read and could converse knowledgeably on a wide range of subjects and he had an encyclopaedic knowledge of folk music.

If travel broadens the mind, then Pat's must have been broader than most, for he had free-lanced as a singer and dancer all over the world and his personal experiences added a touch of authenticity to his singing. His ability to talk about various South African dialects gave colour to a performance of Bantu folk song in the same way that his ability to speak the idiosyncratic French-Canadian language did when he sang a French Canadian lumber song.

Pat came from a very musical background. His mother "Holly" knew Cecil Sharp well and had been largely instrumental in getting his work as a folk-song collector recognised and had worked unstintingly for the development of the EFDSS and the building of Cecil Sharp House. Pat grew up in a musical and cultural environment where folk music was important and the love he developed for it was not diminished by his talent as an oboist or his Cambridge music degree. His decision to become a free-lance musician was taken in the full knowledge that it would not make him rich.

As a performer he will best be remembered for his distinctive voice, wide repertoire and ability to conjure up an unusual song for an occasion. This could be a haunting Indian lullaby, a moving performance of "My coffin shall be black" or his tongue-twisting version of "Four and Twenty Fiddlers" where everyone would hang on eagerly to see if he would make a mistake and so have to buy drinks all round, but he never did!

Those of us who first met Pat on SfP courses will remember his folk sessions where we sang one piece after another, some with guitar, others unaccompanied, and will remember being infected by his enthusiasm. The songs would often be preceded by some anecdote or other because he loved to stimulate your imagination. We will also remember with great pleasure his dance sessions, where he would hug his accordion to his chest and call the steps. American square dances, complicated basket dances, Scottish reels and many more would keep us going for ages and you knew that the laughter and enjoyment he generated would spill over into other sessions and help to make the week a success.

His sense of humour was boyish and contagious. He delighted in relating incidents about one or other of his colleagues who had been caught in a compromising position and would chuckle conspiratorially whilst introducing us to a risqué round by Purcell. His skill as a "round-smith" was almost always used for fun and he wrote dozens of catches which played on the name of someone present. The syllables would be placed on different high notes so that when the victims stood in the centre of the singers they could hear their names ringing out clearly at the top.

Every year brought a new enthusiasm! The year where he paraded a constant supply of fluorescent socks – with ties to match; the next when a dancing marionette with clicking heels accompanied his singing; the year of the alp-horn on which he played Brahms at 7 a.m. as a morning reveille, and which he somehow managed to pack into his mini-car along with vast amounts of music, his large accordion and himself; the many bottles of malt whisky he brought one time, collected from various distilleries whilst researching Scottish folk song, and from which he distributed liberal doses to all and sundry; ... and perhaps the most bizarre incident of all when, after dancing a final Virginia Reel on a hot night he suggested we repeat it and other dances in the swimming pool! Astonishingly, we did!

In relating these anecdotes, we must not forget the serious Pat. He was a purist in many of his attitudes to music and particularly to folksong. For instance he disliked "A Coeur Joie" taking a bouncy English dance and sentimentalising it in a French version called "Ma Belle Aurore". In dance sessions he used to object angrily when dancers counted themselves in by numbers when they should 'jolly well listen and let the music tell you when to move!'

His work for SfP was prodigious. He was a fine ambassador for us, pleading our cause and acting as a recruiting sergeant on his travels; he wrote lots of rounds and arrangements and offered a fund of advice to our committees. He was a pillar of the movement and helped to build SfP into what it is today.

It is now fifteen years since he died and it is appropriate that we should bring out a collection of his music to remember him by. It is also right that the editor should be someone who knew him well as a child and for whom he wrote "Algy" and other pieces. Our latest publication **"Simi Jadech"**, is a splendid tribute to him and offers choirs a number of attractive and unusual songs to add to their repertoires. It is published with the blessing of the EFDSS and, as Pat intended many of the pieces to be danced as well as sung, we hope that a small booklet of the accompanying steps will be produced in the not too distant future.

Through his music Pat lives on and we hope that "Simi Jadech" will bring back memories for those who knew him and, for others, give a small insight into his character.

(from SfP Summer Newsletter, 1992)

The website for "Simi Jadech" says the book contains "Dance, songs and rounds arranged by Patrick Shuldham-Shaw, edited by Elisabeth J. Wild".

Pat Shuldham-Shaw travelled the world to research folk music and to collect melodies, many of which he subsequently arranged for choirs and for Sing for Pleasure. His genial personality and warmth attracted many friends, and this book includes some of his most popular pieces which illustrate his twin loves of folk dance and choral singing." Contents:

1.   Juliana.
2.   Going to Boston.
3.   Simi Jadech.
4.   Balquidder Lasses.
5.   Three Rhythmic Rounds (In Athens, Liszt and Brahms, Furiante).
6.   Come, My Love.
7.   Old Joe Clark.
8.   Two Dance Rounds (Waltz, Fandango).
9.   Dick's Maggot.
10.   I've Been to Harlem.

On the contents page, **Elisabeth J. Wild**, the editor says –

For many people, the strongest memories of Pat are of him playing his accordion to lead the dancing sessions on our courses and of him accompanying himself on his guitar. This booklet includes some of his most popular pieces which illustrate his twin loves of folk dance and choral singing. It is intended as a tribute to a wonderful man, who shared his music and his life so generously with those around him. Although still greatly missed by his friends, his spirit lives on in the music he left with us.

Elisabeth Jill Henderson-Wild – now known as **Jill Henderson** gave her memories by telephone – Pat Shaw was a great friend of their family and she can remember him always being around when she was a child. As she was only ten when he died, Jill always called him Uncle Pat and was quite convinced that she would marry him when she grew up – a running joke in their family. One little song Pat made up for Jill was

> Algy met a Bear
> The bear met Algy
> The bear was bulgy
> The bulge was Algy

At SfP Summer Schools, Pat would take choral sessions and the conducting course during the day and in the evening, he would call country dances – accompanied by his accordion. Jill remembers how these country dance sessions were great unifiers, bringing everyone together from the youngest to the oldest. Virginia Reel was her favourite dance and, as with others, her memory is of Pat being very light on his feet and a person of immense fun. He would ring up their home when he was near J38 on the M1 and say that he would be arriving at their house in twenty minutes and then stay over with them. He was always very welcome and he always brought Pontefract cakes for her mother as she loved them.

Jill can recall the Alpine Horn and lime green shirts and socks at SfP summer schools plus the time when even his Mini was lime green much to her delight – with the horn sticking out of the back. She can still remember the devastation and sense of loss when she learnt that Pat would not be coming any more.

STANDING CONFERENCE FOR AMATEUR MUSIC (SCAM),

As well as his work in Folk Music and SfP, Pat Shuldham-Shaw was a member of the Executive Committee for the Standing Conference for Amateur Music where he represented the EFDSS. His work for choirs and instrumental ensembles included many of his own compositions, notably carols and rounds.

Marjorie Fennessy sorted Pat's music for the SCAM in order for it to be published by Sing for Pleasure in the future. This was seen not only as an invaluable addition to SfP repertoire, but also as a very worthwhile and continuing memorial to Pat for his many friends both in Sing for Pleasure and SCAM.

Pat wrote about his introduction to the International Folk Music Council in his autobiography (see chapter 1).

J. K. Owens was the chairman of the Standing Conference for Amateur Music. These comments are extracted from his tribute to Pat Shaw at the memorial service at St. John's Church, Hampstead, London, 9 December 1977.

In talking about Pat Shaw, it is hard to know where to begin because he was a man of so many parts and known to so many people.

Pat joined the youth subcommittee of the Standing Conference for Amateur Music in 1966 and the executive committee in 1967. He brought enthusiasm and warmth to every meeting. He attended regularly, in spite of a busy life as a free-lance musician, and it was always a pleasure to look up and see his smiling face at the table.

He was particularly concerned with one aspect of our work, Sing for Pleasure, which we started with the assistance of A Coeur Joie, the French movement which

Pat during a SfP course

had spread all over Europe. Pat eventually became vice chairman, his particular role in Sing for Pleasure being to produce sheet copies for the members and to help make decisions about publication in general. This he did with his usual enthusiasm and, indeed, he wrote or arranged many pieces. He was working on a book of dance songs for SfP and his book of carols, Gloria, was a great success.

Pat always enjoyed conducting; he was a member of SfP summer school staff for many years and directed it three or four times. It was always a great pleasure for me to watch him conduct, because his style was especially rhythmic. His dancing feet, his swaying body, as well as his hands, brought music to life in a remarkable way. I haven't been to many SfP courses, but I remember the accompaniments to evening folk dances, the alpenhorn, the celebrated occasions when he dressed as a ballerina in a tutu and performed some amazing steps before an astonished audience. It was the first time I ever saw a ballerina with a beard.

It is probably for the gift of infectious fun that I remember Pat most – and, of course, for his delightful, unpredictable acts. Pat would not have wished to be serious, but I must say a few such things in conclusion. For his scholarship and knowledge and his research work (especially, most recently, in Edinburgh) – all in the field of folk song – we will always respect him. For his support of SCAM and Sing for Pleasure and his encouragement of music making, we are greatly in his debt.

For his unparalleled generosity with time, energy and even money; for his sense of fun and for his inspiration to us all, we give him most grateful thanks.

8. PAT IN SHETLAND

The war had been a difficult time for the Shetland Isles. Perhaps difficult in a different way from on the mainland – with such a small population and such integrated families, every loss had widespread ramifications. Many men were in the merchant navy and losses were great – *it was a "heavy" time.* The islands were heavily involved in watching the northern passages between the mainland of Europe and Iceland and ensuring that Shetland would not become an alternative entry point for a German assault on Great Britain. At the height of operations, some 20,000 service men were stationed in the islands, easily outnumbering the local residents. Shetland became a restricted area and no one could get in or out without an official pass. The "Shetland Bus" regularly ran from Scalloway to bring members of the Norwegian resistance to Shetland to continue their fight.

So when Patrick Shuldham-Shaw arrived in Shetland for a holiday in 1946 after his release from the NFS (National Fire Service) he could have been one of the first visitors. There he *found a whole mine of uncollected folk music* (his own biography see chapter 1) and resolved to return on a collecting trip. However, in his manuscript books, the first tunes collected are dated July 1946 – these being four from Mr Barclay of Mid Yell (two from manuscripts in his possession), two songs from Mrs Sandison of Mid Yell and four tunes from Laurie Davie Robertson of Herra, Mid Yell. The bulk (fourteen) of the 1946 tunes collected came from John Stickle of Unst – one of which was a Norwegian tune, MTB Waltz (for information on MTBs look on the Shetland Bus website). The journey to Unst is, even now, through Yell.

Pat would have arrived in Shetland by **June 1946** as The Shetland Music Festival was held in the Town Hall, Lerwick, on 25, 26 and 27 June. (Shetland Times 21 June 1946) Pat must have attended this as, on the last day,

> Mr Laurence A. Robertson won the Shetland Fiddle Music prize. The judge 'was most enthusiastic over the flexible wrist and fine fiddling of the Herra, Mid Yell fiddler' *(report in Shetland Times 4 July 1946).*

Laurence "Lell" Robertson remembered in 2008 how, when he arrived home from this competition – having remained in Lerwick for a few days – he found Pat Shaw on his doorstep. The tunes mentioned above were collected in Mid Yell on 2 July – Laurie Davie Robertson being Lell's father. So Pat had found the tip of his "mine of folk music" as well as a life long friend in Lell Robertson.

By 10 August 1946, Pat was recording folk songs from Switzerland for Children's Hour back in London. Even now, over sixty years later, the trip to Shetland from London by air can take the best part of a day and by sea it is an overnight sail from Aberdeen so a full 24 hour trip with the train to Aberdeen included. Trips between the islands are now very easy with many sailings per day. The oil money revenues were very well spent on improving the roads throughout the islands and by the acquisition of superb, efficient, car ferries between the islands. Before this, some islands only had a boat service once a week or else people had to use a passing fishing boat!

1947. In his autobiography Pat says he spent five months in Shetland in 1947 mainly collecting, but this length of time must have been in two visits. His manuscripts show he was collecting in Bressay on 27 January. Bressay is the nearest island to Lerwick so this fits in well with the thought that he would want to be there for the Up Helly Aa – Shetland's Fire Festival – which happens each year on the last Tuesday in January. From 1 February, he was back with John Stickle in Baltasound, Unst and then on to Haroldswick and back to Mid Yell. In early March, Pat went to Out Skerries – the most Easterly islands which even now is a journey of 150 minutes from Lerwick in a modern ferry boat. In 1949 there was only one boat a week, so once there Pat would have stayed for a week.

On 17 March, Lerwick Choral Society in conjunction with Lerwick Amateur Orchestral Society were giving a performance of Handel's Messiah in the Town Hall in Lerwick. Pat was to be involved in this performance as he was playing the oboe – he told us in his autobiography that he was a *fairly proficient oboe player* in the University Musical Society whilst at Cambridge, 1936-1939. 1947 was a particularly bad winter with snow still lying in parts of Shetland till the end of May, which is unusual. The tenor soloist was weather bound at his home seven miles from Lerwick and it was announced at the beginning of the programme that

> Mr P. Shuldham-Shaw, at a day's notice, had stepped into the breach doubling where possible on the oboe. The hero to the rescue was warmly applauded at the outset.

The Shetland Times write up of the event on 21 March continued

> The valiant substitute tenor, Mr Shuldham-Shaw, gave no evidence of a last minute approach to the position and interpreted all his commitments with feeling and in pleasing voice. To sing such a solo as "Every Valley" and then rush back to the orchestra to prove an asset on the oboe is an achievement of note.

Messiah 1947 Concert in Town Hall. Orchestra (left to right): Mary Garriock, Tom Anderson, John Goodlad, Beatrice Hunter, William Sandison, Fred Tait, T. M. Y. Manson, Sandy Bennet, James Spence, Julia Sutherland, Robert MacKay and Elizabeth Smith. Choral members (top row): Jim Clark, Mimi Peterson, Anna Brown (Robertson), Jessie Smith, Nell Harrison, Jennie Gray, Miss Garriock, Daisy Conochie, Bill Rhind (????), Stewart Smith and Willie Anderson. Second row: Cissie Smith, Frances Smith, Mrs Petrie, Joan Brain, Peter Robertson, Tom Pottinger, Mervin Jones, Murdo MacLean, Lissie Ratter, Geira Burgess, Lena Mouat, Mollie Odie, W. Robertson and John Manson. Front row: Hetty Robertson, Elizabeth Barclay, Marjorie Manson, Mrs Attie Smith, Eddie Henry, P. Shuldham-Shaw, Doris Hunter, Miss Boyd, Maggie Blance, Ronald Robb, Kitty Gray, L. Sinclair, J Rogerson, A. W. Smith and Lolly Dalziel. *(Courtesy of Mrs H. Hurlock)*

The newspaper the following week noted that

> Members of Lerwick Choral and Lerwick Amateur Orchestral Society, with their friends, met at a whist, supper and dance in the Masonic Hall, Lerwick on Wednesday evening when the principal guest of honour was Mr P. Shuldham-Shaw. The President of the Choral voiced appreciation of the services of Mr Shuldham-Shaw, who had rendered such great assistance in the recent production of "Messiah".' Later during the evening "a solo was given by Mr Shuldham-Shaw" and, during the dance, he "gave a selection on the piano-accordion."

This could have been one of the first times he played his accordion in public as he had taken up playing this instrument, *to the disgust of his serious minded friends* while in Shetland and came to regard it as his passport and ice-breaker when on collecting trips.

By the end of March and early April, he was collecting in Whalsay and then Fetlar and South towards Lerwick via John Stickle in Unst (when he first collected King Orfeo – see chapter 6), and Gossaborough, Yell – to the Scollay family.

At the Town Hall, Lerwick on 30 April, Patrick Shuldham-Shaw gave a "Recital of Folk Songs of Many Nations" accompanied by Miss Jean Boyd LRAM who had been the conductor of The Messiah and was the music teacher at Lerwick secondary school. Miss Boyd subsequently accompanied Pat on many occasions in Shetland. The Shetland Times was fulsome in its praise for the evening. In the 2 May 1947 edition it was described thus

SONGS OF MANY NATIONS
Delightful Evening for Town Hall Audience.

For nearly two hours a large audience listened with delight to a one-man recital of folk songs of many nations. The singer, Mr Patrick Shuldham-Shaw introduced the songs, translated them where necessary, and sang them in their native languages.

Mr Shaw has a charming personality and the ability to hold an audience spellbound with his extempore remarks, revealing a complete personal knowledge of folk music and a deep understanding of the people whose songs he so charmingly sings. Those of us who have yet to get beyond the first lessons of a French grammar and who have no linguistic ability in other tongues, lost little when the singer turned his fluency into unfamiliar channels. Interpretation was complete in every item, and his humorous introductions which preceded them were often an entertainment in themselves.

A musical world tour commenced with two French songs, moved to Ireland, where of three songs "She Moved Through the Fair" was notable if only for a lovely performance of an old and much loved ballad. The two German songs which followed were in marked contrast; the first a night-watchman's song with the ponderous tone of clock chimes, the second a charming light air which, Mr Shaw explained, was really a girl's song.

The American contributions were "The Rebel Soldier", a riddle song which compared with an English riddle song later in the programme, and a laughter-raising item "The Deaf Woman's Courtship". Mr Shaw was at his best here.

A Swiss song and two Dutch songs led home to a Hebridean air, "The Cockle Gatherer" which gave Mr Shaw an opportunity to use the Gaelic. "The Four Maries" is a little heard but lovely piece, the choice of which adds to our personal regard for the singer. A song of the 1945 period with a humorous turn caused us some uneasiness when it started – fortunately not ending in the manner which army experience had led us to regard as traditional.

From Wales the singer chose a farmyard song which, locally, would bear the title of "Da Flekked Coo" and a lengthy Yiddish song added further linguistic laurels.

"The Unst Boat Song" in the original Norn was the first of three Shetland songs which gave Mr Shaw an opportunity to show how he has profited from his stay in the Isles. His introductory apologies for lack of local dialect ability were soon proved unnecessary as he gave "In a moarnin o' Mey'o" and went on to amuse his audience with the one and only musical relic of the Picts. The language of the "peerie folk" presented no more difficulty to Mr Shaw than the other tongues he had already coped with, and a humorous story of the source of this "ballad" caught the audience off its guard.

A goat herding song from Norway, a Danish counting song, an Icelandic lullaby, and items from Sweden and Finland brought the tour back to British shores.

"The Death of Queen Jane" is a solemn ballad which Mr Shaw dramatised to perfection. An English counting song followed, a counterpart to the American one earlier in the evening. Finally, a Sussex song with a gay lilt and catchy words.

When Lt-Col Shearer voiced thanks to Mr Shaw and his able accompanist, Miss Jean Boyd, he spoke for the audience without exception, and a further song was the much appreciated response from Mr Shaw.

To entertain for nearly two hours and in many languages is an accomplishment of note, and to this was added Mr Shaw's pleasing and thoroughly trained voice. At the piano, Miss Boyd was a skilled and sympathetic accompanist whose contribution to an outstanding entertainment was appreciated by all.

The proceeds, amounting to £17 0s 9d, go to the Gilbert Bain Hospital.

During May 1947, collecting continued around Lerwick and he was billed as taking part as a singer in a "Shetland Concert" put on by the Shetland Folk Society on 9 May. The evening included recitations, traditional tunes and talks on

Shetland folklore. The programme was repeated a few days later at Vidlin on the central mainland. The Shetland News wrote a review of the concert:

> Mr Shuldham-Shaw played on his oboe four of the tunes he has collected during his four month stay in Shetland – three collected from Mr John Stickle, Baltasound (Friedemann Stickle's Trowie Burn, a tune of unusual rhythm called Doon da Roof, and Da Bride's a Boanie Ting, and the Fetlar melody Winyadeppia, collected from Mr Walter Shewan).

The second trip to Shetland in 1947 was in September when his manuscript book shows tunes and songs collected from Unst, Fetlar, Yell and Lerwick and Bobby Johnson recalls his second visit to Skeries – see later.

Christmas Day i da moarnin
or, Da day dawns

Tune noted by Pat Shaw from John Stickle, Baltasound, Unst, Shetland.
This tune was traditionally played early on Christmas morning in the house of Buness at Baltasound. The great Shetland fiddler, Friedemann Stickle, whose portrait still hangs in the house, was paid an annual retaining fee for playing it and the tune has been preserved in his family. There are other tunes of the same name to be found in Shetland and elsewhere, but musically they have no connection with the above; nor have I come across versions of the above under other names.

*PNSS ***

---

*   Pat Shaw in English Dance and Song, November 1950.

1948 saw Pat in Shetland in May and June when he again travelled extensively throughout the islands collecting both from old friends like John Stickle and some new contacts.

The Folklore Society gave a concert at North Roe – reported in The Shetland Times of 21 May which recorded that

it was a piece of rare good fortune that Mr P. Shuldham-Shaw, happening to be at present in Shetland, accompanied the concert party to North Roe. He delighted the audience by singing some of the "finds" made by him in his folk-lore researches.

23 June saw a Recital in the Garrison Theatre – another "Folk Songs of Many Nations" but this one included "Shetland Songs collected lately". The Shetland Times reported:

Accompanied by Miss Jean Boyd LRAM Mr Shuldham-Shaw again shows himself to be a singer of wide resources, from pianissimo, as in "Robin's Last Will" to rousing vigour of the most robust numbers. His powers of vivid interpretation made every song delightfully understandable, even when in a completely unfamiliar tongue – Icelandic or West Indian or Yiddish.

Three Shetland Songs, "Bere and Bursting", "Lament for a Sailor", and "Da Key-Wife", had only recently been collected by the singer, and had not been sung in public before.

As on a previous occasion, the evening was really a musical tour of the world, and many of the items were personally arranged by the artiste.

Thirteen different countries (if one includes Shetland as a separate entity) were represented in the programme which included the following items:
France – The Ballad of Jesus Christ and Au Clair de la lune;
Ireland – Down by the Sally Gardens, The Spanish Lady and She moved through the fair;
Germany – Nightwatchman's Song;
Netherlands – Little children picking berries;
Scotland – Hame cam oor guidman and The Robin's last will;
USA – Cherry tree carol, Black is the colour and The Nightingale;
West Indies – Ogoun Belele and Lim;
Greece – Yonder in the church and Yaroumbi;
Shetland – (all arranged by P. Shuldham-Shaw) – King Orfeo, Unst boat song, Bere and Burstin, Lament for a sailor, In a moarnin o Mey'o, Da Key wife, Fetlar lullaby and Hyltadance;
Wales – Milking song and My sweetheart is like Venus;
England – The Willow Tree Carol and Nutting Time.
The entire proceeds of the recital go to the Rehabilitation Fund.

During 1948, a piece in the Shetland News notes:

Shuldham-Shaw Records – We learn that Mr P. Shuldham-Shaw has had a number of original compositions of his own, dedicated to Shetland, recorded

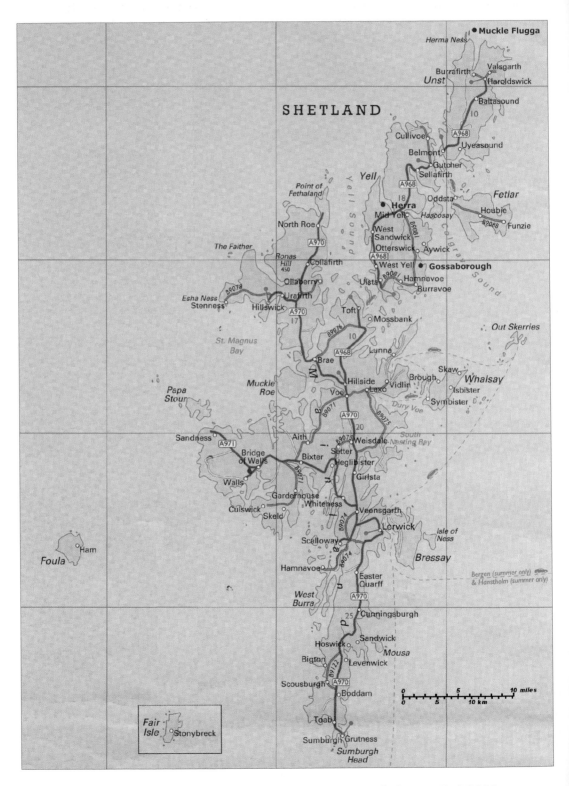

Reproduced by kind permission of © Collins Bartholomew Ltd 2008.

on one of the semi-private "Vinylite" plastic records by the Traditional Players, who comprise Miss (sic) Nan Fleming-Williams (violin), Mr Shuldham-Shaw himself (piano-accordion), Mr Brian Fleming-Williams (Guitar), and Mr Geoffrey Ginn (drums). The compositions mentioned, grouped under the collective name "Shetland Isles" comprise **Jackson's Escape from the Trows** (composed for Mr Robertson of Tresta, Fetlar), **Da Herra Boys** and **M.V. Earl of Zetland** composed aboard that vessel during one of the food relief trips in March. On the other side of the same record the Traditional Players render three jigs of other composition for the American dance "Portland Fancy". A limited number of the records will be sold in Lerwick by Mr David Robertson, Harbour Street, who will advertise their prices and arrival in due course.

1949 Four tunes are recorded in the manuscript book as collected on 15 February 1949 and, as he was playing for Marjorie Fennessey's 21st Birthday party in London on 11 February, he could not have been in Shetland for Up Helly Aa. No concerts or recitals are recorded for around that time so maybe this was mainly a holiday trip. He was back again in August 1949 notating from Laurie Fraser of Papa Stour. Then, on 22 August, Mr Shuldham-Shaw and Party gave a concert in Mid Yell Public Hall. This is the first time the "and party" was noted and so presumably is the first time Nan and Brian Fleming-Williams went with Pat to Shetland. The write up of this event in The Shetland Times reads –

In Mid Yell Public Hall on Monday, Mr P. Shuldham-Shaw and his party generously gave a concert in aid of the Mid Yell Men's Social Club, and the proceeds amounted to over £30. A well attended dance, to music of local sources, followed the show.

The same edition of the paper reported:

Recently more than half the population of Papa Stour met in the school to enjoy a social evening, organised especially at the request of Mr Patrick Shuldham-Shaw, who was on a visit to the isle and who particularly asked for a performance of the traditional Papa Stour sword dance, which was admirably performed under the leadership of Mr Alex Johnson. Mr Shuldham-Shaw delighted the audience with Shetland folk songs and other requests, including the piano-accordion selections.

(See Pat's account of this visit in his notes on the Papa Stour Sword Dance at Appendix 9)

Recollections from **George P. S. Peterson** –
George was a member of the crew on the boat which went across to Sandness from Papa Stour to meet the bus which had come out from Lerwick. On board the bus was George's Mother – Martha who had been out of the isle for an eye appointment. Another person who had made the trip from Lerwick that day heading for Papa was Pat Shuldham-Shaw. Gideon Sinclair from Sandness who had come to the pier to meet the boat was aware of the stranger standing close by, and thinking he wouldn't understand the dialect, then commented to Martha that they would have no fear if the boat should sink on the way across to Papa, that

they would just grab hold of this man's beard, to which she replied "the beard will maybe come to me!" They both laughed heartily until they realised – to their embarrassment that Pat was laughing as well and had understood them perfectly.

George remembered the schoolroom being cleared of the desks, etc. to make room for the occasion and that a lot of people from the isle came to proudly watch the sword dance being performed for Pat. It was led by Alex Johnson and Lowrie Fraser was the fiddler, with George being one of the dancers. Pat also entertained during the evening by singing and playing the accordion, and had with him a bottle of whisky which was passed around much to the enjoyment of the sword dancers and others, enhancing his popularity. Pat stayed at the Manse in Papa for several days during his visit.

Pat later requested the Sword Dancers to come across to Sandness so he could record them. There was a crowd of Sandness folk at the hall, and as it was darker at night by then, the hall was lit by tilley lamps. The microphone was attached to one of the tilley lamp hangers from the roof to get a better sound, but when Pat listened back to the recording he could hear the hissing of the lamp in the background – much to his amusement.

The rest of the manuscript book records one tune and two songs from John Stickle at the beginning of February 1951 – this could be a visit to coincide with Up Helly Aa. Then one song from Tina Shewan of Fetlar – which says collected in Aberdeen 8 April 1955 – and three further undated tunes.

Our searches through the Shetland Times archive produced nothing further although more time could have been spent there if only it had been available.

Certainly it seems that the Fleming-Williams and Pat went to Up Helly Aa on many more occasions. When Pat was working in Edinburgh, from 1972, he would have been able to go to Shetland much more easily, not only because the distance was less but he was travelling around the country much less. **Hamish Henderson** wrote in his obituary for Pat –

Eventually he became so much part of the North Isles scene that he was several times invited to play an official role in the flamboyant Viking ceremonial of Up-Helly-Aa, the Shetland New Year.

Altogether Pat noted 92 items from John Stickle.

John Stickle's grandson, **Henry Henderson** (picture on page 112) who lives in Lerwick, is justly proud of his grandfather and remembered well how, when Pat arrived whilst Henry was visiting the family home in Unst, Pat would give Henry a huge hug, calling him Peerie Henry (little Henry – he was then about ten years old). Pat wrote **Sweet Maggie Stickle** for Henry's aunt, John Stickle's daughter, and Henry is quite convinced that **Margaret's Waltz** was also written for her. Though he did ask why it was called a waltz as it is always played as a slow air in Shetland – as he demonstrated using the fiddle which had been constructed around a fiddle back which had come ashore with Christopher Friedemann von Stickel who jumped ship and landed on Unst still clutching his fiddle – probably in the 1770s. Christopher married two local girls – first one from Unst and then, after her death, one from Yell and never returned to Germany. His direct descendent was the John Stickle who Pat met and whose grandson is Henry who spoke of his memories of Pat. Henry having played the slow air, Vic played **Margaret's Waltz** as a waltz as we know it in the South for the dance of the same name. Henry decided he preferred it as a slow air as played by Aly Bain and Willie Hunter. Henry has a tape which was recorded in the front room of the house he still lives in which is of an instant session which happened after one of Pat and

Nan and Brian Fleming-Williams concerts in Lerwick. Henry can also remember Pat teaching Portland Fancy at a dance.

Henry was the first in Shetland to talk about the tune **Rosemary Brown** which is again played as a slow air in Shetland but a waltz further south. It is felt by Shetlanders that you can put "more feeling" into a slow air. The last time Henry saw Pat was in 1973 in Edinburgh.

Henry gave the words of a song written by Pat in 1950 which he sang in the Balta-sound Regatta Concert in 1950. Henry, aged ten, played his fiddle in this concert.

I wish I were an Unst midden slue
I wish I were an Unst midden slue
If I were an Unst midden slue
I'd never get up till half past two
I wish I were an Unst midden slue

I wish I were a Fetlar russie foal
I wish I were a Fetlar russie foal
If I were a Fetlar russie foal
I'd bury my head in a rabbit hole
I wish I were a Fetlar russie foal.

I wish I were a sheep thief frae Yell
I wish I were a sheep thief frae Yell
If I were a sheep thief frae Yell
I'd jump on my motorbike and ride like hell
I wish I were a sheep thief frae Yell

I wish I were a keeper o da Mucklc Flugga Light
I wish I were a keeper o da Muckle Flugga Light
If I were a keeper o da Muckle Flugga Light
I'd drink Hom Bru till I was tight
I wish I were a keeper o da Muckle Flugga Light

Unst Midden Slue – meaning dirty lazy people. A midden is a large pile of cow's manure on the croft!

Fetlar russie foals are ungroomed year old colts with their first coats hanging in unkempt masses about them

Yell sheep thieves simply means thieves.

The Muckle Flugga Light is at the very north of Unst and is Britain's most northerly lighthouse.

These are nicknames for the inhabitants of Shetland districts and were first recorded in the late 19th century.

Apparently people found these words very amusing and were not bothered about them.

Elizabeth Morewood from Mid Yell told more about Rosemary Brown. Pat stayed with her adopted family when in Mid Yell. She was adopted when she was six years old and never seemed to get over that fact. Apparently she was forced to learn the fiddle – so perhaps Pat wrote her a tune of her own to try to encourage her. When old enough, she married against her adopted parents' wishes and went to Australia. Nobody hears from her now so perhaps she never knew how well her tune is regarded.

Henry Henderson

Elizabeth Morewood

Elizabeth is of the time when secondary pupils had to go to Lerwick to school and so she was not at home except during the holidays and therefore has not many direct memories of Pat in Mid Yell. Though she does recall that he went into her school in Lerwick and up to Miss Boyd's – the music teacher's – room. Miss Boyd became Pat's accompanist when doing Recitals in Shetland. Jean Boyd started the Music Festivals for schools but Elizabeth does not remember Pat being involved in them. At the start of them, just after the war, not many adults were competing – even Lell Robertson had to be persuaded to enter when he was nineteen years old in 1946 and Pat heard him and went to Yell to visit him. Elizabeth was only the second pupil in Shetland to do Higher Music – she is a singer. Pat came into Miss Boyd's room once when Elizabeth was having a lesson and he remarked upon her lung capacity. Although she took part in "The Messiah" she does not remember much about rehearsals and Pat was not always there for practices. *He was more brought to mind when he visited the girls' hostel – fifty girls so when a man came in it made your eyes open and he was noticed.*

Elizabeth can remember Pat at an Up Helly Aa in 1949. There are several squads of men – all heavily disguised – each squad having a musician. One came in with a chap playing an accordion, who had a heavy beard – it was Pat Shaw with an extra beard on top of his own. A neighbour re-called Pat striding into the dance after Up Helly Aa, singing a lullaby.

Elizabeth explained why some Shetlanders appear to have stronger accents than others. Apparently, children are taught that when they speak to someone not from Shetland who can't understand the dialect or speak it, it is only polite to speak so that they can understand you. Elizabeth's mother was born in Edinburgh and so she was brought up almost bi-lingual and then her husband was from Yorkshire. Pat, of course, had no problem with the dialect and she can recall, at the back of her mind, that he did use the dialect.

Her memories, although not many, are very fond ones – she recalls hearing about him being all over Yell and knowing everybody – he would just turn up on doorsteps. He seemed to attend all the local dances which were held fairly regu-larly and usually taught some dance or other – Elizabeth recalls the Swedish Masquerade which they often did after Pat had gone. He was also very interested in the square dances done at that time but Elizabeth does not know where they originated from or when they arrived in Shetland. A neighbour recalls a Box Social in Burravoe where Pat was the judge and he ended up buying her box so they ate the supper together. (The ladies each took a decorated box containing a supper to the dance. The men bid for the boxes and spent the interval eating the supper with the lady of the box.) *Back then, they would get up a concert or a dance for no reason at all – they had more leisure time as now everyone is in employment, some on shift work, most have their own cars and televisions and don't go out so much.*

When he was in Shetland Pat was involved in many things and he took to the usual means of transport – motorbikes. He obtained an Ariel motorbike from Lowrie Stickle of Unst and Elizabeth's brother vaguely remembers something about an accident. There was no other way of getting around – Elizabeth can remember being one of five on the back of a single motorbike once – she was the one right at the back! The roads then were mainly tracks and there was only one boat a day from Yell to the mainland and then a long slow bus ride to Lerwick – Elizabeth was always sick on that bus.

Elizabeth's brother, James Barclay, recalls that he and Pat spent quite a lot of time together, most probably discussing who was a musician and where the next dance was to be held! He remembers them both rowing across the voe to visit Johnny Smith, a boat-builder who liked fiddle music.

Some of the first tunes in Pat's manuscript book were obtained from manuscripts in the possession of Mr Barclay, Elizabeth's father.

Lell Robertson in the 1940s

Lell Robertson gave his memories in 2008. He told the story of Pat being in Yell before Lell got back to the island after his win at the music festival in 1946. Lell had been detained in Lerwick by the BBC who asked him to give a recording playing the fiddle. He and Pat then became great friends through the music. At that time, Lell had an old Triumph motorcycle and he took Pat around to visit some older players so that he saw the styles of playing and the versions of some of the traditional tunes. Pat wrote **Lell's old Triumph** for the cycle. The Herra, where Lell was born and brought up, is a small district. At the time of his visits there were only a few boys in the district and Pat got to know them all. Hence the composition **The Herra Boys**. *My Dad's name was Laurie Davie Robertson and at that time I was playing on his fiddle. Again this gave the title to the tune* **Laurie Davie's Fiddle**. *Pat also composed an air for me which he called* **Lell frae Yell** – *frae being dialect for "from". I am now 81 years old but still get great pleasure from playing my fiddle.*

Sadly, Lell died 13 July 2009. – His obituary written by Laurence Tulloch for the Shetland Times includes – *Lell's ability (on the fiddle) was recognised at an early age. When he was nineteen he won a talent competition and he was always in demand at concerts and gatherings. Sixty years ago the renowned collector and composer Pat Shuldham-Shaw recorded Lell and his father and, indeed, Shaw composed a tune for Lell.*

Mrs Ann Robertson is Lell's wife and lives in Herra, Mid Yell in their home. They did not get together and marry until after the period of Pat's most frequent early visits to Shetland and so she does not have much memory of him.

Margaret Scollay is Lell and Ann's daughter and a fiddler. She is a performer and composer as well as an inspiring teacher. It was Margaret who confirmed how Pat came to be made an honorary Shetlander. There is an annual Young Fiddler of the Year competition for Shetland schoolchildren organised by the Shetland Folk Society. Competitors must play tunes that are either traditional or composed by people in Shetland. In order for Pat's tunes to be used, it was decided by the Folk Society that he should be given this status.

Laurie Davie's fiddle is now played by Margaret's son, Ross Couper – Laurie Davie's great grandson.

Ian McAlpine was more interested in boating regattas than the music although he is a fiddler himself. He was one of the group formed by Tom Anderson from the people coming back to the islands – The Hamefarers – later known as the Forty Fiddlers or the Forty Frenzied Fiddlers. Ian remembers Pat mainly in North Yell – at the sessions after the Regattas, with a notebook and pen sitting at the side noting down the tunes. Most people played by ear – tunes they had learnt from listening – so the fact that Pat could write the music down as it was played and then, even more astonishingly, instantly play the tune back to them was a marvel mentioned by many others as well as Ian.

Ian recalls that people talked of Pat as a very urban and sophisticated man after his concerts in Lerwick. He feels that Pat did contribute largely to the preservation of the Shetland tunes. He also recalls Pat on a motorbike on the bad roads.

Ian spent the years 1969 to 2000 in South Africa and, whilst there, played for a morris dance group – he thinks he was probably the only fiddler in Africa! He was not surprised to learn that Pat was quite an international traveller and spoke to people in their own language or dialect as he did in Shetland. Ian put a name to the practice of not speaking in dialect to visitors – Knapping (with a hard clicking K) – though he said it could also be thought of as putting on "airs and graces".

Ian also prefers to play both **Margaret's Waltz** and **Rosemary Brown** as slow airs.

Mary Ellen Odie (picture on page 116) lives in South Yell and recalled her memories of Pat at the Old Haa Museum in Burravoe. Also present was **Rena Nisbet** whose grandmother was Mrs Andrina Sandison who sang two songs for Pat when he first arrived in Shetland. The songs are in the beginning of the manuscript book. Rena's father was present during the interview but he did not talk.

Mary recalls 1947 as being a *year to die for – glorious summer weather and the war was over at last – what more could a young girl want?* She too could remember Pat teaching Swedish Masquerade and remembered that her sister had said that Pat was a great partner to dance with – *he always put you in the right place.* Apparently Maggie Stickle said the same of Pat as a partner and they, according to Mary Ellen, *were two of the best dancers on the islands.*

Mary did meet Pat, she saw his band – with Nan and Brian Fleming-Williams – playing in Mid Yell but her family would not let her stay for the dance. However, she remembers how nice he was and how he got into the swing of Shetland and spoke the dialect. Mary was obviously taken with Nan and was saddened to hear that she stopped playing in her later life.

He was very popular, great fun and everyone enjoyed him immensely. If he had anything on any of the young men, he would announce it from the stage. He was also a good collector of music, he knew what he was doing – you could tell he had a more serious, academic side. Mary felt that he made many life-long friends in Shetland and can remember the annoyance when *some peevish woman said 'are you sure he is not a spy?'* This she put down to his black beard and jealousy as everyone was talking about him, but it shows how the influence of the war was still uppermost in people's minds. His manner soon shattered such thoughts.

On being shown his autobiography, and seeing that he had an Irish father and that his mother was a professional singer, she felt *he had it made!*

Maggie Ann Nicolson (picture on page 116) was a Scollay before her marriage and comes from Gossaborough in Yell which was where she first saw Pat. She was the youngest of the family, having four elder brothers – the **Gossaborough Lads**. Maggie Ann's family lived in a croft and, as is the way with crofts, they kept a pig for bacon and sides of ham would be hanging up in the kitchen. She can remember her mother taking down the side of ham and cutting off a bit to fry in the pan. Pat put the microphone over the pan to hear the sizzle of the bacon frying. Electricity started to come to some areas in Yell just before Christmas 1967 so most of Pat's visits were when Tilly lamps were still in use.

Maggie Ann did not go on to high school in Lerwick so she was at home for Pat's visits to Yell. She can remember the concerts with the Fleming-Williams when Pat played the accordion, his lovely, soft, singing voice and the fact that he was a lovely dancer. He told them his mother was English and a musician and singer. She also recalls how lovely he was, how he made many friends and was so very humorous with a twinkle – and such a charmer, they had so much fun with him. *He was amazing, we all loved him. He was a very talented man and lived a very interesting life and just loved the music in all its forms.* Her brother could never get over the fact that he could write the music down and immediately play it back on the accordion. When her brother Peter was playing fiddle he always tapped time on the floor with his foot but they had no carpets, only lino on the floor. So when Pat was recording him, he took her mothers shawl and folded it up to put under his foot so that he could keep time without interfering with the recording.

Pat would ask if there were any musicians or fiddlers and just go and visit them. He was interested in the tunes passed down father to son which were not written out. He could write them out as they were played which was a marvel to everyone. Maggie Ann felt that he was the first to be seriously interested in collecting Shetland music and felt that he gave the lead to Tom Anderson, who had a recording machine, to do more collecting. Eventually, Pat also acquired a recording machine but it was very big.

If there were any entertainments going, he wanted to go – he was very interested in the way of life in Shetland as well as the music. Pat was very good at languages, with his agile mind, he could pick up anything, he was on the ball all the time. He had the ability to make himself at home which meant he did fine in Shetland as Shetlanders are not standoffish. He would ask if there was anything he didn't know as he wanted to get it right.

She had thought he might have been a school teacher as it always seemed to be summer when he came to Shetland.

There are memories from two members of the Johnson family from Out Skerries – the most Easterly islands of the Shetland group. **Peter Johnson** is the younger of the two and was thirteen years old at the time of Pat's visits in 1947 and now lives in Lerwick having been a fisherman. **Robert Murray Johnson**, Bobby, still lives in the family home in Skerries and we were fortunate enough to visit him there. Bobby was seventeen when Pat was on Skerries. Bobby remembers that Pat came twice – the second time being just before Bobby went to do his National Service in November. As their memories overlap somewhat, they are together here.

Pat arrived on the Earl of Zetland, the regular weekly ferry boat which stayed in Baltasound in Unst overnight on the way to Skerries. Apparently the Mate on the boat – Willie Sinclair – was a great character who would have enjoyed Pat's company and they would have had a great evening together. Bobby thought it very adventurous to travel all that way and cannot recall much luggage though he remembers the accordion and he thought a recorder (perhaps his oboe for the Messiah?)

Mary Ellen Odie

Maggie Ann Nicolson

Bobby feels that Pat could be more relaxed in Skerries as there was so much more going on in Yell. He recalled how Pat did a lot of walking around the island and he can remember him on top of a hill, singing. Pat also did a lot of visiting – he was interested in people and their lives and picked up the accent very well – he talked like a Skerries person. As there is only one mile of road on Skerries Pat had no need for a motorbike here.

The Johnsons had five children – Bobby and Peter had three sisters, Joey, Agnes and Mary. Neither of the boys played but Joey was a church organist and Agnes would try the fiddle *to their amusement*. They did have a harmonium and a piano in the house – although there was not much time for frivolous activities.

Peter explained how fishing was the main industry *so those who were musical were not always available to play their tunes or spend much time listening to Mr Shaw. However I do remember two evenings when we were treated to folk music, these were memorable evenings having lived through WW2. The island was without dance hall facilities, the schoolteacher at the time was Donald MacAskill who agreed that a social evening could be held in the school building which doubled up as a church meeting place. At the social evening Mr Shaw played many tunes and sang many songs from many areas of the British Isles, he also taught the grown ups new dances, one sticks in my mind being Portland Fancy. We enjoyed a very pleasant evening, some change from the past six years of blackout and the gloom and trauma of war.* At that time there were over a hundred people living on Skerries and most would have attended such a treat. Some amusement was caused to the boys as they watched their mother dancing *as she and her partner always turned the wrong way.* Peter thinks Bobby is a good dancer.

Bobby took us to see the Church that had once doubled as the school. He showed how the partition was across the main body of the church and confirmed that the social evening was on the second visit and that Pat was set on having it and organised the whole thing – he sent Bobby to ask the teacher if they could use the space. Peter was at school during the day so Bobby came more into contact with Pat.

During his time on the island Pat went into the school which had over twenty pupils of all ages with one teacher dealing with the whole age range. Pat taught folk songs from Cornwall in SW England – Peter particularly remembers singing "Crickle Creek Girls do you want to go to Somerset" and other rounds with the words written out on the blackboard.

Andrew Anderson and his brother Johnnie, also their cousins Davie and Lollie, all came to visit. The piano accordion was not known at that time and later Lollie Anderson brought the first piano accordion into Skerries – The Johnsons and the Andersons were two main family names on the island and are all cousins. Peter

The church/school as it is today.

recalls how *Mr Shaw's musical ability sticks vividly in my memory in that he could write down a tune as the fiddler played it and then play it back on his accordion – that was amazing.* Pat noted two tunes from Andrew Anderson.

The family home is not a croft – it has no land. It is a concrete house and, having been built in 1928, was much newer than most and had more rooms. Bobby felt this would have been one of the reasons they were asked to house Pat during his visits. Both men felt that their mother could cope very well with having a stranger staying with them. She never got into a fluster, having worked in a big house in Lerwick where she had to do everything – from cooking and washing to presentation. She was an excellent cook and would have worked out all the menus in her own mind. The stove was coal fired. Both men, and Peter's wife Christine, found the thought that Pat might have liked to try his hand at cooking amusing. In Skerries, men did not do anything like that – the women did everything in the house. They cooked and baked everyday, baited the lines for fishing, milked the cows and looked after the croft if they had one. They would be up at five and by eight making butter and cheese with the nappies on the washing line if there were a baby in the house. If the man was a fisherman then the woman would have to pick limpets off the rocks for bait as well. Both men felt that life was very hard for women in those times but the role of the father was to earn the money by catching fish in all the seasons which was also hard – and the children did their bit from an early age. Mealtimes must have been lively events in this household and Bobby remembers Pat sitting down with them whilst Peter thinks not.

Peter and Christine Johnson

Bobby has a wonderful story of Pat's generosity. When he was staying with them for the second time, Bobby was waiting to go to do his National Service. When he was younger he had

Robert Murray Johnson ("Bobby") holding the watch Pat gave him.

been given a watch as a Christmas present from his grandfather's people. The watch stopped just before Pat arrived on Skerries. It had been sent to Birmingham to see if could be repaired but, whilst Pat was there, it came back through the post as not being worth repairing. After Pat left, the mate of the boat came to Bobby the next week with a box for Bobby and inside was Pat's own watch as a present for him. It was a "Romer" model watch and had 852961 stamped on the back. But the watch had rather a sad end. Bobby was working with the plough and tractor one day and took off the watch and put it into the top pocket of his boiler suit. Come the weekend, work clothes were put in to soak in water – and that was the end of the watch. Bobby had used the watch all the time he was doing his National Service (see picture on page 117).

Neither man could recall Brian and Nan Fleming-Williams but they never saw Pat on the Mainland – indeed would never go out of the island for a concert. Communications were very bad then between Skerries and Lerwick but now you can go to Lerwick for an evening at the Garrison Theatre.

They remember a man with a beard with a great sense of fun and a twinkle in his eye.

Cavy Johnson was fairly young when Pat travelled most widely through Shetland in the late 1940s and early 1950s. What most sticks in his mind is how his grandmother referred to him. She had a great talent for getting words wrong and this included people's names. She called him Tweetim Shay. Cavy also wrote the famous story about Aly Bain and **Margaret's Waltz** – in the dialect – *When Shuldham-Shaw was visiting Tammie Anderson one night, a very young Aly Bain, now a musical legend himself, was also present, and was persuaded to play a few tunes on the fiddle. At one stage he said 'Dis is a peerie tune I juist heard, I dunna keen da nem, but I laek hit a lok.' And he proceeded to play* **Margaret's Waltz**. *When he finished Shuldham-Shaw smiled and said 'I'm glad you liked that. I wrote it.'* Aly's recording of **Margaret's Waltz** in the 1980s was enormously popular in Shetland, and is still often played.

Margaret Anderson gave her memory of Pat by telephone. She is now 76 and lives in Unst. She left school in 1948 but both she and her sister can recall Pat Shaw visiting their school – Livister School on the East of Whalsay – in the mid 1940s. He was collecting in Whalsay in March 1947. They can remember two songs he taught them whilst he played the piano –

"Crickle Creek Girls – do you want to go to Somerset/Crickle Creek Girls do you want to go to town" and "Who Killed Cocky Robin" – this was basically the same story as Who Killed Cock Robin but with different words and tune.

Like everyone she knows *the beautiful tune* **Margaret's Waltz** *which he wrote whilst in Unst.*

The story behind **Jackson's Escape from the Trows** was given via **Elizabeth Nicolson.** Jackson was the nickname of John Robertson whose wife, Ann Mary Robertson, is now 92 years old. Apparently, after visiting the Robertsons, Pat had to walk back to where he was staying along a very dark road. Jackson insisted that he should accompany Pat to save him from the trows, the little people.

Aly Bain recalls:

I never met Pat when he was in Shetland. At that time I was too young. I learned about Pat from Tom Anderson when I first went to him for lessons around 1959. During my early days with Tom his interest was mainly in Scottish music and we spent much of our time together learning slow strathspeys and the playing of J. F. Dickie. However, Tom was leader of the Folk Society Fiddlers who met now and again to play at special Shetland nights. The band consisted of mainly older play-ers like Peter Fraser, old Willie Hunter and Willie Anderson. I was two generations younger than most of them and had never heard music like it before. I knew then that I had found something special and the more I learned about our own fiddle music the more Pat's name came up. He had collected music from all of them and many more throughout the Islands. There is no doubt that Pat inspired Tom to do the same thing and so in my opinion Pat was the saviour of much of our fiddle tra-dition. I often thought then about this Englishman and how he ended up in the middle of nowhere collecting music no one seemed to care much about any more. Many years later after I had moved to Edinburgh I got to know Pat through the School of Scottish Studies. We became friends and shared some time together. We talked of course about the music and the Nordic influence running through our fid-dle tradition. I went to the School and heard many of the old recordings and looked through his notes and music he had written down. We would visit each other for dinner and play tunes together. We had something else in common, we both liked to cook curries. Pat was a great cook and pretty much an expert on whisky which was another thing we had in common. Pat was great company and I enjoyed our times together. Just after I got married in 1974 he came for dinner one evening and after another curry we started to play tunes together. I had just come back from a tour in America and thought I had found the perfect tune for him to learn. He sat there and listened to the tune, I told him it was an American waltz called **Margaret's Waltz**. *When he told me he had composed the tune I nearly fell through the floor. Years later I recorded* **Margaret's Waltz** *and it became the track most played on Scottish radio for three years. I wonder what he would have thought of that. We had some fun together. I remember one day we were in the University staff club with some friends including Hamish Henderson. The conversation got round to malt whisky and who could tell which was which. The conversation became somewhat heated and ended up with Pat and Hamish sitting with their backs to the bar while we bought them various malts to see if they could name them. I think we bought them twelve different malts. It was a serious affair. Pat didn't drink his: he just put them to his nose. In the end Pat got almost all of them correct and Hamish was a poor second, and was not amused. It all ended up with Hamish singing songs and we had a great day. Shortly before his untimely death Pat sent me copies of all the music collected in Shetland along with notes. I got this whole heap of papers one day through the post. Many of the tunes were obscure with a note underneath say-ing Halling or Springer, some of them incomplete. When I let friends from Norway and Sweden look at them they understood what they were and were amazed to find this music still alive in Shetland. I wish now that I'm older Pat was still around as there are many more things I would like to have asked him about, but that wasn't to be. All of us in Shetland have a great deal to thank him for. He is remem-bered in Shetland with great affection by all who knew him. He was indeed a friend to our Island.*

Violet Tulloch also spoke about the strong link between Pat and Tom Ander-son – she recalled that they spent many long evenings together. Violet thinks the recording Aly and Willie Anderson made of **Margaret's Waltz** was the best re-cording of the tune. They kept the chords basic – *not like the fancy chords used by the Americans.*

Pat certainly met **Tom Anderson** at the production of the Messiah in March 1947 as the picture shows Tom leading the orchestra though it would be highly likely that the two would have met on Pat's first visit to Shetland. Tom was working as an Insurance agent at that time and used his travelling around the islands to do some collecting of his own. In an interview with Brian Smith in October 1990 Tom Anderson said that Pat Shaw's advice to him had been that he and his wife would be very foolish to go back to New Zealand when he had the opportunity as he would be letting Shetland down *because there is a hidden treasure here* – though Tom also said that *there's so few people in Shetland as ever saw that.* Henry Henderson recalled that Tammy was very reluctant to revive Shetland fiddling but that Pat persuaded him.

So Tom Anderson, on his retirement in 1972, became the first fiddle teacher in schools, travelling around Shetland to do so. Before that he had taught individual pupils such as Aly Bain but this was the start of his teaching career for the Shetland Islands Council, which led to him teaching Catriona Macdonald, another of his famous pupils.

The Shetland archive has recordings of Tom Anderson talking about Pat Shaw, Pat Shaw singing and Pat talking about his collecting in Shetland.

In "Haand me doon de fiddle" **Tom Anderson** and Pam Swing – in acknowledgements say of Mr Patrick Shuldham-Shaw –

We are indebted to the late Mr Pat Shuldham-Shaw. Mr Shaw came to Shetland in 1947 and became very interested in the musical tradition. Over the years 1947-51 he wrote down, and in the latter two years recorded on tape, many tunes and songs in Shetland. He published in the EFDSS FMJ articles of music on the late John Stickle of Unst. His death in 1977 left a vacuum in the Folk World which will be hard to fill.

Ian Holland – *The last time I met him, which was in the last year of his life, I mentioned that I was moving to Shetland and he suggested that I should contact Tom Anderson and Willie Hunter when I arrived. In my first month in Shetland I went along to a hall with the hope of attending a meeting of the Lerwick Accordion and Fiddle Club. When I knocked on the door it was opened a chink and the voice from inside said 'you can't come in as this is a private club' and I was also told I couldn't join as there was a waiting list for membership. But when I said 'Pat Shaw asked me to contact Tom Anderson and Willie Hunter', I was immediately invited in and signed up as a member! Both were at the club that night and both said 'Anyone who is a friend of Pat Shaw is a friend of ours'.*

This is an indication of how well known he was even in the remotest extremities of the country and of the esteem with which he was regarded by other prominent figures in the folk music world. Tom Anderson was a teacher and collector of Shetland traditional fiddle music and a close friend of Pat Shaw, and was mainly responsible for the revival of traditional fiddle playing in Shetland. Two of his pupils who have made names for themselves nationally and internationally as traditional musicians are Aly Bain and Catriona Macdonald. Willie Hunter, who also taught, was highly regarded as one of Scotland's leading fiddle players and, when working in the London area in the early 1950s, played in McBains Band.

During my time in Shetland I have met several other people who knew Pat Shaw during his visits here in the late 1940s to collect traditional music and dance and everyone without exception spoke of him with fondness and of his gift for friendship.

In "The Fiddle Tradition of the Shetland Isles" by Peter Cook published by Cambridge University Press in 1986, Patrick Shuldham-Shaw has several mentions. Pat's publications on Shetland music and John Stickle in the FMJ of the

EFDSS are mentioned but Cook is also critical of Pat's notation of the music. Talking of the "Shaulds of Foula" recorded in Yell, Peter Cook says that –

> although it was played halfway between a jig and a reel Pat wrote it down unambiguously in 6/8 time. ... Pat implies that there was a difference between musical intentions of the fiddlers and what they actually performed, thereby turning his back on the possibility that they meant what they played.

Pat wrote articles about Shetland for the EFDSS Folk Music Journals:
Folk Music and Dance in Shetland Vol. V No. 2 1947
Folk Songs Collected in the Shetland Isles Vol. V1 No.1
A Shetland Fiddler and his Repertoire – John Stickle, 1875-1957, Vol. IX No. 3 1962

PAT'S TUNES for Shetland places and people taken from his Manuscript books Comments labelled NFW were made later by Nan Fleming-Williams.

Nan's Waltz (c.1947)
NFW *Pat composed the tune for me on our first journey up to Up Helly Aa in January. Pat, Brian and I and Pat's cousin Muriel went on this occasion. He wrote Earl of Zetland at the same time because I played them both at a concert. They became smash hits overnight.*

The dance Nan's Waltz was composed for Nan much later, when she and Brian were leaving for Malta.

Snow on Valafield – Valafield is in Unst

Da Trows o' Swarta Hoalla – Swarta Hoalla is in Unst

Gold above thee, man

Hoy Villa – the name of John Stickle's house in Baltasound, Unst

Sweet Maggie Stickle

NFW *Maggie was the daughter of John Stickle from whom Pat did much of his collecting of Shetland folk music*

Muckle Flugga – the most northerly lighthouse in the British Isles

Daft Laurie

NFW *Laurie was John Stickle's son – Maggie's brother*

Laurie's Lament for the Home Brew

Laurie Davie's Fiddle – for Laurie Davie Robertson (Lell's father)

Mid Yell Voe

Auld Johnnie

m.v. Earl of Zetland   March
m.v. Earl of Zetland   (variation)

NFW *these are the inter-island boats that ran from Lerwick up around the islands as far as Balta Sound on Unst and back.*

Da Red Pants o' Muckle Rø – the Nona United Boys of Whalsey – these were a dance band

Jackson's Escape from the Trows – see Elizabeth Nicolson's story

NFW *The Trowies were the Little People and believed by some to be the remnants of the Picts, who at the coming of the Vikings fled into the hills and only came out at night to tend their flocks.*

Patsy's Jig

The Herra Boys – the young Robertson men of Herra, mid-Yell
Gossabrough Lads – for Scollay family, Yell
Rosemary Brown – see above
Lell frae Yell – for Lell Robertson
Atlantic Jig
Birse her till she pesters – 'squeeze her till she squeaks'
Da Skerries Waltz
Da high-neckit gansie
NFW *I remember Pat writing this, but can't bring to mind why. It's his Shetland phase, so belongs to that collection of his tunes. I think it meant a polo-necked jersey.*
Lell's Old Triumph – for Lell Robertson's motorbike
m.v. St. Clement – another inter-island boat   March
Maggie's Peesterin Twins
NFW *Maggie Stickle – now Mrs. Peter Williamson, she moved to the south of England*
Bobbie Tulloch's Two-Stroke – Tulloch is a Shetland name
s.s. St. Magnus – these five are all ferries between Shetland and then Scottish mainlands
s.s. St. Claire
s.s. St. Rognwald
s.s. St. Ola
Lord Curzon.

On the ferry to Shetland for Up-Helly Aa Pat, Brian and Nan Fleming-Williams and Pat's cousin, Muriel

9. PAT IN HOLLAND

Before the war, there were English country dance exams in Holland and those who had not passed the advanced level dared not even show their faces at advanced classes, let alone dance there. The teachers at that time were Thora Watkins (then Thora Jacques) for country and Miss Sinclair for morris and sword.

The first thing that registered most about Pat Shaw was his accordion playing.

In **December 1973** the Vereniging Nederlandse Volkdansstichting (NVS) – the Dutch Country Dance Society – issued a **Pat Shaw Jubilee edition** of Dansnieuws, their Newsletter, to honour the 25 years that Pat had been leading the Christmas Course in Holland. It contains the following article:

25 Years with Pat Shaw by **Henk Wijnmaalen**, honorary chairman:

The Volksdansvereniging (NVS) began activities straight after the war and, just as before 1940 (as the Dutch Institute for Folk Dance and Song), they needed English teachers.

Richard Callender came in 1948 for the third time and brought Pat Shaw as musician to the Christmas Course at Scouts' Farm in Ommen.*

The appearance of an accordion was something new for us, at least playing for country dancing.

We had been used to a wind-up gramophone, piano, violin but often a single recorder (whether well-played or not) which many found the ideal instrument for folk dancing.

Then there was Pat Shaw with his instrument, and what an instrument! It was a revelation for most of us and a special stimulation at the general dancing in the evenings. In addition the change of melody during a dance was new to us and gave us extra lift.

Besides his mastery of the accordion, we discovered his great interest in song and he was asked to sing when no singing teacher was available for a course. I don't need to write more because we all discovered this many times. My modest opinion is that this was a great success not only for his choice of songs but his way of putting them over.

At a time when we had no funds to invite several teachers to a Christmas course we asked Pat if he could also teach. He immediately agreed and for a fee I hardly dare mention. This was a dance and song teacher and musician altogether for a single (small) fee. He understood our precarious financial position and we will always be thankful.

Pat Shaw experimented on our courses, not only with recently (re)discovered dances but also with his own dances which he tried out with us and later

* Richard Callender died suddenly in November 1949.

used in the Albert Hall Festival in London. In some ways he found us better subjects for experiment than his own countrymen.

Pat has his own style and opinion of the dances and steps and this is visible in the NVS. Sometimes a new dance was quickly mastered, another time he became annoyed when it didn't go as he wanted. He could shout at us but later apologised for getting on his high horse.

Pat Shaw has left his mark on the NVS but only in a good way. He has certainly succeeded in improving our poise and style which we sometimes forgot in our enthusiasm.

When we see how varied and inventive he is, we realise what a great support he has been for us. We hope to see him leading our courses many times more in the way he has done for a quarter of a century (that sounds a long time!), dancing, singing and playing.

It is never too much for him to help us; even after days of hard work, because we do chatter during the classes, he takes up his instrument and plays in the band, providing our musicians with inspiration. And when, dog tired, we flop into an easy chair, all we want to do is to hear him sing or lead us in song.

The familiar song "What would the world be without women" I would paraphrase as "What would the NVS be without Pat". I hope I have shown what Pat Shaw means to us. On behalf of everyone "Many thanks, Pat".

"Pat Shaw as seen by the Dutch Folk Dancers" was the title of the album which was presented to Pat during the 1973 Christmas Course to mark this long association. Many of his Dutch friends contributed stories and thoughts to the album. Here are a few excerpts:

Nel de Vries, who together with her late husband was one of the first dancers wrote:

Then came Pat, young and spontaneous. He revived the Playford dances we had so enjoyed with Thora before the war. Pat taught in a subtle musical way which made you one with your partner and the music so that every dance was a physical and spiritual experience.

I remember a course in Oosterbeek where Pat, Nibs and Mr Ganiford did the teaching. The ball in Arnhem was a high point from my dancing years. Also a course in Drakenburgh near Hilversum at which Thora, Pat and Mr Ganiford taught. I learned a lot about teaching from Pat and have taught many of his dances. You can see, Pat stamped his mark on our courses. When he's MC'ing a ball, you dance and everyone does their best and it doesn't disintegrate as it sometimes does with other teachers.

Johan van Beemen a committee member almost from the beginning and for many years extremely active in organising excursions for the many English visitors on the courses wrote:

I remember the first time I met Pat Shaw in Holland. He was in the company of Richard Callender at the station in The Hague where they arrived after their crossing from Harwich to Hoek van Holland. I followed Richard's advice when I had invited Pat to come and teach at one of our Easter courses. To my surprise he told me that he already knew me. Before the war I had attended EFDS courses and as Pat's mother was a well-known musician, interested in folk music, she played her part at these courses and Pat, in his mother's wake, saw me there. Pat soon became popular among the Dutch folk dancers in spite of (or through) his boyish appearance. What a change when after a few years he grew a full beard which caused much laughter among the dancers. I remember when Pat started to conduct the general singing he said, while pointing to his beard: to prevent unnecessary questions from the ladies 'I tell you that it does not prick.'

Once upon a time Pat visited me after a course before returning to England. After a while my daughter, still in her teens, was so bold as to ask him if he would sing for us and without keeping her waiting he delighted us all by singing an English folk song. This willingness to help and please his pupils has been one of his characteristics and so it is not surprising that the Dutch dancers are looking forward to his 25th visit to the NVS courses.

Piet Swart writes about his first meeting with Pat Shaw:

Scouts' Farm Ommen. Pat and Callender came a day late in the evening because the plane had been delayed by fog. These two stocky figures made a strange impression on us. It was the first time Community dances had been introduced and the first Community Dance Books sold. This led to intense discussion between lovers of Playford and the followers of Community dancing.

During the dancing, Pat sat in a loft with his accordion. Callender stood on the ladder and gave instructions in a sort of Cockney English. He wanted morris danced with complete abandon in leather-soled shoes in the farm living room. I only had boots with leather soles and apart from that gym shoes (you see how untrained we were!) We did Royton morris in boots. I had blood in my shoes at the end! My brother and I didn't see the New Year in, we just slept!

Kees Nieuwaal, ex-chairman of the NVS remembers his first course with Pat:

The first NVS course I attended was one with Pat. I was very impressed with the "advanced" Dutch dancers; I had hardly any contact with them, they were above my level.

Even so it was a good course with a fantastic Ball in Hilversum at the end. We had plenty of contact with the English ladies. Pat taught and you could, I believe, attempt to obtain one or other certificate. Although our class did their best, Pat seemed to have a problem. There was one participant who had very different ideas about rhythm; she shot up in the air when we had our feet firmly on the ground. Pat stared as if at a natural phenomenon.

Another, older, woman had a strict individual non-conformist view of dance figures. At the end of a figure, she was in the right place at the right time but everyone else was all over the place. Pat amiably brought her into line. Luckily he could recover himself at the Ball.

On the couple of occasions I experienced him as teacher it struck me that he gave the dancers the feeling that they could do it and this improved their dancing. On one occasion I observed him listening to a participant who was trying to interpret the music in his own way. He spoke an amiable word of thanks. Very clever because you believed he meant it.

Bernard Anten wrote:

Thank you Pat for all the fine hours you have given us in these 25 years; for the trouble you have taken to convince us not to walk figures but how we can enliven a dance and its music with body and soul. That's it. That's how we are under the spell of the dance. That's how after more than thirty years dancing the simplest dance can give lasting pleasure and why we hope for ourselves that we can continue until we drop. Let that be many years yet!

A big leap brings us to the younger generation represented here by **Hettie Thielmans** who wrote:

BANG! Not afraid (bang means afraid in Dutch – ed.) but with a bang: so I landed in the middle of the Easter course at the NVS. It was a wonderful experience as I remember, 1968. The course was led by Peter Dashwood, the band was a mixture of English and Dutch players, the atmosphere, the pleasure and dedication of everyone gave me an enormous kick. During the course I became aware of Pat Shaw's fame and people said: 'this is nice, but you must come to the Christmas course, we've got Pat there'.

As the Henri Dunant House was close by, I came to the Christmas course, I saw and Pat conquered. The course was magnificent.

It's strange that not only do you yourself strongly experience the song, dance and music phenomenon but you see how everyone else experiences Pat's presence. Nothing can go wrong with Pat. Everyone radiates pleasure because of the fine dance programme he has chosen which I'm sure he has worked at for months because we Dutch can be so critical.

I can still see him in the late evening after the coffee break when everyone has flopped in a chair standing and singing songs with us. First we learned the tune, then, it became a round. He handed out the parts and then as the four-part music was heard, you could see him enjoying it with a big smile. That's one of the finest things I experienced with Pat: he so enjoys what he creates; that is his and that's what he loves.

That's why he asks for complete concentration and nothing is so relaxing as being tired after such exertion. No doubt that Pat influenced dancing in the NVS. Most important for him is the atmosphere, the harmonious movement of the dancers and good, correctly played music. The dances which made the most impression on me are the Dutch dances from English books. They were written or adapted by Pat and one of those is Juliana. I hope that Pat will not use this Jubilee to say farewell to the Dutch dance scene. I wish him a long and happy life and *bok di lupa* (good luck).

English musicians often accompanied Pat to Holland and they were also given the chance to contribute to this book, **Brian and Jan Willcocks** wrote (in English):

We've known Pat for quite a few years now; but does one know Pat or experience him? He excels in so many ways and since his achievements are so widespread it is hard to know where to begin.

His musical abilities? Conductor, composer, singer, instrumentalist, teacher, dancer... he's all of those, but it doesn't stop there. Oh no.

He also learns other people's languages so that he can sing a South American song or read the instructions for Bartok. Pat also knows people everywhere. In all countries of the world Pat seems to know somebody – and that's a lot of friends! And as he travels, he picks up more than just the musical traditions. Pat's constant battle with his waistline is made very hard because of his comprehensive knowledge of the good food of many countries, – and his ability to find some way of eating it again when home once more. To discuss food and wine with Pat is to enjoy a geography lesson, and to partner him when he organises a meal is an interesting and delicious experience.

About ten years ago, motoring from a course in Bangor, Wales, to a Welsh dance rendezvous, Pat suggested a picnic in the mountains en route. 'I'll get the things' he said 'and we'll share the bill when we know how much it is.' On a beautiful day, in fantastic scenery, we followed Pat along crazy roads until we found a nice place to stop. Then we had lunch – or rather LUNCH, Lunch, Lunch. We ate and ate things until we could hardly move.

That's what Pat's enjoyment of life is all about. He's never halfway in anything. Whatever he does, he lives it 110% and we'll always think of Pat that way.

And **Bep Mulder** (now Koopmans) who, with a lot of help, put the album together knows Pat in many forms, witness her contribution:

I first met Pat in 1955. In the following years I got to know Pat as the bearded man, a bit podgy, a man who wore colourful ties and shirts, a single dark blue suit and a very long grey winter coat! Sometimes he came in a Mini, surprisingly just big enough to carry him and his baggage.

I know him as someone with enormous knowledge of languages, countries, eating and drinking, classical music, folk music, folk dance and folk song. As an excellent cook, host and driver, a helper with solving (Dutch) crossword puzzles, pantomime dancer, accordion player, guitar player (and how many other instruments?), singer and composer (sometimes of, for me, illegible music). I know him as a lover of Chinese food, whisky and gin, Poulenc and cats, of people ... and LIFE! As a very engaging and fascinating man who inspired us all. That's how I see him because he's "A Jolly Good Fellow"!

Lies den Dunnen included a story in her piece:

When you think about the first times Pat Shaw was on the staff of NVS teachers, a lot of memories come to mind. Think of Pat and you catch a merry feeling hovering between dance and its variants on the one hand and singing and music on accordion, piano, lute, guitar, banjo etc. on the other which enthralled us deep into the Christmas nights.

How long ago was it that we celebrated his 10th Christmas course? Wil Hoving made a speech and presented a large Christmas cake with ten candles. After putting out the lights, Pat did a round of honour in his well known "poignant step" balancing the cake in his right hand showing it to all the participants, his gaze fixed on the flickering candles. To the sound of cheers he blew them all out at once. Once again it was a Christmas course with an atmosphere that only Pat could create.

This was 1959, the same course on which he earnestly passed round his snuff box. It looked brown and didn't make you sneeze.

The beginning of one course too is fixed in my memory. It must have been soon after 1953, at a time when the car was a luxury and a rare form of transport and which few committee members had. Pat had an aunt who lived in Aerdenhout and took the opportunity of visiting her before coming to the course in Zeist. The NVS was not very well off and a participant who knew Pat was asked to collect him in Amsterdam and bring him to Zeist (I think it must have been the first course at the Dunant House). Pat arrived by train in Amsterdam from Haarlem where I had the honour of welcoming him. It was a bleak winter's day and the almost empty train came in at platform 5 west, well outside the covered part of the station. A warm but hasty greeting followed. He had a guitar and a very heavy case. The guard beckoned us to follow him to the luggage van and handed us fourteen pieces of luggage consisting of musical instruments, cases and bags as if it was all part of the NVS service.

There we stood on the deserted platform with four hands and seventeen bags around us! Luckily I managed to find what must have been the only porter in Amsterdam. We took what we could and left the rest on the platform (you could in those days) and the porter made several journeys up and down steps to platform 2 east. He had no trolley let alone a motorised one and we paid him 75 cents with which he was well pleased because he thanked us three times and came running up when the train to Utrecht arrived twenty minutes later. Here followed the same procedure as before but in reverse order. But he never got the heavy bag from Pat's hand. There was something about it!

While we were waiting for the train, Pat told me he had some work to do on music for the BBC because it had to be in London the following day. The porter had brought us to the D-train. That's what you do with a foreigner, don't you? In the restaurant carriage we had a table where Pat could write without too much shaking. They were not yet open for dinner but by ordering a coffee we could sit there. Pat didn't want anything and sat obsessively correcting large sheets of music and adding arrangements. I had to drink some of his coffee to avoid it spilling on the music.

Amsterdam to Utrecht is only 35 km and didn't take long so that I wondered how long this would go on until at Maarssen the job was finished. He produced a large sturdy envelope from his bag in which the papers had been sent to Aerdenhout. He interchanged sender and addressee and now we had to get it in the post. The BBC had omitted to send sticky tape, scales and Dutch postage stamps.

For the third time (for me) we followed the luggage van procedure. Another 75 cents for the porter who assisted the taxi driver's attempts to get everything stowed. This didn't succeed and the cases had to go on the roof rack and the "m'sic" inside. I asked the taxi diver to take us to the Puntenburg post office right next to the old school where we had danced for years. The taxi drew up at the door and the former dance room was a sorting office in full swing. Pat and I slipped in through a half open door. We had agreed to make it clear that he was an Englishman and to underline that it was "very important" for the package to arrive in time for a radio broadcast. It was not difficult to find someone to take us to the main post office. Nowadays they'd expect a robber under that beard but in those days there were no robberies and beards were exceptional.

Through a back door, past a garage, a bike shed and cellars we were conducted to the saviour official to whom, just as to his colleague, the BBC had a good name. After passing through a taping and stamping machine, Pat's package of music was on its way to London by way of the night boat to Harwich. 'I can't do any more for the gentleman.' It all cost a mere ƒ1.20 considerably less than the taxi to Zeist which had had to wait outside with all the baggage.

Another flash of memory. Who can still remember the Easter course on the Pietersberg in Oosterbeek where the English staff were William Ganiford, Nibs Matthews and Patrick Shuldham-Shaw? The ball at the end was in the Musis Sacrum in Arnhem. An absolutely huge hall but there were over a hundred participants. During one of the intervals there appeared three unrecognisable dressed up vagabonds in the middle of the floor. From a corner one could hear a tune played by Tom Wisse and the three performed a high-spirited boxing dance in the Shaw tradition. It was a variant on the German Rüpeltanz which we knew from our youth movement before the war.

Although Pat played his role as a crippled tramp extremely well, he was the first to be recognised by his beard. The other two, supple and brisk as experienced morris dancers, entertained this musical tramp so well that we only knew who it was when we ascertained that the English staff were not among the spectators.

Four pictures from the 1973 Christmas Course (Pat's 25th). Clockwise: Pat inter-viewing a model of himself, Pat playing a Dutch barrel organ ('I think we've found an instrument you've never played!'), Pat leading the singing of a round and Pat welcoming his partner.

Lastly in this anthology from 1973, a contribution from **Jaap and Dini Krug**. They express the feelings of many when they write (in English):

Thank you very much for...
* coming to Holland year after year
* introducing such a large variety of beautiful dances
* giving so many Dutch girls the nice feeling of a beard
* making Dutch people sing
* being at breakfast every morning
* giving us the knowledge that there is nothing at all against working on a dance so long as this dance is worth doing all the work on
* keeping us awake on the third morning
* opening the door of the large building near Drakenburg
* lessons in South African
* making the number of dancers at the Christmas courses increase so much
* lectures about the difference between "Bokma" and "De grauw hengst"

(strong drinks)
- always starting your lessons on time
- giving us the possibility to see ties in beautiful colours
- coming in perfect condition from "De Zon" or "Old London", (nearby pubs)
- the courage you needed when you gave Mr Beveridge his original form back
- teaching us the jewels that you found in forgotten collections
- giving us a feeling of superiority when noticing that not everyone is able to learn Dutch
- waking us up at the Pietersberg ("us" including Tom Wisse)
- a lot of friendship!

Pat composed **The Dancing Dutch** for the Christmas Course in 1973 to celebrate the 25 years of his visits.

Friends from Holland went to Hampstead for the Memorial Service and then wrote tributes in Dansnieuws in January 1978. That edition also contained a facsimile of the four-page service sheet from the Service of Thanksgiving on Friday, 9 December 1977 at Hampstead Parish Church.

Dini Krug, Jaap and Dini Krug were close friends of Pat Shaw. Jaap is one of Holland's most popular teachers and has composed many English dances –

[The service in Hampstead] was a happy gathering. A little church with many colourful flowers.

Many of Pat's dearest friends.

Pat himself was present in his tunes and songs.

Many people were invited to tea by Daphne afterwards and again you felt the presence of Pat as a proud and happy host among all his good friends. It was a "service of thanksgiving"; it was decidedly not a leave-taking. Pat will be with us for many years to come.

Dini's reminiscences were translated from the Dutch by **Fried de Metz Herman** who added – *This has lost a bit in translation, but I did try to keep as close to the text as possible. Daphne was Pat's (and my) landlady in Hampstead, London.*

Pat was the best and happiest host I have ever known. He loved treating his friends – be it to food or music or just conversation. *

Ria Mathey-Boin – *Hampstead is surrounded by hills and even the street leading to the Church rises steeply. It is a small and simple Church quite appropriate to Pat. Music is playing as we enter, not Psalms but Pat's own dance music. There is a huge crowd – all Pat's trusted friends. Psalm 150 made a particular impression with words like "Praise the Lord on the lute and harp, praise Him with cymbals and dances". A psalm wholly appropriate to remember Pat's life.*

Douglas Kennedy remembered Pat as a man who brought strength to the dance in England and abroad with his unbelievable energy. And from the tribute by the chairman of the Standing Conference for Amateur Music (J. K. Owens CBE – ed.) it appeared that Pat had also done a lot of work in that field and made quite a name for himself.

The service ended with the singing of Lord of the Dance. The service was short and simple in the style of Pat Shaw.

When the call went out for reminiscences for this project, people from Holland responded to the call for memories:

Trijn Nijdam recalls – *Pat first appeared in Holland as a musician on a Christ-*

---

*   Taken from the CDS magazine.

mas course. He arrived just before dinner. We went to our rooms to change and there was suddenly the sound of dance music on an instrument we had never heard before – an accordion! We were used to dancing to the piano and flute, played by very good musicians, but the drive we were given when Pat played for our dancing was a new dimension. Amazing.

After this first visit he came to Holland as a teacher, composer and singer. He came more than twenty times and on the twenty fifth occasion there was a huge party in his honour with a barrel organ playing dance music. A big band was formed by members of NVS and Pat was presented with a "Book of Friendship" filled with many, many pages written by the Dutch dancers and many other souvenirs of his visits. After he died this precious document of friendship and admiration was given to the EFDSS but NVS now has it back on loan and at Christmas courses, in a quiet corner, we can look back on those memorable years.

He always brought new dances, music and songs from different parts of the world with him. He tried out new dances, using the Dutch as guinea pigs. He generously gave the Dutch teachers the chance to copy his dances and the music. At that time there were no photocopiers so every spare moment was spent writing till our fingers turned blue. But at the next event, when Pat had left, Cor Hogendijk and I were able to teach some of the new dances: a joy for all.

Co de Haan – *I remember an incident when Pat became very angry, which didn't often happen. He was explaining a dance; it may well have been a new dance, which he wanted to try out. Something went wrong with the teaching. We started giggling because it kept going wrong. Pat was not happy (we didn't realise it) and suddenly lost his self-control and let rip with a loud voice. A deathly silence fell and you could have heard a pin drop. We realised later that our behaviour had let us down. We were generally quite chatty and teachers from England weren't used to that. In the many years that I experienced Pat's teaching, this was, fortunately, the first and last time that there was any confrontation and it was entirely our own fault.*

Jaap Krug – *When in 1948 Patrick Shuldham-Shaw came to Holland for the first time, he came as an accordionist to play in Richard Callendar's class at the Christmas course. I remember how their coming brought a sudden change of atmosphere. Pat's playing gave the dancers a push that was new to them. It was a wonderful week. And how we were surprised when, during the demonstrations on the last evening, we suddenly saw our musician performing enormous capers in a morris dance.*

*It was about a year later that Pat suddenly had to replace one of the teachers and he was wonderful. After a couple of years the number of dancers at the Dutch courses had come down to some tens and the Dutch committee realised that the only person who could possibly change this was Pat. After that he taught at all our courses – sometimes at Easter and always at Christmas – and soon the Christmas course was overbooked every year. And so we learned to know and to appreciate Pat in all his periods: in his square dance flavoured time, in his "traditional" period with a lot of rant step, during his year of enthusiasm for South Africa, and above all during his Playford era, when he researched and studied the old dance collections, often making wonderful discoveries. And above all we enjoyed Pat's own creations. He created a number of "perfect" dances, always combining music and movements in an ideal way. He was extremely productive. An example of this productivity: A Dutch dancer had given him some small books with old Dutch tunes, a number of them showing clearly the influence of English dance music. Within a couple of months he had composed dances to these (about fifty) tunes. **New Wine in Old***

Bottles *was the result.*

Pat loved coming to Holland and the Dutch really loved Pat. The Dutch dancers were willing to work on a dance and every course brought them something exciting. No wonder that on the occasion of his Jubilee in 1973 dancers and friends came from all over the country. In these years a number of new dances (Pat's Tradition, Our English Dancing Master, etc.) were devised in his honour and new music (like "Musician's Melancholy") was written for him. Pat was a great dancing master and for the Dutch a real friend.*

Geertje Luit – *The first time I met Pat Shaw was at a Christmas course of the NVS (the Dutch Folkdance Society). He was teaching us for several years in Zeist between Christmas and New Year. I liked the Playford dances very much. Between the dancing lessons he was often singing Christmas and other songs with us.*

He was a very good teacher and also a very good musician and singer. I remember an evening when he was singing a song of the Scottish Highlands. I will never forget his voice that sounded as if he was staying between the Scottish hills! He often played the accordion as well as the guitar. When he was teaching us he was always pulling down his pullover, so that it was inches longer at the end of the course.

Our daughter also went to the courses, she told me that one year Pat would no longer teach morris dances, because the dancers were not able to learn a special morris step!

I think he has been a very important man for the EFDS.

Aatje Vink – *I must have been nine years old when my parents took part in a Christmas course in Zeist, Holland, where Pat was teaching. Already at that age I adored him. I remember going round during the coffee break with the sugar bowl. Pat kindly told me in perfect Dutch: 'Geen suiker'. That I can recollect this so vividly in my 59th year shows how much Pat impressed me.*

Later on when I was seventeen years old I spent six months in South Woodford together with my friend Adry Zevenbergen. The two of us were au pairs and we liked English folk dancing.

We attended monthly Playford classes led by Pat on Monday evenings in Cecil Sharp House. Especially for us he taught the dance "Queen Juliana" (the former Dutch Queen). We felt ever so special.

I got the same feeling again on the Christmas course in Holland in 1973. I had taken my future husband with me for the first time. Before the very first dance Pat wanted to show something to the dancers and he picked me to show it.

I was very upset when Jaap Krug phoned me to tell Pat had died. I didn't want to go to our Christmas course that year.

Elsy van Loo remembers going to courses with Pat Shaw but, because her English was so bad at that time, she never held a conversation with him. The courses with him were not only dancing but there was also an hour's singing every day. Songs she remembers are "Patpourri" and "Deep Blue Sea" and at least one from South Africa.

The Dutch courses were so linked to Pat Shaw that reminiscences of them came not only from Holland:

Ken and Helen Warren (now living in Oak Ridge, TN) – *Patrick Shuldham-Shaw, that most versatile musician, dancer, teacher, author, composer and chore-ographer from the British Isles, numbered among his many friends and admirers a group of avid dancers across the English Channel in the Netherlands. Among*

*   Taken from the CDS magazine.

Shaw's long-standing and dedicated services to the dancing community, and one that is probably little known, was his annual Kerstkursus in Holland.

For many years Pat Shaw arranged to spend the week between Christmas and New Year's Day with his circle of Dutch friends, teaching old and new dances. We were living in Germany at the time and were invited to participate in his year-end workshop at Zeist, Holland, in 1973. It was a very special celebration planned by the Dutch group, Pat Shaw's 25th-anniversary dance workshop, when he brought fellow-teacher June Wilson Lay and Brian Willcock's dance band from London for the occasion. During that week at Zeist, Pat Shaw taught morris dancing, Scottish reels and strathspeys, advanced contras, sword dancing and Playford. June Lay filled in with sessions in more Scottish dancing, Flamborough sword and an assortment of traditional material.

The last evening was the jubilation occasion. The programme of dancing was arranged to commemorate Pat Shaw's several "periods" in chronological order: musical period, South African period, square dance period, traditional period, and creative period. The total number of dances invented or composed by Pat Shaw is large, indeed. "We danced only a handful that evening as part of the celebration; those which I can recall now are **Margaret's Waltz**; **The Real Princess** (composed in honour of Princess Margaret), "The Wives Victory" (not yet in print in 1973), **Angenietje; Little Agnes** (set to an old Dutch tune), and, of course, "The Twenty-Fifth Jubilee Contra", or "Twenty-Five Years in Holland", composed especially for the occasion.

The evening featured specially composed music by one of the musicians, many thank you gifts to Shaw from friends, a telegram from the British ambassador, and the awarding of copies of a new book on contradances, **English or Double Dutch**, to the planners of the jubilee festivities. The author, C. J. Hogendijk, was also present. During refreshments an old, hand-operated organ, fed with perforated paper strips, produced very lovely tunes. The NVS had borrowed the organ from the Utrecht museum for the party.

Patrick Shuldham-Shaw left his mark wherever he went, making priceless contributions to the world of folk music and dance.*

Brian Willcocks again (of the Ranchers Band) – who was musician at Zeist on many occasions:

The NVS – Nederlandse Volksdans Stichting – courses at Easter and New Year were held at the Dunant Huis at Zeist, near Utrecht. Pat would put the very enthusiastic Dutch dancers through their paces in traditional, 18th century and Pat Shaw material. I was fortunate for a number of years to be asked to lead the music for Pat, who always brought along some sort of "special", either of his own devising or collected in, say, Shetland or whatever. The very competent band, "The Exiles", was led by Jelle Dijkstra. They needed no urging to get to grips with Pat's exports and did credit to his very fine material, which, although generally quite sophisticated, 'fell under the fingers' rather well. This surely is a mark of quality, as the melodic line of his tunes generally develops logically, but always with freshness and without clever-clever harmonic or rhythmical devices. If only today's would-be emulators would take this on board.

Pat would often ask me to test-drive some new stuff, and being hidden away in Holland was ideal for keeping the cat in the bag until publication time. I still have the pre-publication pages of **New Wine in Old Bottles** which he handed me for trial purposes. Pat was no hater of fusion!

---

*   Taken from the CDS magazine.

Mike Wilson-Jones (from England) – *I have lots of happy memories of sharing the Christmas course at Zeist with Pat. I was a bit flabbergasted to be asked by Nibs (Matthews, early seventies, I guess) if I'd like to go over for the course and teach morris, sword and Scottish, as well as take some English beginners dancing, while Pat took the advanced. Always a hectic four days with four sessions in the mornings, four in the afternoons, plus a share of the evening's calling! Pat always had his supply of songs and rounds to fill the intervals and for late evening. Of course, that was where he tried out his* **New Wine in Old Bottles** *dances, and I still have a signed copy of the loose leaf version. I believe it was also where he first tried out his* **Quartet**. *Mary (Wilson-Jones) recollects being in his advanced class and learning these.*

Mary Curling (from England) – *My earliest memories of Pat Shaw go back to 1960, when with my friend Muriel Moxham née Kennett, we joined a week's dancing, workshop and sightseeing group of approximately two hundred in Holland. The course was led by Pat Shaw, together with the late Thora Jacques, Nibs Matthews and two Dutch callers. During the coffee breaks the group, together with their notebooks, gathered around Pat as he entertained with his singing and guitar, the Dutch in particular making the most of the opportunity to question him. They really couldn't get enough of him.*

Ken Kane (from England) – *When Paul Bumstead and I were having a short holiday in Amsterdam we met up with a local group of dancers whose main dances were English. Pat knew them very well and often went to guide/teach/lead/encourage them. One could easily see how much they loved and respected him. I guess that this was how it almost always was when people grew to know him well.*

Pat inspired many to write dances. In Holland, probably the most well known to do so is Cor Hogendijk who wrote dances **for** Pat Shaw – **Macfriesian March**,* "Pat's Tradition", "P.S. Jubilee Dance", "Our English Dancing Master" (in December 1977). Anton van Renssen wrote "Pat's Visit" and it was he who gave Pat the tune books which he used for **New Wine in Old Bottles**.

Probably the best known Dutch dance composer is Fried de Metz Herman who has now lived in America for many years.

Pat's Dutch Dances

In 1960 **Holland as seen in the English Country Dance 1713 – 1820** was published by the Nederlandse Volkdans Stichting. This was 'a selection of twenty Country Dances with references to Holland in their titles which were taken from various English sources, selected, edited and described by Patrick Shuldham-Shaw for the NVS.' (1st edition 1960 – 2nd edition 2002). In the Foreword Pat wrote

Some time ago while idly looking through a copy of Volume III of Playford's "English Dancing Master", I came across a dance called "Holland's Ginn". This, I thought, should be of interest to country dancers in Holland and I resolved to try it out on my next visit.

In the same volume I then found "Zealand" and "Batavia" and I started wondering how many more dances there were with references to Holland in

---

* The tune "Macfriesian March" was written by Pat for Cor. There was a joke about Cor's "tartan" being black-and-white as he came from Friesland (black-and-white cows!)

their titles. After looking at all the collections of country dances that I could find in the library at Cecil Sharp House, I had a list of about thirty, from which the dances in this book have been selected. Some have been omitted because either the music or the dance was not of great interest; some because up to now I have not been able to find an adequate interpretation of the dance and some because as yet I have not seen the originals – I only know they exist somewhere.

I would like to acknowledge with gratitude the encouragement I have had from various members of the NVS; the patience of many dancers in England and in Holland on whom I have tried some of these dances out; the assistance I have received from the library staff at Cecil Sharp House at all times during my research and the historical information and advice so freely given by my friends Dorothy and David Hellings.

I hope this collection may be of interest to country dancers in England as well as in Holland and that some, at any rate, of the dances will give pleasure to dancers in both countries.

New Wine in Old Bottles was first published by the NVS in 1974. In the Introduction, Pat wrote –

Many years ago I was given by a kind friend three small collections of old Dutch songs and Country Dances. At the time I thought many of them were quite attractive but I laid them aside and thought little more about them. Years later I came across them again and took them over to the Nederlandse Volksdansstichting's Christmas course in December 1970, during which I put a dance to one of the tunes and taught it to my class with fair success. I decided that the tunes were all interesting enough and between New Year and Easter 1971 I "set" all the others in the three collections and a few other Dutch song tunes as well. (Many of the dances were composed in bed at night, which may account for a certain nightmare quality about some of them!) I started trying them out on my long suffering friends on any occasion I thought I could get away with it. I received much encouragement and was urged to go ahead and publish them. So here they are, including one **(The Waters of Holland**, first version) which I had made up for my Dutch friends some years previously.

These are all essentially connoisseurs' dances. They are not intended for ordinary social hops. (It isn't that sort of music.) They vary considerably in formation, tempo, style and difficulty. Some are very straightforward, some are real teasers and it is hoped may provide a challenge to those who really like something to get their teeth into; but may I say that in no case did I deliberately attempt to be difficult. The ideas I had simply worked out that particular way and frequently when trying them out, I was astonished that pretty expert dancers should find things that I had thought fairly simple, even if unusual, as tricky as they did.

Nearly all the dances are influenced by the work of the English dancing masters of the 17th and 18th centuries. I have used most of the movements that were then current but have embroidered and extended them. For example, the usual Playford "formula movements" of leading, siding and arming will be found in most of the set dances, but seldom in their original forms. A few new movements have been included here and there, also some new ideas of progression in the longways dances.

In this day and age when country dancing is no longer the only occasion on which a young man can talk to his girl unchaperoned, dances in which there is little activity for some of the couples are not popular. In this collection nearly everyone is on the move most of the time, and I have tried to keep a reasonable balance between what is fun to do and what is nice to look at. It is hoped that at any rate some of these dances will be visually attractive for the onlooker as well as satisfying to the dancer.

Pat goes on to write notes on style and tempo –

The only plea I would make is for plenty of flow; plenty of push off the back foot and a good full-blooded movement of the whole leg, no dancing from the knees downwards only and no creeping diffidently about.

Writing about the titles and how he has tried to indicate an approximate difficulty of each dance and the actual notation of the dances, he says –

...in order to save space and therefore cost, I have used the same type of abbreviated notation that I used previously in **Quartet.** Of this, one reviewer remarked that it looked like a knitting pattern. (The main difference is perhaps that in dancing you cast off rather more frequently!)

Finally, I hope that at any rate some of the dances may give pleasure. Even if they may be found difficult, none of them is impossible with practice and some are really simple indeed.

Marjorie Fennessy wrote of this publication –

Pat had been given two or three books of old Dutch tunes (around 18th century). When he was 54 he decided to compose 54 dances to go with some of the tunes to give to the NVS (Nederlandse Volksdans Stichting) – the Dutch dancing Society. I typed them out in a shortened version (i.e. RHTn for right hand turn), which was very difficult to type, but Pat wanted to save paper. He kept changing his mind – he always thought he could do something better. This meant many re-types until I eventually said I am not typing these dances any more! It was photo-copied and collated by him – quite a mammoth task – loose sheets in a folder. Pat in his Foreword wrote "and finally an enormous thank you to Miss Marjorie Fennessy, not only for doing all the typing of the script, but for all her encouragement, kindly criticism, prodding and general help throughout the whole operation."

The book was re-published in 1996 by NVS as a bound book in the usual form of notation.

10. PAT IN WALES

Padrig Farfog (Bearded Patrick) is his Bardic Name.

Pat Shaw was involved in reviving the Welsh Folk Dance Society in the 1960s working closely with Lois Blake, then President of the Society. Mrs Blake took him to a course at Pantyfedwen, Borth. This was the first of many such courses and the start of a productive and harmonious association between Pat and Cymdeithas Ddawns Werin Cymru. As well as becoming a member of the Executive Committee of the Welsh Folk Dance Society for a number of years, Pat researched many dances and tunes and composed several others.

Felicity Blake, Lois' daughter wrote after Pat died – *When I first met Pat, he was in his late twenties. Already he had established himself as a collector and singer of folk songs, and he would disappear to remote parts of the world where he would sing for his supper, learn the language and collect tunes and songs. He had a delightful tenor voice and I remember him singing "Blow the Wind Southerly" long before Kathleen Ferrier made it famous. Songs such as the "Foggy Dew" are sung in different versions all over the world, and Pat collected and sang many of these.*

Not only was he a fine singer, he used to be a vigorous dancer and was a member of the English morris team at many international folk festivals. At Venice in 1947, I remember him sitting in the "Vaporetto" steaming across the lagoon, wearing a flowered straw hat and his morris man's breeches and hose. As we crossed, the sound of his piano accordion drifted across the water.

Although something of a loner, Pat had countless friends. During the last twenty years he worked extremely hard arranging, recording and composing folk music as well as performing. To do this work, he often sought haven at the home of one of his friends. Most of us have memories of how he would arrive, unannounced, carrying gifts – a saucepan or a brace of ducks – and bringing three weeks' washing. He would stay a few days or weeks, working hard, enjoying peace and quiet, playing scrabble (but always taking a long time to get the long words), and then maybe it would be a year before he came again. We felt privileged to be on his visiting list.

Pat encouraged music-making wherever he went, and many choirs and folk bands have cause to thank him for the workshops and courses he ran. Perhaps one of the ways we could pay tribute to him might be to do more to encourage folk music-making in Wales. Welsh folk dancers will be constantly reminded of Pat and all he gave us – records of dance music played and arranged by Pat, arrangements of folk dance melodies and composition of tunes.

Babs Salter, also of the Welsh Folk Dance Society, continued the theme of the joy of having Pat visit – *It was a very large key for the small cottage nestling at the foot of the Berwyns where we lived. Pat knew where it was hidden, and we often came home to find him catching up with his sleep or washing his accumulation of laundry or amusing himself with his artistic spirograph pictures which he presented to lots of his friends around Britain. He loved the peace and quiet of our home. He was a keen gardener and his greatest love was clematis. There are ten different varieties around the walls of Tyncelyn where there is plenty of room, all carefully planted by Pat, but the pocket handkerchief garden at Abernethy House (Pat's home in Hampstead) was his pride and joy, packed as it was with countless plants.*

Whenever he was tutoring on courses or giving concerts within reasonable and sometimes unreasonable travelling distances, I could be sure that car loads would arrive with him at Tyn Celyn for bara brith and raspberry jam teas. He was a wizard with a map and if a road was unsuitable for vehicular traffic that was the one Pat would follow. Friends who took the road with him in fear and trepidation would be delighted with some unusual building or just an enchanting view. U-turns in the middle of Manchester traffic were not unusual, and, as he never took a direct route to his destination if it was at all possible, the last part of the journey was usually hair-raising because of time being short.

Although he was latterly unwell, I didn't hear him grumble or complain. Sickness did not deter him from fulfilling his engagements, even though after one such gig pneumonia kept him in bed at Tyn Celyn for a fortnight. To the end he worked, danced and sang. That is the way I'll always remember him. He was a good friend and I was happy that he was mine but much more fortunate to have been his.

Some of his most interesting Welsh dances were composed at Tyncelyn. (Babs Salter's Home) **Tŷ Coch Caerdydd** was danced first with the aid of a few chairs in the red-tiled kitchen there, as was **Flowers of Chirk** for Jack Salter and **The Delight of the Men of Llay** for Betty Davies, both composed in the 1960s.

Frances Môn Jones from the Welsh Folk Dance Society recalled – *I first met Pat at the Royal Festival Hall, London, in a concert of folk music of all nations. Later that same year our President, Mrs Lois Blake, brought him to our folk dance course at Pantyfedwen, the first of many such courses and the beginning of Pat's association with Cymdeithas Ddawns Werin Cymru.*

Pat playing the alpine horn at Tyn Celyn Cottage in the Dee Valley, Llangollen, home of Babs Salter's first husband Emrys Jones (who is Betty Davies' Uncle). The Mini is Pat's. It is thought that this is where Pengwern Valley Galop and the Flowers of Chirk were composed.

From Pantyfedwen it was usual for him to come and stay with us at Llanrhaeadr ym Mochnant, a village nestling in the foothills of the Berwyns which he came to love so much. Often I would drive him to the top of the Berwyns, to a spot between Llangynog and Bala, leave him there in the early hours of the morning, and Pat would spend the day roaming the hills, walking miles, arriving home late in the evening exhausted but completely relaxed and thrilled with his day. It didn't matter how many times a year he came to stay, a visit to the Pistyll, our famous waterfall, was always a must. It was here that "Dawns y Pistyll" came into being. The first time we tried it out at one of our courses, I can still hear Pat, with a naughty twinkle in his eye, telling the story of our meeting with Evan Jones, an old shepherd, who remembered the dance being performed, etc., etc. This was accepted by all present except for Gwyn Bangor who raised one eyebrow and gave us a very quizzical look. How Pat enjoyed that little episode.

So many incidents took place, some comic, some sad. I would like to tell you of one particular visit. One never knew how many instruments Pat would bring with him or what kind of instruments. It always amazed me the amount of luggage a Mini would hold. On this occasion, plus the usual accordions, guitar, masses of music, out of the car came, of all things, an Alpine horn. Pat had come to practise among the Welsh hills. One afternoon during this visit, another friend called – Dr Mostyn Lewis – complete with Tibetan horn. After a time I went to prepare tea leaving the two discussing Tibetan folklore and song. Suddenly the peace of the summer afternoon was shattered by the most awesome noise which reverberated from hill to hill. The villagers came rushing out of their homes, probably thinking the end of the world was nigh. My friend helping me prepare the meal dropped a bowl of eggs making an omelette on the floor. Fred the builder who was repairing a plastered wall dropped the hammer through the wall creating a bigger hole than had previously been there. All this because Pat and Mostyn were trying to play a duet on Tibetan and Alpine horns quite unconscious of the turmoil they were causing.

Pat was unique in that he was equally at home in the Royal Albert Hall, London, or the village hall in Llanrhaeadr ym Mochnant, where he would play for our twmpathau.

I Padrig Farfog	*To Bearded Patrick*
I ddawns a chân cyfrannodd	*To song and dance he gave*
– yn helaeth,	*– in abundance,*
A'i dalent fe'n swynodd;	*And charmed us with his talent,*
Cain oedd y ceinciau nyddodd,	*The airs he spun were dainty*
A'u rhoi i'n gwerin yn rhodd.	*And he gifted them to our folk.*

E. Cicely Howells from the Welsh Folk Dance Society felt a poem in Pat's memory was justified:

He loved a jig, did Pat Shuldham-Shaw,
A jig with a tuneful tune,
An air to be hummed all the dancing night through
And whistled the following morn.

He showed with his hands
How the feet should go.
In time to the fiddler and band
And gently he'd sway to its rhythmic command,
Coaxing from all a glide and a flow
As the sequence of dance was planned.

Pat cannot die in the hearts of the Welsh,
If they dance Powell's Fancy and Sawdl y Fuwch,
With the stepping and speed he would choose,
Playing with harpist and fiddler
Our hours to amuse.

Miss Bedlington's Fancy must now join the rest,
Meillionen and sweet Abergenny,
An elegant trio for long evening dress,
Putting grace and courtesy to the highest of tests.

It is thank you to Pat, who saw the great need
And gave us his music and dances to lead

Onward and outward towards all that is true,
In our tradition and culture for me and for you.

It is sad – Oh! so sad, that his years were so few,
For a man and musician like Pat Shuldham-Shaw,
Who so readily shared the gems of his store.
It is sad – Oh! so sad that we will meet him no more.

In the Welsh Folk Dance Society's Annual Report of 1977-78, the Secretary's Report contained the following words about Pat –

Pat Shaw, spent his life steeping himself in the folk cultures of the nations with which he came into contact and being intensely thorough in his interests. It is not surprising that when Pat came to Wales, he learnt our language and researched the soul of our folk songs and dances. A man, sincere of character and a perfect gentleman at all times. It is sad to realise that we shall never again see the old familiar signature at the bottom of his letters – "Pat Sh-Sh".

Mavis Roberts (Mavis Williams) remembers that Pat researched many dances and tunes for the Welsh Folk Dance Society and when interpreting a longways dance he would often teach a complementary movement for the second couple. This greatly enhanced the dance and increased enjoyment for the second couple. When he taught "Hoffed ap Hywel" for the first time he offered a selection of steps to suit the slip jig, many of which are still danced.

In October 2007 Mavis said she *first met Pat Shaw when he came to the University College of Swansea to help the folk dance team. We were known as Parti Prifysgol Abertawe and we were preparing to dance on a Welsh TV show called "Amser Te". This would have been around 1961. Pat was teaching us to dance "Fair Caerffili", we used to practise in a large lecture room (Room 16) and Pat wanted us to try an alternative tune (one not published with the dance). In fact he chose "Ymdaith Caerffili", a tune which completely changed the character of the dance. He believed the dance had its roots in the morris tradition: to demonstrate this he danced across the hall still wearing his enormous accordion, leaping every third step out of four. He seemed to cross the length of the hall in a few bounds. Dawnswyr Tawerin still dance this dance to the tune "Ymdaith Caerffili".*

Pat gave us so much help with our dancing. He taught an open flowing style which I have always favoured even though in Wales we are asked to dance the Llanofer based dances in a very different style. He would call out from the stage 'move, boy' or 'dance from here' and pat his imposing chest. He also encouraged quiet involvement of "posts" in the social dances. He talked to us about many things in the folk world. Quite often people will disagree about the pace of a dance: Pat disliked a dance to look laboured, and suggested that a dance containing, for instance, clapping, should be danced at a comfortably crisp pace to avoid laboured clapping. In his early records with Nan Fleming-Williams the pace of **Tŷ Coch Caerdydd** *and* **Sawdl y Fuwch** *is quite brisk!*

Our current team, Dawnswyr Tawerin, evolved from Parti. Prifysgol Abertawe and it was our habit at the time to attend the Sidmouth Festival whenever we could. We would sneak back midweek to dance in the National Eisteddfod and then return to Sidmouth for the second half of the Festival. Pat had written the dance **Tŷ Coch**

Caerdydd *as a competition piece for the 1966 National Eisteddfod and, having won the competition, brought the dance to Parti Prifysgol Abertawe at Sidmouth. He had not seen his dance performed so he taught it to us that evening and it all flowed perfectly, no alterations were required! So perfect was it, that we danced it the very next day at the Festival Concert, it has been a favourite in Wales ever since.*

I shall always be grateful to Pat for the expertise and enthusiasm he shared with us, from his teaching and accordion playing to his research and his many compositions. I have personally tried to dance as many as I can, have never forgotten his lessons and can picture him quite easily even though I was, at that time, very much in awe of him.

As has been mentioned, Pat researched old traditional Welsh dances and collected, composed and arranged many airs for dances so providing instrumentalists with a wealth of tunes to add to their repertoire.

Dwynwen Berry – *I was at school in the late 60s when I first went to Welsh Folk dance courses. I was impressed and charmed by this dancing bear of a man, very light on his feet when dancing but immensely knowledgeable and able to convey his enthusiasm and knowledge to us. I didn't know enough at the time to realise the breadth of his knowledge and how lucky I was to be at those courses. I was probably one of the youngest there when the dances he composed,* **Sawdl y Fuwch** *and* **Tŷ Coch Caerdydd** *were first danced by the society members – dances which have now become a well-loved part of our tradition and am so glad now to have had that experience.* **Sawdl y Fuwch** *is still one of my favourite dances – it somehow seems to flow so well and is such an enjoyable dance – it's a great interpretation of the Llangadfan tradition. I don't think I ever spoke to him personally – I was probably too overawed and shy – not that he was unapproachable but I just remember seeing him dance and teaching us with such gusto, he was able to convey his enthusiasm and his ideas about folk dance so clearly.*

His contribution to the folk dance movement in Wales, as in other parts of the British Isles, was a very valuable one.

Tricia Collins (Babs Salter's daughter, née Jones) recalls – *He often stayed in Llangollen, where, away from the telephone and all other means of communication in the 1950s and 60s, he would, first of all relax a little and then compose and create new dances, such as* **Pengwern Valley Galop** *and* **The Delight of the Men of Llay***.*

Back in London, Pat continued with his busy life, publishing music, arranging folk music for the Albert Hall weekend, leading the Sing For Pleasure Choir, preparing teaching work and of course, recording songs and dance music for us to enjoy.

Mary-Jo Searle believes he worked with Swansea University Welsh Folk Dancers (Parti Prifysgol Abertawe) and others. Dancers from Swansea University went on to found Dawnswyr Tawerin. Pat wrote the dance **Tŷ Coch Caerdydd** for the Swansea University team This dance uses the figures from the Llangadfan traditional collection and is set to the tune with the same name which is similar to the 9th edition Playford tune Red House. The dance is now an established part of the repertoire of almost every Welsh Dance Team.

Pat also wrote the tune **Coleg y Brifysgol Abertawe** (University College Swansea) which is published in Blodau'r Grug by Cymdeithas Ddawns Werin Cymru,

Over the years Pat's input to the Welsh music scene was prodigious. Some highlights:

- In 1944 he gave two recitals in Cardiff, presumably whilst in the Fire Service

- In June 1963 he appeared on Welsh television (TellyWelly) – in Cardiff with the Whirligigs (Dawnswyr Chwyrligwgan) led by Marjorie Fennessy, dancing Welsh dances
- Whilst in December of the same year, there was an Anglo-Welsh Folk Song Recital in the Library at Cecil Sharp House in London with Esmé Lewis where they swapped English and Welsh folksongs
- In 1964 he led a course at Bangor University which ended with a dance at the end of the week
- In September 1964 – As Padrig Farfog – published "Six Easy Dances"
- In 1967 the Whirligigs danced on the forecourt of Waterloo Station, London. They were dancing Welsh dances in "Welsh" costume but were not supposed to speak – except Mervyn Clayton, who was the only one who was Welsh and so had the right accent
- In August 1966 Pat composed **Waterfall Waltz** and was thrilled when it won 1st Prize at the National Eisteddfod (Port Talbot) Competition for a Twmpath Dance
- In 1967 he published Four Welsh Barn Dances, which included **Waterfall Waltz**
- In 1971 his researches of "Welsh" dances were published as "Four Social Dances"
- In 1978, posthumously, Calan Clwt y Ddawns 2 (A Selection of Welsh Dances) stereo record was published.

Intricate Pat-turns

*This is a copy of an article which appeared in an EFDSS newsletter, reproduced by kind permission of **Hilary Warburton** – now Blanford. This course of Pat's dances was run by Nicolas Broadbridge in April 1994. Hilary attended and collected memories of Pat from participants during the weekend.*

Many members of the English Folk Dance and Song Society visiting Cecil Sharp House earlier this year may have been intrigued by a poster in the foyer advertising "Intricate Pat-Turns" to be taught by Nicolas Broadbridge on 15-16th April 1994. More intriguing still to them was the fact that the poster was from the Welsh Folk Dance Society, advertising the weekend at Llandrindod Wells of dances which most of them would think of as being English as they were written or interpreted by an Englishman, known to them as Pat Shaw. However, Pat was known to the Welsh as Padrig Farfog and spent much of his time in Wales, often staying at the house of the recently retired President of the Welsh Folk Dance Society, Alice Williams.

So the day started, in Welsh, which was somewhat daunting for the English teacher, now resident in Scotland, and the two musicians, Vic Godrich and Vi le Maistre. I think we, that is the English, were all a little surprised at the depth of feeling for Pat and the emotion of their remembrance of him. Nic taught a number of Pat's own compositions and many of the seventeenth and eighteenth century dances which Pat either revived or revised.

Constantly, the dancers recalled Pat and what he had done for Welsh dance and their feelings were summed up at the end of the day by Alice Williams. I doubt whether anyone, sadly least of all Pat himself, has ever heard such a eulogy to Pat and his life's work. There is something about Welsh oratory that the English can never match. Perhaps it is because we rarely show our emotions in public life. Perhaps it is the timbre of the voice. Whatever it was, it was a wonderful experience to be there and to listen to Alice. And even more wonderful for the visitors was the warmth of the applause for Nic and particularly for Vi and Vic. A real standing ovation, as we had never heard before, brought tears to our eyes.

Alice Williams told me later that she had first met Pat at Pantyfedwen, Borth, on a Welsh Folk Dance Society course. Much of the Welsh dance tradition had been lost, apart from a few figures and some clog steps so in the Society's early days most of the teachers were English. The dancers started with some dances published by Playford and Walsh, which were re-published by W. S. Gwynn Williams. Some of the material published by Gwynn Williams had been found in the British Library by an English-woman, Lois Blake. In the late 60s Felicity Blake, Lois' daughter, brought Pat to Pantyfedwen, where initially he was another English observer. He quickly realised that the Welsh were becoming a dancing nation again, but that there was a dearth of dances.

Pat had also met Frances Môn Jones when she played the harp at an Albert Hall Festival and he was impressed by the musicality and musicianship of the Welsh. From then on he became embroiled in the Welsh dance move-ment. He transcribed numerous dances that might have had Welsh connec-tions, such as "Caernarfon Castle" and "Lloyd's Whim". He composed dances, using traditional figures and old tunes, and **Waterfall Waltz** and **Red House of Cardiff** won first prize in their sections at the National Ei-steddfod held at Port Talbot in 1966. Realising that the Welsh musicians were not used to harnessing their music to dancers, Pat led workshops for musicians, he wrote musical arrangements, and frequently stayed with Frances in her home in the Berwyn mountains. He became a familiar figure, wearing one or another of his international hat collection, blowing his Al-penhorn on the mountainside as if there were a rising in the valleys.

Alice also recalled Pat's wonderful sense of humour; how he had laughed at the thought of adjudicating with her, as Mrs Albert Shaw, at another Ei-steddfod, which sadly was not to be, and the happenings on the day of Pat's Memorial Service in Putney. She had journeyed to London, travelling with Tom Cook from Chester and was due to give a short address at the Service. On her journey home her high heeled fashion boots were so painful she had to resort to asking a fellow traveller to pull them off for her. Oh Tom, oh Tom, where were you in Alice's hour of need? For at Chester she could not get her boots back on again and so had to walk barefoot to her car. As she did so she looked up at the stars, remembering how she had earlier sat on a Hampstead tombstone to write her tribute, having started her day by going to Wrexham to give an interview about Pat, and later travelling across Lon-don to Cecil Sharp House, then to Holly House. 'I hope you know what bloody bother I've been in today for you,' she said. And she heard him laugh, all the way home to Ellesmere Port.

Such then were the memories that many of the dancers brought with them to Llandrindod Wells this April. The day ended with a brief AGM for the members, then dinner and a dance, where we continued to dance Pat's dances, interspersed with some Welsh dances, and the band just grew and grew. We finished, by request, with a really wild Welsh **Levi Jackson Rag**, twice through.

But if you'd like a really wild coincidence, just read on, for the night before I finished writing this I was at a concert of Shetland and Norwegian Fiddle Music at Cecil Sharp House (and very good it was too). There I met an old friend, Alan Humberstone, whom some of you will know as the pianist in McBain's Band, or as the pianist in the massed bands at the Albert Hall Festivals or as one of the pianists at "Beginners" at Cecil Sharp House or, well, I wonder? For as we chatted away I told him of our wonderful weekend in Wales. 'Oh yes,' he replied. 'when Pat did an early broadcast on Welsh radio about Welsh Folk Dancing he took me with him to play the music on the piano.'

In **May 1976, the Welsh Folk Dance Society** held a week-end at Halsway Manor. The Newsletter – No. 2 June 1976 – contained a write-up of the event:

The course was led by the master himself, and the members of our Society who were present were even more impressed than they had previously been by the intricate mind (and the amazing dances produced by it) of this amazing man who started composing before entering his teens.

Dr Aled Rhys William of the University of Salford wrote to Marjorie Fennessy in May 1979 – *I can't contribute much in the way of information except that I enjoyed his company at several Welsh Dance Society courses in the mid-1950s and was very impressed by his remarkable knowledge not only of Welsh dances but also our folk songs. His singing of them to his own accompaniment was delightful to hear, and he had a great feeling for the rhythms and cadences of the Welsh language. It was a pleasant surprise to meet a "foreigner" who knew so much about our culture, and who valued it so highly among the other cultures he had made his own.*

"DAWNS" is the magazine of the Welsh Folk Dance Society. In the 1976-77 edition, Pat Shaw wrote on presenting dance on stage –

... Many of our dances are of this type which were for pleasure and to have a good time. It is a pity when all the fun and naturalness is ironed out by trying to get too much effect on stage. We must try to keep the feel of the social dance first and foremost. We must keep it happy and not let stagecraft eclipse the real dance.

... If theatricality reduces the dance quality then one should not be in favour of it, because it's the dance that matters the whole time and it's the dance quality that is the most important thing.

DAWNS 1978-79 – a piece of writing about two dances composed by Pat Shaw –

Sawdl y Fuwch.* This dance was composed by Pat Shaw who based it on traditional dance figures and used a traditional tune. He brought it in note form to an English Folk Dance Society course in Carmarthen where he decided to work it out. Many of the dancers who were used as guinea pigs came from the Llangollen Folk Dancers, so he dedicated it to them.

Blodau'r Waun or **Flowers of Chirk**. This was composed by Pat Shaw using a traditional tune. When staying at Tyn Celyn, Llangollen, he often visited the night class in Chirk school or went to the folk dances where he would call and teach. He came to know the people very well and named this dance after their group. The word "flowers" was used because the class teacher was a nurseryman – Jack Salter.

In 1991, Marjorie Fennessy sent Pat Shaw's Welsh music to Amgueddfa Genedlaethol, Cymru – the National Museum of Wales in St Fagans, Cardiff. He had written quite a few Band parts of traditional Welsh tunes and these are now available for anyone to use from the archives.

WELSH DANCES, TUNES AND PUBLICATIONS

1960s
- **The Flowers of Chirk** for Jack Salter
- **The Delight of the Men of Llay** (Difyrrwch Gwyr Llay)
- **Helen's Fancy** (Hoffed Helen)

1964
- as Padrig Farfog "Six Easy Dances"

In the Foreword to this book Pat said

Whether these dances are truly Welsh in origin is open to question. They are no less Welsh than "Lord of Caernarvon's Jig", "Oswestry Wake" and many others. What will make them Welsh is the style in which they are danced. The country dance style of late 18th century England should be forgotten and Welsh steps and holds should be introduced where possible. Accordingly in interpreting the original instructions, (which are given here so that others may make their own interpretations if they so wish), strict accuracy has given place to something more in keeping with the Twmpath, where it is hoped these dances may be found a useful addition to the repertory, and original movements have sometimes been replaced by the nearest equivalent in the modern Welsh idiom. It must be remembered also that certain figures e.g. "Allemande" and "Right and Left" changed considerably during this period. This explains why the same instruction in the original has been interpreted in different ways.

1966
- **Waterfall Waltz**
- Published **The Delight of the Men of Llay** – Welsh Betty's Dance
- **Pengwern Valley Galop**

---

*   This translates as the Cow's Slip but we know it better as the Cow's Heel.

1967
- **Red House of Cardiff** to the tune "Tŷ Coch Caerdydd"
- "Four Welsh Barn Dances" published which included **Waterfall Waltz**

In the Foreword he said,

What gives a dance its sense of nationality is the style in which it is performed, rather than the actual figures, and whenever I see these dances performed by Welsh people, they have looked just as Welsh as the few dances of undoubted Welsh origin.

1971
- Researches of "Welsh" dances published as "Four Social Dances"

1978
- "A Selection of Welsh Dances" Stereo Record published posthumously, Calan Clwt y Ddawns 2. Pat had been very involved with this. He played accordion, guitar and flageolet and sang. The band played his arrangements of tunes he had collected "Sweet Richard", "Miss Williams' Fancy" and "Milford Haven" and his own "Richard's Wife" and "Mince Pies".

The book "Something old, Something New"/"Hen a Newydd" contains all but three of Pat's researches/compositions. Those missing are his **Carlam Nant Pengwern/Pengwern Valley Galop**, 1966. (Pengwern Valley is part of Llangollen), **The Delight of the Men of Llay** (for Betty Davies) and **Helen's Fancy**"

Alpine horn with Pat!

11. PAT IN AMERICA

When Pat died, **Fried de Metz Herman** wrote in the January 1978 edition of the CDSS Newsletter* –

'The sad news came to us during Thanksgiving 1977. The Nederlandse Volksdansstichting (our Dutch counterpart) informed us that Pat Shaw had suddenly died in Weymouth, England.

For us, his friends, it is a stunning blow. We have lost an exquisite musician, composer, choreographer, dancer, musicologist, singer, lecturer, teacher, writer, and above all, friend.

The Dutch dancers have known Pat since 1948 when he came to Holland for the first time. They recognised his monumental worth and he was asked back year after year.

For the sole purpose of attending Pat's well-known class, "Another Look at Playford", I went to live in London for a year. How we all enjoyed those sessions! And how happy I was to be there.

Pat was an outstanding human being, born with great talent, working intensively to develop that talent and using it to try and make people happy. He has succeeded gloriously.

He did considerable research on English, Scottish and Welsh dances and dance tunes. The English Folk Dance and Song Society showed its appreciation by awarding him the Society's Gold Badge in 1971.

Even during his lifetime, his name had become an adjective. We have all heard of a Pat Shaw dance or of a dance in Pat Shaw style. And so his life's work in the furthering of people's happiness will continue. May it never end.

Pat enjoyed his stay in the United States tremendously and was always saying how much he wanted to return for a further visit. Pinewoods was something very special to Pat; witness his creative **Between Two Ponds**, a book with fourteen new dances, especially written for and generously donated to the Pinewoods fundraising effort.

On the 9 December, 1977, at 2.30 p.m., a memorial service was held in his Parish church, St John's in Hampstead, London. Many of his friends for whom the distance is too great were not able to attend. But in the spirit, we, friends for so many years, were there.

What a great privilege it has been to have known Pat. What joy he has given and is still giving.

---

*   Taken from the CDS magazine.

Our deep sympathy goes to Christopher Shaw, who writes "I have lost a brother who was always a tower of generosity, good humour and good music."

Pat Shaw visited America only once, in 1974, but he truly made his mark with the members of the Country Dance and Song Society of America (CDSS). In his time there, he spent two weeks on the staff at Pinewoods Summer Camps dance weeks. He then toured around the US until the end of October. (See the programme of dances Pat taught at Pinewoods later in this chapter – Ed.)

CDSS informed its members of this forthcoming visit and Pat's availability for engagements from 26 August to 31 October.

Mr Shaw is a long-term Member of the EFDSS. He has done a great deal of research into the Playford dances and has, as he says, "fairly strong views" about them. (They are most interesting!) He has also created many dances and hopes to bring about fifty new dances with him this summer; the music is newly composed also. He is, in addition, thoroughly acquainted with the traditional country dances. One of his specialities in sword dancing is the Papa Stour dance from Shetland which he learnt in the islands, and he has a fine background of morris dancing.

Mr Shaw is currently at the School of Scottish Studies in Edinburgh; he writes that he is "working eight months of the year on a vast (13,500 texts, 3,300 tunes) collection of north England and Scottish folk songs collected by Gavin Greig and James B. Duncan about the same time as Sharp." His normal repertoire is, he says, "largely international", and he is very well known as a performer of folk songs. He has also done a lot of work in schools with folk music "as a lead to general musical education", and with this has used play-party games extensively.

As one may see, Mr Shaw has a wide variety of subjects of interest to CDSS members. He is an excellent lecturer and can be counted upon for a most interesting workshop or session. He has given us no indication of what he would like in the way of a fee; if hospitality and travel expenses can be guaranteed, he would probably be happy with whatever the centres or groups could manage. He is particularly anxious to lecture on the work he is doing in Scotland.

Memories of that time in Pinewoods are still fresh for a number of people. A general memory is how much Pat's singing was loved by the people in camp – particularly the 'Goat Song' when he paced back and forth in front of the group as he sang, still wearing his accordion although not playing it.

Gene Murrow (musician and dance teacher) – *Pat visited the States in 1974. During that summer, he spent two weeks at Pinewoods Camp, at what were then called the "Dance Weeks". These were programmes combining English country dance, American contras and squares, morris, sword, and folk song sponsored by the Country Dance and Song Society of America (CDSS), under the direction of May Gadd who had been Director since arriving in the US in the 1920s.*

An important feature of the Dance Weeks, no longer part of Pinewoods workshops these days, was a weekly demonstration by a select group of dancers, plus staff. I was there as a 27-year-old staff musician, playing oboe, recorders and accordion for dance classes, for the demonstrations and for the evening parties. May Gadd (Gay) was still active as director of CDSS and as programme director for the workshops.

I recall a combination of excitement and trepidation about Pat's participation in the programme. On the one hand, he was clearly an accomplished teacher, singer, leader, choreographer, and researcher and quite a celebrity. On the other hand, his reputation for upsetting the apple-cart preceded him, and Gay in particular was a bit nervous about how he might affect the pursuit of English dance in the US as she had nurtured it for so many years. Pat lived up to the advance billing on all counts.

On the bandstand, we all were thrilled by his accordion playing and interpretation of the English repertoire. His playing had great zest, energy, danceability and creativity. Frankly, I don't remember much about his dance teaching or calling in the evenings (I wasn't calling then, and not even dancing that much, being on the bandstand most of the time). I believe Susan or I have some old Philips-standard cassette tapes of his calling that I made that year, which I might be able to find.

Two incidents do stand out clearly in memory:

One was the famous Scotch-tasting party when, one afternoon, he invited some people in for a pre-dinner party. Upon arrival, we found an open suitcase with several bottles of single malt Scotch opened and an assortment of cups. Apparently, he had brought over all this liquor from the UK and was going to convince all us Colonists of the superiority of single malts over the blended whiskies normally consumed here. So there we all were, crowded into the cabin, holding our little cups, sampling one single malt Scotch after another, with Pat extolling each of the makers qualities! The party became rather riotous in short order.

The second was Pat's contribution to the weekly demonstration. I think Gay was hoping he would organise a brilliant country dance demo or sing some of the chestnuts of the English folk revival ("Lark in the Morn" or "Seeds of Love" etc.) which meant so much to her. Instead, for both weeks, and despite her not too well concealed discomfort, he insisted on singing a Welsh ploughman's work song. At the appropriate time in the demo programme, he strode over to one end of C# pavilion. He was quite large, as you know, both in actual stature and in presence/carriage. Then, throwing his head back, he almost bellowed this powerful, rough-cut working song in Welsh as he slowly strode back and forth across the pavilion as if he were ploughing a field. We all didn't know quite what to make of it, but he obviously was having a grand time.

Looking back, I think I understand his motivations. The English folk revival had gone through many changes and challenges (we seem to be at such a spot again today with our ageing "Playford" groups while the ceilidh scene seems to be thriving). Pat was enormously creative and dedicated and I think he wanted to keep things alive and off-balance a bit – to keep it fresh and interesting – and I think he relished his somewhat "bad boy" reputation. All of that contributed to his making a strong impression at Pinewoods and to the change in direction of America's approach to the English dance which led to our tackling new reconstructions of old dances and the creation of the large body of country dances composed by Americans.

Kate Van Winkle Keller (dance teacher) – *"Pat Shaw at Pinewoods in 1974"*

My recollection of Pat's visit to Pinewoods is very, very vivid, because he came just at the moment that Joy Van Cleef, Chip Hendrickson, Ralph Sweet and I were discovering and reconstructing authentic early American material and working with Wendy Hilton on the appropriate footwork and technique for eighteenth century dance. We had met with great resistance to our efforts in the country dance world. We were looked on with much suspicion and bitterly labelled "anti-Sharp". Joy already knew Pat and had corresponded with him so we knew he was a kindred spirit. He too was looking at the interpretation of the old dances and how they would be affected by authentic technique and information in period manuals. We had shared materials with him across the pond.

The atmosphere at Pinewoods in 1974 was polarised. Chip and Pat were on the staff, Joy and I were campers. Pat spent several days after camp in Manchester at the Van Cleef home so we had plenty of time to share feedback. There were some who wholly supported what Pat and we were finding and many others who felt that, by taking a "second look" at Sharp's reconstructions of early dances, Pat was ruining country dance forever. While our work with early American dance was of mild interest because of the forthcoming bicentennial in 1976, neither his nor our ideas about technique were welcome either.

Naturally, Pat's wonderfully warm nature and ability to present his work won many over to his point of view and created a demand for more such classes and workshops, but it would be many years before "taking a new look" would be generally accepted without a good deal of criticism. Today, with so many sources easily available, it seems almost automatic that we look back at the original instructions when we have a question about a figure. Thanks to Pat and those who followed him, we now dance many old dances much more closely to the way they were danced when they were first devised.

We have not lost Cecil Sharp's beautiful dance interpretations – they are still untouched – we dance them with pleasure and his figures and technique have become a prized tradition, certainly as Pat would have wanted it. But Pat's vision and willingness to brave entrenched and deeply held loyalties gave us a new world of country dance, historically a much more accurate one, for which we are all forever grateful.

Jacqueline Schwab (musician, leader of "Bare Necessities") – *I attended Pinewoods Camp for two dance weeks the year Pat visited America and Pinewoods. He startled the attendees (and America's English Country Dance world) with his fresh view on Playford, his innovative choreographies and his overflowing cornucopia of other artistic creations (his* **I Sat Next to the Duchess at Tea** *round comes to mind). He charmed us with his thoughts on dance. I vividly remember him talking about a "moment of poise" between the phrases in his reconstruction of the dance "The Spring" (Thomas Bray, 1699). I still use that phrase in my own teaching, even though its elegance does not match my own language, since I believe it captures the simultaneous sense of flow and phrase punctuation that English dance can have. Pat's charismatic presentation of his work swept us away and inspired the whole new generation of choreographers in America. (I co-wrote a dance "Hudson Barn" in the 70s, a dance that has been on many ball programmes, and I realise now that I might not have written it or my several later dance reconstructions, if not inspired by Pat's work.) It was only later, when I visited England in the mid-80s, that I came to understand that Pat's work had not been immediately respected or credited, at least from what I heard. That might have been a natural chain of events, but Pat presented his work so confidently and brilliantly, that he drew us into his world, with (in my memory) nary a clue that it might be considered controversial.*

That fall (September? October?), Pat gave the first musicians' workshop that I attended, in the living room of dance leaders Arthur and Helene Cornelius. At the time, I was truly a greenhorn dance pianist – I'm not sure I had yet played for a dance evening. Pat gave us a lot of practical information about the art and craft of playing for English country dancing, as well as a sense of his joy in playing for dancers. He had a great sense of humour – he played for us his killer version of "The Boatman", which he renamed "The Grounded Boatman", which ground to a halt a few measures into the piece. Pat's encouragement and information helped launch me (then a young, shy, undeveloped musician) on my long dance musician's journey.

I was too shy and tongue-tied to talk much with Pat, but I remember conversing with him about his music typewriter, an unusual gadget in those days. I was also interested in Scottish folk song and believe I talked with him a bit about his work with the Gavin Greig "Last Leaves" collection. I also remember (and still own) his creation of 'words' to "Dick's Maggot", inspired by the Swingle Singers. (See pages 154-155. – Ed.)

What a gift to the world he was!

Tony Barrand (Singer, Dancer and Recipient of CDSS Lifetime Contribution Award, 2008) Tony has three indelible and cherished memories of Pat for which he believes he will be forever in debt. The first concerns the Christmas Concert and will be found under that heading. – *I didn't actually meet Pat until the summer of 1974. My singing partner John Roberts and I had been hard hit by the morris dance bug while teaching English songs and ballads in 1973 at a "Folk Music Week" run by the Country Dance and Song Society of America (CDSS). We saw a group of men doing a Cotswold morris dance as entertainment in an evening country dance party. This revealed the type of display dances alluded to in Pat's Christmas show. "Have to learn how to do that!" So the next year we went to "English Dance Week" also run by CDSS at Pinewoods camp in Plymouth, Massachusetts.*

My second memory, then, is that "Massachusetts" was the first word Pat Shaw said while introducing himself to the camp in August 1974. "I didn't know what to expect" he went on "I thought I might see piles of false teeth laying around". This was met with puzzled silence. "Massachusetts", he said again. More silence. "MASS O' CHEW SETS", Pat the pun master said slowly and more loudly, as one would to foreigners without good command of the English language. He laughed heartily; his audience produced a muffled groan, the standard American response to a pun, an unloved form of humour.

The rest of the week, I revelled in getting his take on the radically different Papa Stour sword dance he had collected, with its challenging "loom" and "tunnel" figures and delighting in learning from him many of his own composed dances. What a teacher he was! His clarity and humour became a model for my own teaching, albeit one that set the bar very high. Though I have never liked singing rounds very much, two of his own among the many he sang that week: **I Sat Next to the Duchess at Tea** *and* **To Stop the Train** *simply won't go away.*

But the third piece of indebtedness came from the education he gave to John Roberts and me, after lunch and before dinner, sampling from the one dozen or so bottles of single malt whisky. On one or two occasions, he invited May Gadd (known affectionately at Pinewoods as "Gay Mad") to enjoy the riches. It doesn't get much better than that: garnering the subtleties of single malts ("smooth", "sharp" and "peaty") and listening in on the stories of those two links back to "Mr Sharp" and the early days of the revival of interest in English music and dance. Now that was the major gift I still have from meeting Pat Shaw. How I wish there could have been more.

Bruce Hamilton – *I met Pat when he came to Pinewoods camp in 1974. His arthritis kept him from dancing much, but he still wowed us. He introduced* **K & E** *by teaching it at one of the evening dances – to a roomful of people who'd never done it before. He got us singing and dancing "The Noble Duke of York" and "I've been to Harlem" as party games, and we later danced "Dick's Maggot" to a 4-part arrangement he taught to a group of singers. He showed me that a reel can be played "as a hornpipe" when he taught Kate's Hornpipe. He sang "Admiral Benbow", played "The Birks of Invermay" for me when I needed a strathspey at Show and Tell, and entertained us on the kalimba. All this between teaching the finer points of his dances during the day and regaling us at late-night parties.*

This was 31 years ago (this was written in 2005) *and I remember those things clearly (and still sing "Admiral Benbow"). What a generous teacher he was and what an impression he made!*

Marshall Barron – *Pat Shaw was one of the most loveable people I ever knew. His warmth, generosity, charm and joyousness touched all those near him. I feel privileged to have been his friend. One time on the path of Pinewoods Camp, going to breakfast, I greeted him, gave him a kiss, and said 'How are you?' 'Better.' 'Better than what?' 'Better than I was a minute ago'.*

Once the evening's entertainment at the Pinewoods Camphouse was a home-made movie of morris dancing. Something malfunctioned and the tape started to pour out from the reel in a tangle. Pat leapt to his feet, came to the front of the hall and kept the roomful of people happy for an hour. He sang, he taught us rounds, he created choral singing by teaching parts to the basses, to the tenors, to the sopranos, and then singing verses above this choral underlay. A wonderful rich texture. (Afterwards, rather shyly, he said to me 'Do you think that I am being overexposed?' Later, I tried to make up a clever verse about the pleasures of being covered with a "PatShaw [sic] work quilt" – patchwork quilt, (if you say it quickly!).

Joan Carr Shimer (Pat wrote **Quite Carr-ied Away** or **Joan Transported** for Joan) – *Pat was a vibrant person, overflowing with music and the joy of music making. He is unforgettable. That summer at Pinewoods he gathered a small group of us to sing dance music – something none of us had ever done before – or ever since, I believe. We sang "Dick's Maggot" and "Balquidder Lasses" for the entire camp to dance to in the evening. Such a joyful experience it was!*

It is an honour to have a dance of my own by Pat!

Pat also wrote **The Shy Mer-chant** or **Jack's Serenade to Genny** for Jack Shimer's first wife, Genny Shimer.

Susan St Germain (Murrow) – *Pat's visit to Pinewoods in 1974 – my memory of Pat Shaw conjures up a cheerful chap who brought a wonderful assortment of new dances and songs. I was terribly shy in those days and we stayed out at Cottey House (in the Boondocks) so I wasn't part of the "in-crowd" who got to know Pat on a personal level. In general, I don't think anyone who was there at Pinewoods that summer will ever forget Pat Shaw, the "force of nature" that was with us in 1974.*

George Fogg also knew Pat very well, having him as a house guest for a spell. May Gadd often asked him to house the English staff leaders either before or after the Pinewoods camps. For a while he thought he should call his house "Pinewoods Camp Half Way House".

Dick's Maggot

Dick's Maggot

optional alternative for 1st A bars second time through

then on to 2nd score of previous page as before. ✳

Introduction if required.

(Hum)

(Hum)

(Hum)

(Hum)

© Copyright Pat Shaw Feb 1972

George also sent this entry from the diary of **Louise Winston** which he came across when sorting out her effects:

"Abbreviations: wi = with; gp = group; wkend = weekend

Saturday August 3, 1974

(Pat Shaw - being picked up @t Bus Sta)

Sunday August 4 1974

... Top country class, C# – the top group's split in 1/2 wi those staying 2 weeks having Gay in C# Minor, while the rest of us – a big hall full, having Pat Shaw in C# (11 :15 –12:00). He did an excellent job. Taught American Seat (A Merry Conceit) with Gloria Berchielli as my man; Boatman – with Chris Walker (Pat's version - siding replaced by side by side as in morris – into line & back right shoulder, then L: last fig, had Lady 2 circle with the end men, then her partner cuts in & hand turns her; then he circles with the other 2 women, then she cuts in & turns him – more interesting than the present one; then a 5-C dance of Pat's **The Rose of Tankerton** – 1st fig only – I with Julie Drexler; then traditional one, Kate's Hornpipe, a duple longways very near to a Strathspey – I with Shirley Drexler. Then reviewed **The Rose of Tankerton** ... 8:00 –10:15 – dance – ... Pat Shaw led several very easy, lovely dances"

PAT SHAW – 1st Dance Week – Pinewoods 1974

The Spring	Bray 1699 original bass – 1 minor alteration.
Bartlett House	Bray 1699.
Monica's Delight	
Merry Conceit	Kynaston 1710 + D Vol.II originally 6/4 now 6/8.
The Boatman	
Kate's Hornpipe	CDM 7.
The Pursuit	Dancing Master Vol.II.
Mr Beveridge's Maggot	Dancing Master 12th & 17th Editions.
The Rose of Tankerton	

PAT SHAW – 2nd Dance Week – Pinewoods 1974

The Scotch Measure	Bray 1699 original bass.
	Tune believed to be composed by Purcell.
The Health	B music: Everal de Jersey.
The Sleepless Swain	
Up on a Lofty Mountain	
Ludlow Castle	DM Vol II – 4th Edition. 2 notes in B music – bars 3 & 4
News from Tripoly	DM Vol I 12th Edition.
	(or Manage the Miser Vol. and Edition uncertain).
The Tatler	John Essex 1710.
The Lover's Luck	Thomas Bray 1699.
The Wives Victory	Thomas Bray 1699.
Derry Down Derry	Tune: Balquidder Lasses in Royton Tune Book.
Portsmouth	
The Country Farmer	as in CJS Book VI. Set XX Tunes.

PAT SHAW – Evening Dances – Pinewoods 1974

The Flowers of Chirk	Machynlleth.
Prince Garden	Seàn South (Roddy McCorley) or Kelly the Boy from Kildare or The Macfriesian March (Caller's Choice).
Arnold's Circle	Looking for a Partner and Little Burnt Potato.
K & E	
Valentine's Day	printed in CDS magazine.
Margaret's Waltz	printed in CDM 6.
Upon a Summer's Day	(see changes)
Friday Night Special	in Everyday Dances.
The Welsh Jig	Preston 1793 Six Easy Dances.
Farewell Marian	Four Welsh Barn Dances.
Waterfall Waltz (Caerdroea)	Four Welsh Barn Dances.
Morecambe Bay	alternative tune Billy Barlow in O'Neill.

After Pinewoods Pat spent two weeks in September 1974 travelling around Eastern Kentucky with John M. Ramsay from Berea College.

John M. Ramsay writes – *Pat Shaw came to Kentucky with his portly posture, big accordion and ailing back in September 1974. Berea College's Recreation Extension Office had obtained a grant from the Kentucky Arts Council to have Pat help us enhance traditional songs, music and dance in a region once their stronghold.*

As I drove him around the Eastern Kentucky hills in my old Ford station wagon, we put the seats down so he could lie on his back as we travelled from school to school. It was great fun to travel with Pat. His creative mind was always at work. We played Pinky Stinky, thinking up pairs of rhyming words and then giving each other clever, cryptic definitions from which to guess the rhyming pair. I don't recall any of the word pairs but will always remember how much fun Pat was.

When we arrived at a school, he would strap himself into the heavy accordion, put on his happy face and act as if he felt great. In a way, he did feel great because he was sharing what he loved and was following in the footsteps of Cecil Sharp who had visited some of the same communities 58 years earlier in 1916. By the time Pat arrived, however, most of the traditional folk arts had been replaced with modern culture. Pat did not try to reintroduce the old traditions. Instead, he used his own repertoire of fun folk songs collected from around the world and helped the kids in these still isolated communities to remember with pleasure that they had personally met a funny man from Scotland/England. I recorded a cassette tape of some of his shows. The quality is poor, of course, but it shows how he charmed the kids and got them singing along with him.

We ended the two week tour at the Mountain Folk Festival, Adult Section, held at Levi Jackson State Park near London, Kentucky. The weekend at Levi Jackson was special and Pat shared his many talents with us without stint – he had so much to share and he dominated the Adult Festival that year.

He woke us up in the mornings almost yodelling his goat call song – Oes Gafr Eto (Calling the Goats). He was superb at leading the singing sessions, coached us in a traditional morris dance and led country dances, some of his own composition which was a daring break and came as a surprise to conservative traditionalists who expected only "authentic" material - the "sacred" repertoire at that time. He shared some of his research into songs and dances and charmed everyone.

I taped many of the sessions he led and made copies for the Christmas School

Store so that others could hear Pat at his congenial best.

We had some small amount of funds ($50) left after the Mountain Folk Festival. It is always nice to have some extra funds because they can be used to do extra nice things – like ask Pat, who had been a featured caller at Levi Jackson State Park, to create a dance for the Festival. I "commissioned" Pat to compose a dance for us and presented him with the challenge that it must accommodate the two posts in the main hall at the Lodge House where we danced.

Pat went back to Edinburgh and worked up the dance there.

The following summer the Berea College Country Dancers went to England to participate in the 1975 Tyne and Wear Folkmoot where they were representing the United States. After Newcastle they went on to tour England and Scotland – Pat arranging several engagements for the Scottish visit. John continues – *He tried out **Levi Jackson Rag** on my Berea College Country Dancers in Newcastle-upon-Tyne. He made a couple of adjustments and then presented me with the final copy printed on a single sheet when we met him in Edinburgh a few days later. That sheet should still be in the archives at Berea College.*

The music recapitulated the sounds of both Lewis and Donna Lamb (Appalachian hoedown) and the McLain Family Band (Bluegrass/Beaumont Rag). Both bands had provided music at the Levi Jackson Festival. Musicians found the music challenging because of its unusual progressions, but they liked challenges. We callers also had to learn how to teach the dance: "Ladies, after the do-si-do move in toward the centre for the 5-ladies chain. Gentlemen, be ready to snag the second lady past your partner." It was an unusual dance at the time. It is great to find the dance and tune nominated for the "top ten" country dances.

The arrangements Pat made for my dancers in Edinburgh were stupendous: he was a wonderful host. There was a memorable performance at Princes' Street Gardens, and the tour also had its phenomenal abdominal aspects. Pat prepared a haggis repast at Gladstone's End on the Royal Mile. He recited Browning's (sic – John probably means Robert Burns) Ode to a Haggis and then plunged a knife into the "delicacy", bloated with steam. Lewis Lamb, upon taking a sample bite, asked me what I thought of it. I, having grown up in Pennsylvania-Dutch country, commented that I would have liked it better with the ketchup which had been applied to our "scrapple" when we were kids.

Pat had also arranged for the Berea Dancers to give a performance not far from Edinburgh in a fine, modern, state of the art media centre located in a converted horse barn on the outskirts of the city. The performance was recorded on 8-track tape as I recall. But, before the performance, Pat had himself prepared a spectacular dinner for us. The dining room had rich wall-to-wall purple carpeting which set off the gleaming white linen table cloths. Crystal goblets on the banquet table were filled with elderflower squash which Pat had personally made. Its yellow colour against the white and purple were unforgettable. Have you ever made elderflower squash? It requires collecting a large number of the flowering stems and tediously pulling the petals, stamens and pistils from the branching stems. The flowering parts are then steeped like tea. When did Pat ever find time to make this brew – a tedious job for a troupe of some 26 people – as well as organise and lead our tour?

Pat was at the time preparing the comprehensive collection of folk songs for the School for Scottish Studies. He told me that he had always felt that the tune for "Amazing Grace" was American but had instead found the tune was originally Scottish. He did not have the reference at hand when I talked with him and died before mailing it to me.

Patrick Shuldham-Shaw was a giant in so many ways: a big man with a big accordion and a very big heart. He drove himself to the limit in bringing joy to others and used his wonderful creative talent and love of puzzles in the service of the music and dance communities. Hopefully these assembled memories will inspire others in years to come to share their talents generously in making life a great and fun-filled adventure.

Others have recalled that he was in a great deal of back pain at this time and how difficult it was to get Pat into John's relatively small car. The pain did not, however, dampen his energy and enthusiasm when he was in front of a group.

Alice McLain of the McLain Family Band remembers how specific and exacting Pat was when they were learning the **Levi Jackson Rag** tune.

Hanny Budnick writes – *Some time after his two weeks at Pinewoods in the summer of 1974 Pat came to Philadelphia, Pennsylvania, for a week full of activity. I had arranged for a number of appearances and played chauffeur.*

He arrived on 30 September and, when he left exactly one week later, he had worked with seven entirely different groups, sharing a different kind of knowledge with each, and enriching them all. Tuesday night was a band rehearsal for the budding Fine Companions, the Germantown Country Dancers' musicians. Pat worked with them and taught them to sing on their instruments. Wednesday night he shared some of his own dances with the dancers (and how many of us can boast now of having learned **Walpole Cottage** *and* **K & E** *from Pat himself?). Thursday morning we visited a Quaker elementary school. Pat the ballad-singer with his guitar held the kids spellbound during the assembly programme. Afterwards he went to different classrooms to sing with the little ones, teaching them African songs with kalimba accompaniment, introduce clapping patterns and interesting sounds – and he had admirable rapport with the youngsters. On Friday, Pat visited Swarthmore College for a workshop session on the Papa Stour Sword Dance. In addition he ran a dance party with his own as well as traditional material for the College Folk Dance Club. Saturday was the day of the Germantown Country Dancers' special event, for which Pat Shaw had originally been invited to Philadelphia.*

The dancers learned dances and dancing; Pat's sense for styling, his witty choreography and his original tunes were quickly recognised and then taken in with delight. Did we ever have a marvellous time!

Imagine an afternoon of singing rounds with and by Pat Shaw! That's what was arranged for Sunday, courtesy of the Philadelphia Folk Song Society. Rounds ranging from Lawes, Purcell and Lassus to modern composers, including, of course, Pat Shaw, were sung by a small but enthusiastic group. That workshop rekindled an interest in rounds, canons and catches in our community which has recently culminated in the formation of a Catch Club, and the **Duchess at Tea**, **Smetana**, **Dvorak** *and* **Janacek** *and the* **Flea and a Fly in a Flue** *have started to travel in folk music circles. Monday afternoon Pat lectured to the Graduate Seminar in Folklore at the University of Pennsylvania at the invitation of Kenneth Goldstein. The theme was the revival of ritual dance forms in England, and Pat the scholar and Historian spoke and was available for explanations. Pat also talked about his work on the Greig-Duncan manuscripts in Edinburgh and played English traditional tunes on his trusted accordion.*

The week had passed, and in its course Patrick Shuldham-Shaw had shared himself in all his diverse roles with people of all ages and of many different orientations.

On Monday I delivered Pat to his train to New York City. We Philadelphians were much enchanted with Pat, his enthusiasm, dynamics and the wealth of his knowledge which he so readily shared.

Even before he left, we had decided to invite him again for the following year. Sadly he never got to read that invitation letter and I could never follow up his invitation to visit him in the UK either.

Pat and I had many conversations about the various things he shared with the different groups in Philadelphia, his growing up in country dance circles, his travels on behalf of music and dance – and the differences between the English and American folk communities.

I treasure the memories! My children, Manya, then 13, and Vincent, then 11, remember Pat's visit as well. He was this Englishman who could eat four eggs for breakfast! By lunch time he would be really hungry again.

Marshall Barron, as well as her time with Pat at Pinewoods, recalls *Once at Hudson Guild Farm, at a dance weekend, we two sat at the piano during a quiet time and Pat played and sang for an audience of one. His passion for music, his generosity of spirit and his sweet nature, made this afternoon and my memory of him, something to be treasured forever.*

Fried de Metz Herman wrote in her book of dances, Choice Morsels, published 1989 –

in honour of Pat Shaw with love and admiration

Although all country dancers know some of Pat Shaw's tunes and dances, not many people in America knew Pat himself. He was such a colourful personality with such widespread talents and such a zest for life – it was a joy to know him!

Pat came to the 1948 Christmas Course at Ommen (the Netherlands) where we met for the first time. We had nothing to say to each other as I didn't know English and he didn't know Dutch at that time. But Pat was a born linguist and in years to come he was at home in many languages including Dutch. I always felt that his interest in languages came from the wish to communicate with people.

There are many sides to Pat's inventive genius and this is reflected in the variety of his work. He wrote waltzes, rants, jigs, reels and strathspeys, minuets, choral compositions, church music, rounds and part songs. He wrote marches and lyrical tunes and his dance formations are as varied as his methods of progression.

He did not deliberately set out to make complicated tunes and dances but when he was working out one of his sparkling ideas, he was not deterred by the level of difficulty. It's true that an intricate but interesting dance, set to an enticing tune, will give a feeling of joyful accomplishment when mastered. We see that happen with **Ah Belinda**, **Four Winds** and other dances. Once we get through the whole dance, it is not complicated any more – but just sheer joy!

Pat was a most enthusiastic performer himself, dancing morris and sword as well as English and Scottish country dances with style and grace. He loved the boisterous dances that require stamina. When Pat danced a skipping step he SKIPPED taking all the space he could get. He was no less fond of the slow stately dances and would visibly melt when singing or playing or dancing the lyrical strains.

Pat liked variety. After having sung a ballad that brought tears to our eyes, he would jump up and start a lively music-hall ditty – some catchy tune and clever words. We see this variety in some of his dances: a slow part is followed by a jolly skip-change, then back to elegance.

For Pat the tune was of the utmost importance. He once said to me: 'Get some GOOD tune and any dance will do' – one of his sweeping statements! But it shows how important the tune was for him as the starting point for a dance.

Pat was the 20th century dancing master par excellence. He was precise in his teaching: after four steps you are here, two more steps take you there, etc. He then expected the same precision from the dancers. He was a most demanding teacher and he made us dance better and remember more than we thought we could. He never underrated his audience and expected – and got – full attention.

For many country dancers Pat is THE originator of interesting modern country dances. One hears people talk about the "Pat Shaw Style" and one wonders what they mean by that.

Speaking to the DANCE TEACHER, the "Pat Shaw Style" surely means the perfect preparation before each session. The teacher must be able to read the music and fit the movement to the tune with precision. Pat was strongly in favour of giving a different colour to the separate parts of the dance by using a variety of steps. He felt – and how I agree! – that the step used should reflect the mood of the tune.

Speaking to the DANCE MUSICIAN the "Pat Shaw Style" again means the proper preparation. According to Pat most dances need a second tune. The selection of this second tune was extremely important to him. He had to find (or write) a melody with the same musical feeling as the original tune. But there was another matter concerning the musician that was dear to Pat's heart and that was how the music was interpreted. He felt that the musicians should play for the dance and not for themselves. They have to "give" the dance musically to the dancers. Pat knew to a nicety how to support the melody with well-chosen chords. He gave the dancers a feeling of floating over the dance floor by just one line of something special. Just enough – never too much. He was a most accomplished and sensitive dance musician.

Speaking to the CHOREOGRAPHER, the "Pat Shaw Style" advocates an eclectic choice of steps and movements for a new dance, not forgetting the new step and/or formation, figure, progression, combination of movements, to make this dance different from other dances. A special tune may also make a dance unforgettable.

Speaking to the RESEARCHER. the "Pat Shaw Style" warns of the fact that English Country dances from the 1700s till the present are in reality West European country dances and that Scottish, German, French and Dutch materials have to be studied in connection with the Italian and English sources. One can see how Pat's linguistic and musical abilities were invaluable to his work!

And speaking last but not least to the DANCER. I feel that the "Pat Shaw Style" – means dancing in such a way that the last drop of enjoyment and satisfaction is squeezed out of the tune, the movement, and the company. To be able to achieve this, some work has to be done first i.e. we have to learn to dance! The reward is great! When we have overcome the difficulties, we are able to relax and enjoy all that the dance has to offer.

Pat is with me in the spirit in every dance I dance, in every dance I teach and in every dance I write.

Reproduced with kind permission of Fried de Metz Herman

Dances for American Friends and Pinewoods

Pat wrote many dances for his American friends and dedicated his **Between Two Ponds** booklet to Pinewoods as his contribution to the Pinewoods Camp Capital Fund. His foreword to this collection, printed in 1976, gives an insight into his natural humility about his work and reads:

The idea of this collection came to me while I was in America two years ago. I thought it was a pity that some of the cabins and places around Pinewoods had no dances attached to them as most had. I therefore decided to make a small book of dances to rectify the matter. This, I thought, might be a way of raising some money for the Pinewoods Fund, more than I could possibly afford in hard cash. Inevitably I started thinking of further possible titles, mostly terrible puns (I am sorry, I inherited that form of humour from a Victorian father) on the names of people without whom Pinewoods would not be Pinewoods. Then I thought of various other friends I had made while in the US and the list grew and grew and so I decided to split my efforts into two collections, possibly more if I don't run out of ideas. Here is the first of them, the second will appear, I hope, in about a year or eighteen months' time.

So here is my small contribution to the Pinewoods Camp Capital Fund and it is dedicated to all the wonderful friends I made both at Pinewoods and elsewhere on my visit to America in 1974. The entire proceeds from the sale of this first edition will go to the Pinewoods fund as the costs of publication have already been met. If you all buy it in quantity and there is a demand for a further edition, the profits on that too will go to the fund. Don't forget the price we ask for this little book is a minimum. If you feel you can give a little bit more, it will be welcome and I am sure you will enjoy the dances all the more for so doing!

My apologies to those of my friends who do not appear in this collection. I did not want to put all my best eggs in the first basket! Inevitably too, there will be many for whom I will not be able to make dances; my American friends are too numerous and my creative imagination is limited. I hope they will understand that all the dances without personal references are really for them.

Finally, I must take any blame for the amateurishness of the production of this book. I would like to have given it a more spacious look but that would seriously have increased the cost of producing it. The entire enterprise, apart from some proof reading for which I am very grateful to Miss Marjorie Fennessy, has been done single-handed. I am not a trained printer, though I am trying to learn something about the art. The music was done on a Musicwriter, a marvellous machine that comes from Boulder, Colorado, and the text on an IBM Electronic Composer, the complexities of which I am at present trying to master. So please forgive the lack of polish in the production of this humble effort.

You will find that the dances vary in difficulty. I hope some of them at any rate may give you pleasure. But, even if you detest them all, please buy the book and get your friends to do likewise. It's a great cause.

Pat Shaw
Edinburgh

(I think he collated all the photocopies he had made to sell of "Between Two Ponds" at my house – Marjorie Fennessy)

Sadly, of course the second collection did not come. But **Pat Shaw's Pinewoods** did.

This incorporated **Between Two Ponds** and **Among the Pines**. In 1983, Pinewoods 50th Anniversary Year, **Marjorie Fennessy** wrote a Foreword to **Among the Pines**:

Whilst Pat Shaw had done a considerable amount of work on **Among the Pines** before his death in Dorset, England, on 16th November, 1977, he had, unfortunately, not completed all the music and dances he intended to include. Everything available is printed here, however, even if it is not in the form he might finally have chosen.

Levi Jackson Rag, Buzzards Bay and **The American Husband** were printed as single sheets before his death. He had tried out **K & E, Pine Needles, Camp House Reel, Little Hunsdon, Hamburger Special, The Leiberts' Wedding** and **Pine Cones**. The remainder of the dances and tunes were in embryo stage and I have done my best with their interpretation.

Pat had done nothing more than note down the following titles: The Dewy Fogg, a hornpipe (for George Fogg), The Norman Conquest or The Singer's Victory (for Norman Singer), The Two Sisters or Mireille and Lyndal (for Mireille Backer and Lyndal Brandeis), Chapin's Chaconne (for the Chapin family), Frank's Joy (for Frank and Joy Cleef), The Snore or Hanny's Fancy (for Hanny Budnick) and Blundon's Bourée (for Joe Blundon). It is interesting to reflect on what these would have been like.

What is certain is that he would have been delighted that we enjoy dancing his compositions and that his donation of these dances and tunes in **Between Two Ponds** and **Among the Pines** has benefited Pinewoods Camp, which he visited and so greatly enjoyed in 1974.

Christine Helwig *was one of the leading contributors to English country dancing in America through her active teaching and research. She taught at Pinewoods Camp and elsewhere and was a member of the editorial board of CDS and in 1986 she wrote for the CDS magazine –*

Pat Shaw's Pinewoods – A Variable Feast
Pat Shaw's extraordinary versatility as a composer of dances and music is exemplified in **Pat Shaw's Pinewoods**, dedicated to Pinewoods Camp. This book incorporates the fourteen dances that he composed and published in 1976 as **Between Two Ponds** and twelve new dances and eight tunes that he had planned for a second collection, **Among the Pines**.

The collection memorialises the places, the people and the experiences that Pat enjoyed when teaching at Pinewoods and travelling in America in 1974. His ideas came from many sources; he drew on his vast knowledge of traditional and historic dance forms to create new combinations of figures that are unusual and ingenious. Among the 26 dances, there are sixteen different formations ranging from sets for two, three, four and even five couples to longways, Sicilian circles and a morris dance!

Several of the formations are unique. **Levi Jackson Rag**, for example, for five couples arranged in a U-shape was composed to meet a particular circumstance. This, as we hear from John Ramsay, was the existence of several posts in the centre of the dance hall. Who but Pat would have had the ingenuity to use an impediment such as this as an accessory for a dance? Other dances incorporate a joke. In his travels, Pat was greatly amused by the ubiquitous McDonald's Restaurants on our roadsides. His fertile imagi-

Pat Shaw with May Gadd at Pinewoods Camp, 1974 *

*   Taken from the CDSs magazine as before.

nation concocted **Hamburger Special** in which he teams a figure that recalls the golden arches with the traditional tune "McDonald's Reel"!

Many of the dances incorporate a hidden meaning or reference of special
significance to the person for whom Pat was writing. **John Raymond** has a
unique three trio formation, each trio consisting of one man and two
women. In 1974, that cabin for three was inhabited by Fried de Metz Herman, her husband, Al, and her sister, Noor Derksen, who had come from
Holland for the week. The formation alludes to this housing arrangement
and there is a further subtle reference in the music; the tune (as Pat wrote
to Fried) incorporates several bars of the Dutch National Anthem. Perhaps
this is why he notes *"The tune should be fairly lively but should retain a
feeling of respect."*

Pat's self-confessed addiction to punning was not confined to the plays on
words that characterise the titles of dances. An outstanding example of his
witty use of musical allusions is the mélange of tunes in the music for **The
Leiberts' Wedding.** His own notes read:
> *Music*
> A: "Haste to the Wedding" (bars 1 and 2) merging into "Orange in Bloom"
> for the bride's bouquet (2 to 4), "Haste to the Wedding" version B (5 and
> 6) and "The Joys of Wedlock" (7 and 8).
> B: "The Wedding" (1 and 2), "We'll Wed and We'll Bed" or "Dublin Bay" (3
> to 6), "Mutual Love" to the tune of "The Flight" (7 and 8) and "The Merry
> Meeting" to the tune of "The Handsome Couple" (9 to 12).

In the **Introduction to Pat Shaw's Pinewoods** Christine wrote in 1985:

This Pinewoods edition of the dances that Patrick Shuldham-Shaw composed during and after his visit to America in 1974 includes not only the
dances that he himself published in **Between Two Ponds** but most of the
dances that he had promised to publish in another collection to be known
as **Among the Pines**.

Pat Shaw inspired everyone who came within his orbit during that visit. We
were awed by his knowledge, delighted by his inventiveness and warmed by
his enthusiasm and his wit. His energy seemed endless and his great generosity and joy in sharing his many gifts endeared him to dancers, musicians,
singers and scholars alike. Pat's generosity is exemplified by his dedication
of the proceeds of **Between Two Ponds**, which he published in 1976 entirely at his own expense, to the Pinewoods Camp Capital Fund Drive.

This new publication is also a labour of love that has involved the collabora-
tion of many of Pat's friends and admirers – and as he wished – all proceeds
from its sale will go to Pinewoods Camp.

Marjorie Fennessy brought form and life to the scraps of music and notes
for dances that Pat had intended for his second Pinewoods book. Her presence at Pinewoods in 1983 not only brought Pat's dances to a new generation of dancers but gave her a chance to see the places and meet the people

that were memorialised in the dance collections. It gave many of us an opportunity to study and confer with her about the notations that Pat left among his papers when he died in 1977. Marjorie's interpretations have been made with care and true understanding of Pat's wishes and intentions.

Genevieve Shimer worked directly with Marjorie in choosing the material that could be published and helped with the notes about the people and places Pat had honoured with dances and music in his collections. She also contributed the sketches that enliven the pages and cover of this book. Helene Cornelius made valuable suggestions from her long experience in teaching Pat's material. Marshall Barron provided vital advice and detailed help with the preparation of the music for the second volume and Kate Van Winkle Keller served as overall editor and prepared the copy for printing.

Finally we acknowledge with deep appreciation the kindness of Christopher Shuldham-Shaw in granting us the privilege of publishing the Pinewoods Collections. In his warm letter approving this project, he wrote:

There is no doubt in my mind that Pat intended both collections – whether edited later or not – to be published for the benefit of Pinewoods Camp and it gives me great pleasure to know that his music lives on there.

Pinewoods Camp treasures the gifts and the legacy that Pat Shaw has left to us.

We are grateful to him and to all of the people who have made it possible for everyone to share and enjoy the dances and music that are a lasting reminder of his presence here in 1974.

November 1985
Christine Helwig
for the Board of Directors of Pinewoods Camp

Pat with Helen Kennedy (EFDSS) on his right and May Gadd (CDSS) on his left.

12. Pat on Tour

From the Natal Mercury, 15 or 16 November 1955

Pat, with his flair for languages, was included in many tours to which the EFDSS were invited.

Felicity Blake has already mentioned (in Pat in Wales, chapter 10) a trip to **Venice** in **1947** where she remembers Pat sitting in the "Vaporetto" steaming across the lagoon, wearing a flowered straw hat and his morris man's breeches and hose. *As we crossed, the sound of his piano accordion drifted across the water.*

The first **South African** trip was in **November 1955**. The Union of South Africa was celebrating the Centenary of the founding of Pretoria and had invited the founder countries in Europe to take part by sending representatives, including teams of folk dancers.

The Society's team was led by the Director, Douglas Kennedy with Helen. The musicians were Nan Fleming-Williams, Patrick Shuldham-Shaw, Peter Swann and Jim Coleman. Pat was a musician and singer.

The team left from a dark and foggy Stansted in a Viking 36-seater. There were 21 in the English team and their travelling companions were the twelve members of the Scottish team. It was a 6000 mile trip with an overnight stop in Malta.

After spending a week in Pretoria, a special train carried the teams to various centres in the Union.

Pat Riding an ostrich at Highgate Ostrich Farm, Oudtshoorn, South Africa on Monday 21 November 1955. Pat was lucky. The ostrich had a trick of racing to the pond and then stopping suddenly so that the rider went in head first.

Pat's turn during a party in a guard's van of the train carrying them round South Africa in November and December 1955.

Douglas Kennedy's report in English Dance and Song says that

The flags of Holland and England were received coolly: it seemed as if people remembered that these were the "old gang" of the bad old days.

He records how the English dances were gay and vivacious in contrast to some of the other countries' performances; the morris and sword Dances, the Abram Circle, the clog dancing and the wicker Hobby Horse.

But it was Pat Shuldham-Shaw who completed the conversion of any South Africans who still bore some remnant of grudge against England. He had spent a short time before the trip learning Afrikaans. With his musical ear and previous visits to Holland to help him his accent was almost impeccable. When he announced his English folk song titles in Afrikaans a ripple of surprise rippled through the crowds. He followed his English song with an Afrikaans folk song and even managed to extemporise verses suited to an immediate locality. After his singing the "Roineks" were regarded with a new warmth and respect.

There had been no rain in one stop – De Aar – for eighteen months but the day the teams arrived there was fives inches in three hours. Pat inserted a joke into his Afrikaans song about the Manchester morris dance bringing down the rain.

Whilst the teams were being treated to a trip around Kruger National Park, Pat claimed to have seen a small elephant but the rest of the team felt that, in that green jungle, only a pink elephant would have been reliably visible.*

Marjorie Fennessy – *We were away for five weeks, travelling round South Africa, living on a train, with a very narrow gauge, which meant the train swayed considerably. After Pretoria we*

---

*　taken from reports in English Dance and Song Vol.XX No.4 March/April and No.5 May/June, 1956.

went to Pietermaritzburg, down the coast to Port Elizabeth and the Garden Route to Cape Town. Then travelling North through Kimberley etc. back to Pretoria. We had a day in the Kruger National Park before flying home via Benini and Malta.

A special memory for Marjorie is of Pat looking after the girls:

We landed at Luxor for a night's stay at a most impressive Victorian Hotel on the banks of the Nile. As we were flying on early the next morning in our plane which we shared with the Scots team, after dinner, we decided to hire some carriages to go and see the ruined Temple at Karnak by moonlight. I remember it as a narrow road with a stone wall on one side and the Nile on the other and the driver of each of our horse-drawn carriages dangerously trying to overtake the others at break-neck speed. On arrival at Karnak, lots of "guides" appeared out of the shadows to show us round the extensive ruins. Pat tried – and succeeded – in keeping several of us girls together, like a Mother hen defending her chicks. I don't know where our partners were! It was a memorable experience – the first of many – also visiting Gordon's house at Khartoum on our return journey home.

Following the return of the team, the EFDSS received a letter from the Parliamentary Under Secretary of State, Commonwealth Relations Office. He congratulated the team on the variety and skill of their performances and the excellent impression they made as representatives of this country. He went on to say

I am sure that the member of your party who took the trouble to learn Afrikaans and was thus able to make speeches and sing songs in that language must have brought an additional warmth to your welcome.

There was an EFDSS trip to **Geneva in August 1956**. On this occasion, Pat drove across France with the sticks, swords and hobby-horse as his companions. He met up with the rest of the team at Geneva station. The trip was recorded in EDS as a wonderful experience.

In 1958 Douglas and Helen Kennedy took a team to a Festival at Viana di Costello in **Portugal**. The musicians and Pat travelled overland.

The Society was again invited to **South Africa in 1960** and visited from 29 April till 10 June. Personal memories of that trip –

Jan Willcocks – *I got to know him on a trip to South Africa in 1960. Douglas (Kennedy) was invited to take a team, for the second time, joining other founder-nation groups celebrating fifty years of union of the four states. Pat had taught himself Afrikaans for the previous trip and was known out there as "the red-neck with the beard". He sang with guitar and played accordion for some displays. He seemed to know someone everywhere we went. However, in the middle of the Karoo Desert on our way to Kimberley we stopped on the road for a 'ladies left, gents right'. Not a tree or a bush in sight. Someone was heard to mutter 'Who d'you know here, Pat – can't we use his toilet?' We drove on.*

Rita Knell – *I suppose I only really came in contact with him during our six week tour of S. Africa in 1960. He was a real asset to the group as he could speak on the loudspeaker in English and Afrikaans (and possibly in Zulu? Not that many of them would be admitted to the showground in those days of strict apartheid) and explain what our dances were, where they were collected etc, and be quite amusing. I believe he used to play and sing folk songs from other countries in their language which went down very well. I can't even remember what instrument he had.*

Rita also has an anecdote about Biltong – dried meat – which is in the Memories chapter.

Rosemary Gentleman – *In 1960 I was part of the team, led by Douglas and Helen Kennedy, that went to South Africa as part of a six week international folk dance and song tour (including Pat) where we had more opportunity to get to know each other: we sang at each other on the long tiresome coach journeys involved! He was loved by everyone on the tour, and the audiences, for his humour and versatility. He taught himself Afrikaans which he used to introduce himself and the English Team. He translated "My Boy Willie" into Afrikaans, which brought the house down as did well-known local songs, like "Suikerbosse".*
This is from a Pretoria paper May 1960:

But the man who stole the show was the English folk singer, Patrick Shaw, who delighted the audience by making his announcements in flawless Afrikaans, and singing an Afrikaans folk song...

Keith and Maggie Uttley – In South Africa in 1960 he certainly enhanced our reception by the large audiences by singing in Afrikaans.
There was an EFDSS trip to **Macedonia In July / August 1962**,
Jan Willcocks – *In 1962, for the last week of July and first week of August, I was asked to join a team going to Macedonia just before the end of term. My boss, possibly with South Africa in mind, said no. The team set off without me, by train. I followed by plane to Paris then across Paris to pick up a train. Due to timings I had a day in Paris by myself so was nicely tired by the time I caught the train. Two nights later I arrived in Skopje tired, hungry and a little anxious. Pat was detailed to meet me! He had learned Serbo-Croat especially for the trip. I had never been so pleased to see anyone before! I was dubbed "Janski" from then on.*

When he went on an EFDSS trip to Macedonia in Yugoslavia, he impressed the locals not only with his fluency in the national language of Serbo-Croat, but especially with his knowledge of Macedonian which he had learned before the trip.
Bob Rundle also recalls London Folk's a trip to **Macedonia** in **1962** –
Because of his interest in languages he took an English/Serbo-Croat dictionary and enjoyed speaking the language at every opportunity. At the end of the tour he gave the dictionary to the student who had been our guide and who was pleased to have the opportunity to improve his English. In reply the student said how delightful it made him to be given it!

13. THE ROYAL ALBERT HALL FESTIVALS

As **Marjorie Fennessy** says, Pat was involved in most of the EFDSS Royal Albert Hall Festivals in one way or another up to the time he went to Scotland. But 1968 was the only one of which he was the Producer, thereafter he was a member of the Production Team.

He is listed in the programmes as a member of the band for many years and in 1951 and 1952 as a square dance caller and a caller for the Finale. By 1953 he was billed as an arranger of the music and 1964 – 1966, he was the presenter.

Fond memories of dancing at the Albert Hall Festivals as part of the "London Folk" team were sent in recalling Pat as a hard task master, as forever changing his mind over sequences and for his enthusiasm.

Jonathan Cohen – *Pat was incredibly disorganised. I remember one Albert Hall Festival where Pat arranged the music for the Choir (The Co-operation) in an "à la Swingle Singers" style. This was the Choir singing in four-part harmony, very complex and very interesting to do. (See an example of this in the American Section)*

He would always think of a new idea. If only we did this, that would improve it. We would learn something and suddenly it would all be changed. He was creating constantly. Somebody had to say 'Now look, we have to stop here. For God's sake, we've got to get this done'. He always seemed to be in a panic, like those horrible nightmares where you are trying to get somewhere and you can't. Then he'd start shouting but what you got, in the end, was this incredible inventiveness. He did them brilliantly.

The dancers form the text RAH 1971 to commemorate the centenary of the Royal Albert Hall

Pat made "Amazing Grace" sound like a Western movie score.

It was a panic, everything was always a panic.

For the Return of Albert (A taste of the Royal Albert Hall Festivals) on 10 February 2007 at Cecil Sharp House – part of the EFDSS 75th Anniversary celebrations – I managed to get my Choir together – or they wanted to get back together – as people hadn't seen each other in 33 years or something. We did some of the Pat Shaw stuff and they just remembered parts they were singing from all that time back.

Hugh Rippon recalled – *Pat Shaw spent many hours in the Library researching old dance and tune books. One year Pat had the task of producing one of the Albert Hall Festivals and he unearthed the Shaker hymn tune "The Gift to be Simple" and he devised a dance to go with it. At the dress rehearsal on the Friday afternoon before the show, Sydney Carter (who for a short time had also been a co-editor of ED&S) and I were sitting in the Albert Hall watching the proceedings. Sydney heard the tune and exclaimed 'Ooh, that's a nice tune: I'll see if I can write some words for it.'* As we know, 'The Lord of the Dance' was the outcome so indirectly Pat Shaw was responsible for this song which has gone round the world. Of course we all know that Aaron Copeland had also used the tune much earlier in his piece "Appalachian Spring" but there's no connection with Pat Shaw's discovery really.*

His Shaker sequence lodged in **Joan Harborne's** memory –

My clearest memory, apart from as a caller at numerous dances, was when he was rehearsing us (Sunday Club members) dancing in one of the Albert Hall festivals the year he introduced the Shaker Dance (The Garland Dance?). I think it must have pre-dated his Lord of the Dance which became so well known. I remember his insistence on exactly the right step, which was amazingly hard to do to his satisfaction, and the words "till turning, turning, it comes out right" as his rather intricate "hey" was resolved.

Simple Gifts – Heidi Laufman (now Stridde) when she was 16 in 1975 wrote a dance to "Simple Gifts" Shaker hymn tune. She modestly showed it to Pat Shaw who liked it and wrote **Shakers Follow-on** as an alternative tune.

Marjorie Fennessy's memory adds to this

We sang this Shaker Hymn at the RAH Festival (1962)

Tis the gift to be simple, 'tis the gift to be free,
'tis the gift to come down where we ought to be.
And when we find ourselves in the place just right,
'twill be in the valley of love and delight.
When true simplicity is gained
to bow and to bend we shan't be ashamed
To turn, turn will be our delight,
till by turning, turning, we come round right.

My memory is not too bad, is it!

I may be getting items mixed up, but I think it was the one where we came up the various rabbit holes and each line danced into a tight "ball" in the centre. We then turned abruptly and danced back in the opposite direction, except for one line, who had joined the "circle" eight bars too late! This was to a variant of Simple Gifts as a fast reel.

*   Sydney Carter's words "Lord of the Dance" were published in 1969.

Jan Willcocks sent in many memories – some of the Albert Hall Festival –
He taught us a Carole from Shetland:
Verse: This is guid new even's night
 Chorus: We are all Queen Mary's men
Verse: And we've come here to claim our right
Chorus: And that's before our Lady.

Sung with the correct accent – which Pat could do. That's all I can remember. Pat sang the verse and we responded with the chorus. This was a very old Carole and danced on the floor of the Albert Hall by torchlight (us) and the minimum of light in the hall. (Should have been candles but even then Fire Regulations and Health and Safety reared their ugly heads.) It was quite a different display from the ones the London Corps was usually asked to perform; probably the beginning of the 'set pieces' that were produced later.

I think it was "Hunsdon House" we danced for the Albert Hall Centenary to an adapted lively version of the Hallelujah Chorus, by Pat – naturally!

The photo shows a pentagonal rapper sword lock, similar to the hexagonal EFDSS badge, with dancers at the Albert Hall in 1961.* There were several frustrating rehearsals. Cecil Sharp House dance floor is the wrong shape for a circle.

For after-the-show parties on Sunday afternoon after an Albert Hall show, Pat would write some diabolically difficult tune or dance to test the brains of the survivors of these epics! The Ranchers acquired a reputation, justifiably, for being able to play ANYTHING, and the note written by Pat requesting "Beaumont Rag" was picked up as a challenge. The tune is on the Ranchers' LP "Rags to Rituals".

Fred Grimshaw – *Coming in to the folk dance world as a musician in the late 1960s I had the good fortune to be involved in many of the Royal Albert Hall annual festivals organised by the EFDSS at that time. As a consequence of this he became a*

---

*   Jubilee Suite by London Corps of traditional couple dances ending in set piece "The Lock" devised
    by Pat Shaw. This concluded the first half of the programme.

familiar (and outstanding) figure to me as one of the most important and hard working people who gave such a lot of their time to make these festivals so successful. Many Sundays were spent in Trefusis at CSH rehearsing Pat's musical arrangements under the energetic guidance of Nan Fleming-Williams with Pat being in attendance. I still have some of his arrangements for these festivals, my favourite being one of the overtures which includes the Symondsbury tune with different parts for accordions and violins. For me the outstanding and lasting memory of him is the pleasure I still get from playing his wonderful dance tunes with their rich variety and different styles.

Judy Parry – *I particularly remember Pat's involvement with the 1971 Festival. Pat did a sequence to end the show and I remember the endless rehearsals in January and February where we thought we would never get it right as Pat kept changing his mind. However, needless to say, it came "all right on the night" and we ended with RAH 1971 formed on the floor of the arena – a perfect ending for the celebrations of the centenary of the opening of the Royal Albert Hall".*

David Welti – *I remember rehearsing and dancing to some of his arrangements for the Albert Hall shows. At times he introduced some difficult (musical) tunes.*

Elizabeth Noyes – *My main memory of him was of his enthusiastic conducting, especially at the Albert Hall Festival, which he did in a very lively manner.*

Two Albert Hall memories came from Wales:

Betty Davies – *When he produced the English Folk Dance and Song Society Festival at the Albert Hall in 1968, he included dancers from North and South Wales to represent the Welsh Society. About this time Television Wales and the West (TWW) transmitted a series of programmes on folk music. Pat was responsible for the folk dance content and gave a number of dance groups the opportunity of performing the dances he had chosen, to the tunes that he had arranged, for the benefit of a wide audience. He arranged the tunes included in the Clwt y Ddawns records produced in the 1970s and was also leader of the band.*

Mavis Roberts – *An important occasion for us was the May Day celebration, held at the Royal Albert Hall where teams came from across the UK. I don't recall the date (late 60s?) but I expect others have mentioned it. Pat organised two teams from Wales, one from North Wales and one from the South. The two teams practised separately, the main theme being the fair dances originally danced at the South Wales Cheese Fairs. I remember we danced "Rali Twm Sion" and "Dawns Flodau Nantgarw" among others. The whole display came together on the night for the first time; it was a memorable concert, even the Padstow Hobby Horse was there.*

But the memory of Pat's final appearance at an Albert Hall Festival was sent in by **Mike Wilson-Jones** –

I produced a dance item for London Folk at the 1979 RAH Festival in memory of Pat called "The Dancing Master Revisited". I got Nan (Fleming-Williams) to record an introduction for the piece and had a recording of Pat singing "Streets of Laredo" as the opening to the set.

14. The Carol Concerts

The Christmas Concert at CSH was one of Pat's triumphs. For many, Christmas did not truly begin until after this special evening. No matter that the format was always the same –

Part I "The Christmas Story"

Part II "The Twelve Days of Christmas"

that was what we knew, expected and loved. The Main Hall would be full to bursting, the House would be looking its best festooned with traditional decorations and Pat would weave his magic every year.

Pat wrote the arrangements for the large orchestra and several soloists and conducted the audience singing the carols. For many years Pat was joined by singers Joy Hyman and Jennifer Rice and The Co-operation, a choir directed and conducted by Jonathan Cohen, – a "full chorus (The Audience)" was also billed.

After the Concert, there would be a party thrown for Pat by the landlady of the house in Hampstead where he was a tenant. These parties were famous and **Lynda Smith** can recall going to them in the early 1960s. Other memories –

Jonathan Cohen (The Co-operation) – *We'd rehearse in the morning of the concert. We'd never get through it all! Pat used to do all the arrangements for it and panic his way through it. The orchestra was absolutely huge, because everybody used to play.*

But the great thing was the stuff he did for the Choir. He did a brilliant arrangement of The Coventry Carol, which was incredible – and the middle verse (Herod the King) the harmonies would clash – clash – clash – and the Choir did it! He did a fantastic arrangement of The Cornish Wassail which was just brilliant. He enjoyed having a Choir he could experiment with.

Brian Willcocks (accordionist in The Ranchers Band) – *The annual Carol Concert at C# House was Pat's Tour de Force. He would invite 'external' musicians to join the orchestra (I believe Jonathan Cohen came aboard this way) of usual suspects, and arrange the dots accordingly. Trouble was, because of the time of year, he only knew at the last minute – almost literally – who was going to be there. French horn? Harp? Cor Anglais? More than once I recollect Pat dashing in to the hall full of assembled musicians with the ink on several pages of arrangements still wet. (Actually, Pat didn't dash ...he had fast, medium and slow variants of his rolling gait, involving sideways head and shoulder movement, gaze at long-range and knees and feet flipping inwards. Only Pat could walk like that ...unmistakable.)*

Dr Tony Barrand (CDSS lifetime achievement award holder) – *I have three indelible and cherished memories of Pat for which I will be forever in debt. The first is from a field trip to England in, I believe, 1972 when I attended a Christmas concert that Pat had produced at Cecil Sharp House. First, the story of Jesus' birth was told in traditional songs and then the secular ways of celebrating the midwinter were presented, both to great theatrical and musical effect. It also revealed a complex set of dance and drama customs which I had not experienced as a child in Lincolnshire. Exploring the framework became a central theme of my singing career as I borrowed the conception wholesale for a show called "Nowell Sing We Clear" which spawned six recordings (from LP to CD) and tours for its 30th season this December, 2005.*

(see chapter 11 for other two memories)

COVENTRY CAROL

Pat Shaw

Mike Wilson-Jones – *Lots of happy memories of Pat's version of the Carols at CSH. I have come to realise that he must have taken over the format, at least for the first half, from when RVW organised it as all the original pieces in it were RVW, Holst and Sharp arrangements and collected items – "The Truth sent from Above", "Masters in this Hall", "It came upon a Midnight Clear", "The Sussex Carol", "King Herod and the Cock", "The Bells of Paradise", "O Little Town of Bethlehem", "Come all you Worthy Gentlemen", "The Gloucestershire Wassail" and "The Somerset Wassail". I would love to know if anyone has memories going further back on this.*

Brenda Godrich – *This evening was my first introduction to CSH when I was about twelve. My sister and I were treated to the Carol Concert for many years. She worked as the nursery assistant in an East End school and the nursery teacher danced at CSH, so this treat was my sister's Christmas present. By the time I was nearly sixteen, we decided to take a chance and try coming to the building in between carol concerts and so began dancing on Thursday evenings.*

Vic Godrich – *Pat was a great all rounder and appeared not only as a caller but as accordionist, singer, guitarist and general encourager of all things folk. One of his biggest successes was the annual carol concert which he ran using only English folk carols some of which he had collected himself from the countryside. He recruited a choir and orchestra and arranged many of the carols for them. His ability as a singer made it possible for him to lead the singing and to teach the audience by ear the new tunes that he had collected. I still have in my head tunes that I learned orally from him that will remain there for life.*

§ *The first time he asked me to play in his Carol Concert (possibly 1966) and, although the part was beyond me, Pat was full of encouragement.*

§ *The memorable Christmas Concert which Pat hosted for many years will surely be remembered by most people. I particularly remember his wonderful rendition of "The Cherry Tree Carol" many times.*

§   This symbol denotes an unattributed contribution.

15. Pat through his Letters

Pat's letters are of interest as they confirm his multi-faceted personality – his sense of fun, his use of puns and his more thoughtful, academic side.

As far as possible the ones quoted here are in chronological order – though whilst having a day and month recorded, the year is often omitted, so in some cases this has been guessed at from the content or context.

Where the original handwritten text is included, there is also a printed version for clarity.

To **John Stapledon**, West Kirby Folk Dance Band
? April 1972 on School of Scottish Studies (SSS) headed notepaper. *(Errol on the Green and Morecambe Bay were both composed in 1972 and Pat went up to Edinburgh that same year)*

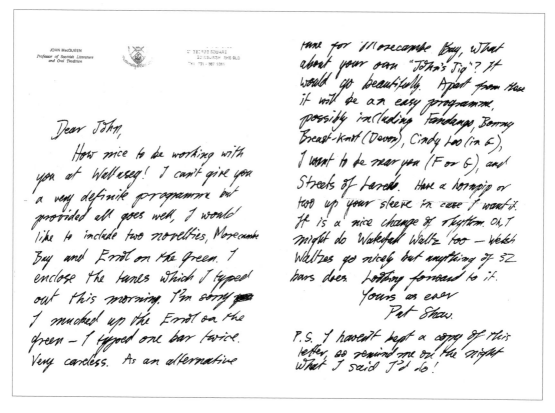

Dear John,

How nice to be working with you at Wallasey! I can't give you a very definite programme but provided all goes well, I would like to include two novelties, *Morecambe Bay* and *Errol on the Green*. I enclose the tunes which I typed out this morning. I'm sorry I mucked up the *Errol on the Green* – I typed one bar twice. Very careless. As an alternative tune for *Morecambe Bay*, what about your own *"John's Jig"*? It would go beautifully. Apart from those it will be an easy programme, possibly including *Fandango, Bonny Breast-knot (Devon), Cindy Loo* (in G), *I want to be near you,* (F or G), and *Streets of Laredo*. Have a hornpipe or two up your sleeve in case I want it. It is a nice change of rhythm. Oh, I might do *Waterfall Waltz* too – Welsh Waltzes go nicely but anything of 32 bars does. Looking forward to it.

Yours as ever

Pat Shaw

P.S. I haven't kept a copy of this letter, so remind me on the night what I said I'd do!

A memo to **Marjorie Fennessy** regarding the dance he was composing for the Whirligigs (her dance group) "Final Fling". in March, 1973. The dance was **The Whirligigs Last Bow**

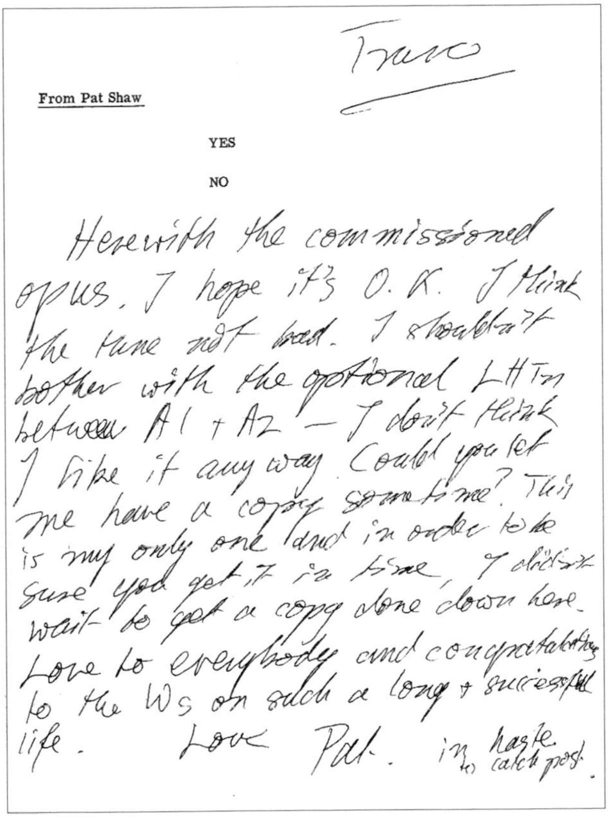

Truro

From Pat Shaw (typed)

YES

NO

(in hand writing)
Herewith the commissioned opus. I hope it's O.K. I think the tune not bad. I shouldn't bother with the optional LH turn between A1 + A2 – I don't think I like it anyway. Could you let me have a copy sometime? This is my only one and in order to be sure you got it in time, I didn't wait to get a copy done down here.
Love to everybody and congratulations to the Ws on such a long and successful life.
love
Pat

in haste to catch post

Bob Rundle's contribution to the project –

1. He used to sign off with "Pat Sh-Sh".
2. I enclose a letter which demonstrates his interest in languages and his humour through wordplay (which we shared). It seems that he's replying to my enquiry as to where I could contact Andrew and Paul Tracey, "stars" of the S. African based musical "Wait a Minim!" that had been at the Fortune Theatre for a few years. I first met them at a party Pat held at his lodgings at Holly Mount, Hampstead or Highgate. I have some photos taken at my place in Oct. 65 when they came to a party of ours, including Pat, Nan and Denis Smith. I expect you have enough photos though. (I've remained closely in touch with Andrew and Paul ever since. Andrew has recently

retired from running the International Library of African Music, finally as professor at Rhodes University).

They started calling me M'bob, hence Pat's "N'dear M'bob", his opening with an Africa greeting (presumably!) and signing off as "M'pat". I'm lost on the meaning of "Phogue tail" (folk tale). References to the Manx man with no tail would be lost had I not been to the IoM and know that Manx cats are tailless.

16th April 1974 On SSS paper
Dear Mbob,

Ngiyathemba ukuthi usaphila. Ngiyakubonga.

Many thanks for the photo of myself. Having seen it I'm not inclined to fall in love with myself! I always thought I was rather good-looking, but I see I am very plain. Thanks also for the Ossianic Phogue-tail! Your flying-cow story is obviously a lot of bull!

Re the Waverley disc (Tom Anderson + Willie Johnson) Waverley have ceased to exist. They were bought up by EMI. Their records are still available at some shops in Scotland. I'll try to see if I can find one in Edinburgh but don't hold out much hope. Peter Cooke, whom I've just rang, says write to Craighall Recording Studios, 68, Craighall Road, Edinburgh, EH6 4RL. They did the original records and they might have a supply and should know where if anywhere, you could get hold of a copy. Have you heard the Bill Leader Shetland Fiddle disc? Nothing like as good a recording as the SSS one and rather too much of the 40 Fiddlers, but definitely of interest.

The Folk Shop at the House (Cecil Sharp) have it in stock.

I've tried to find out about the Tracey's. Peter was at an African music conference two or three weeks-ends ago and it was said there that as far as is known they had no intention of leaving South Africa. Are you sure you put the right Box no.? Try again. Sorry can't help more than this.

I saw Nan + Brian two days ago. They came over for Nan's nephew's wedding near here. Both in cracking form.

There's a Manxman working here (I know he's Manx 'cos he ain't got no tail) who played me a recording of poems + songs all read and sung in Cornish by Brenda Wooton + Richard Gendall. Somehow I wasn't all that impressed.

All best wishes to all of you. How is Roger getting on on the fiddle?

Yours as ever

Mpat.

To **Brian Willcocks**

18th Feb ?? – on SSS headed notepaper

Machines which Pat used for processing the Greig-Duncan manuscripts are mentioned in the Academic Section (chapter 6). Assuming it is the same machine

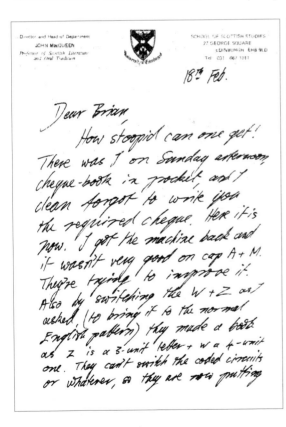

this would be written after 1972.

Dear Brian

How stoopid can one get!

There was I on Sunday afternoon, cheque-book in pocket, and I clean forgot to write you the required cheque. Here it is now. I got the machine back and it wasn't very good on cap A + M. They're trying to improve it. Also by switching the W + Z as I asked, (to bring it to the normal English pattern) they made a boob as Z is a 3-unit letter +W a 4-unit one. They can't switch the coded circuits ar whatever, so they are now putting them back where they were!. Also I'm having the degree sign altered to an asterisk. More useful to me for footnotes etc in reports and as you doubtless know I write Right Hand Star as RH* in my abbreviated dance notations. I shall get the thing back on Friday – all being well.

I enclose a few Willcocks-Rancher type tunes illegally xeroxed – so don't give me away. They're from the book I showed you. and include the printed version of Beaumont Rag. I don't like it as much as Bur (?) MacLain's version, but it might be good in alternation (or altercation) with it. I ain't put 'armonies as you can do that just as well to suit yersel'. 'Ope you like the selection.

Love to Jan + Nicholas. all the best.

Yours as aye

Pat

18th Sept 1975 to **"Skip" Ellacott** on School of Scottish Studies headed notepaper.

On the writing of **Phoenix Rejuvenated** for Phoenix FDC on their 20th Anniversary.

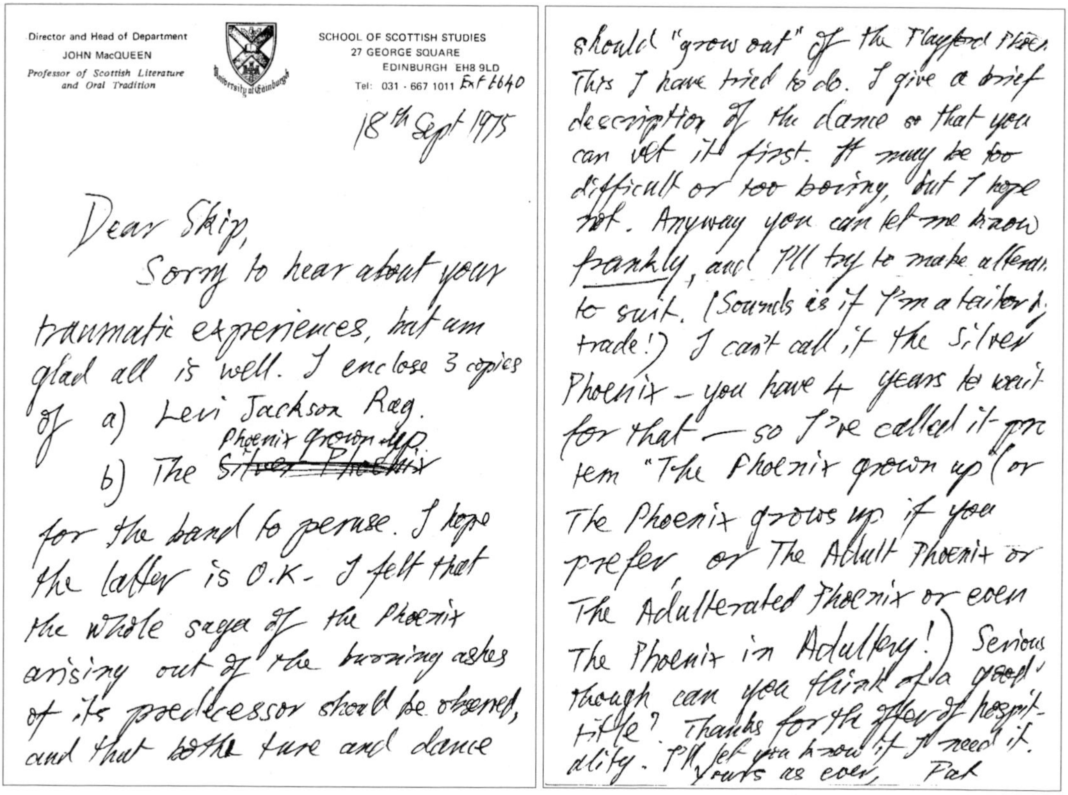

Dear Skip

Sorry to hear about your traumatic experiences but am glad all is well. I enclose 3 copies of

a.   Levi Jackson Rag

b.   The Phoenix Grown Up

for the band to peruse. I hope the latter is o.k. – I felt that the whole saga of the Phoenix arising out of the burning ashes of its predecessor should be observed, and that both the tune and dance should "grow out" of the Playford Phoenix. This I have tried to do. I give a brief description of the dance so that you can vet it first. It may be too difficult or too boring, but I hope not. Anyway you can let me know <u>frankly</u>, and I'll try to make an alternative to suit. (sounds as if I'm a tailor by trade!) I can't call it the Silver Phoenix – you have 4 years to wait for that – so I've called it pro tem "The Phoenix grown up" (or The Phoenix grows up if you prefer, or The Adult Phoenix or The Adulterated Phoenix or even The Phoenix in Adultery!) Seriously though can you think of a good title? Thanks for the offer of hospitality. I'll let you know if I need it.

Yours as ever,
Pat

He includes a hand written copy of the dance:

The Phoenix Grown up.

Longways for 4 couples – all proper.

A1. All forward + back a double (inside hands with partner); 1st Man leads the line of men round the ladies (clockwise, as in The Phoenix.

A2. All lead down + back with new partner; 4th lady leads line of ladies round the men (counterclockwise). All now have their own partners back but the set is upside down. (N.B. The set will have moved over towards the ladies side of

B1. All following the 4th couple, promenade the room. Don't worry the to the left ½ way round to bring the | bit puts this right!) set to its home position, but everyone will be improper. All now set Right + Left to partners, and circle left half way round with neighbouring couple — i.e. 1st with 2nd, 3rd with 4th.

B2. 1st + 4th couples, now in the middle of the set, cast up and down respectively (i.e. cast to the ends) + lead back down or up the middle again, while the 2n + 3rd lead down or up the middle and cast back again; 1st + 4th couples circle left ½ way round + turn partners ½ way onto own sides, while 2nd + 3rd couples (ends) turn partners with both hands all the way round. (Try to make this 2 ½ turns rather than one whole turn, so that it match the middles). Repeat dance three more times when all should be home.   P.T.O.

> As an alternative for the ending, the middles may do the ½ circle left + cross over with their partners without giving hands, and the ends may do a half turn with both hands and cross home again without hands. I think I prefer the first, but you can see which you like.
>
> Please let me know any criticisms. I want to try to get something pleasing to the club members.

Note the alternative ending where he says – I think I prefer the first, but you can see which you like. Please let me know any criticisms. I want to try to get something pleasing to the club members.

Director and Head of Department
JOHN MacQUEEN
Professor of Scottish Literature
and Oral Tradition

SCHOOL OF SCOTTISH STUDIES
27 GEORGE SQUARE
EDINBURGH EH8 9LD
Tel: 031 - 667 1011

3rd November 1975

On 3rd November 1975, on SSS headed notepaper:

Dear Phoenix – now rejuvenated
Many, many thanks for giving me such a wonderful evening last Saturday. I have seldom enjoyed myself so much at an occasion of this kind. So often the MC has quite a lot to worry about though he tries not to show it. On this occasion everyone was so co-operative that I had not one moment's worry.

All best wishes to the club until the time of the next rejuvenation. Incidentally, I _very_ nearly made a disastrous slip of the tongue and called the dance "The Phoenix Regurgitated"! Wouldn't that have been terrible?
All the best
Yours aye
Pat

In 1976, Pat corresponded with **Ivor Allsop** regarding the Papa Stour Sword Dance from the Shetland Isles. Ivor is an authority on the Sword Dances of England. Further correspondence with Ivor on the subject of the Papa Stour Dance can be found in the Academic Section (chapter 6).

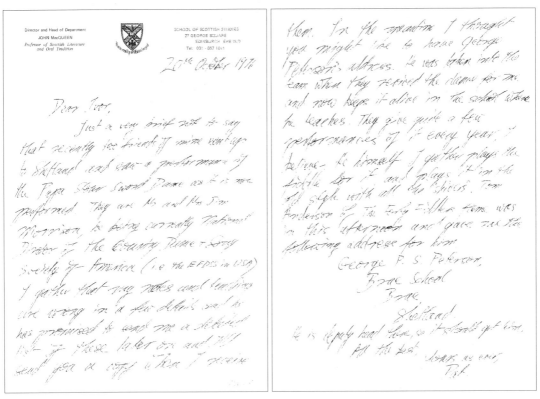

20th October, 1976 on SSS headed notepaper

Dear Ivor,

Just a very brief note to say that recently two friends of mine went up to Shetland and saw a performancc of the Papa Stour Sword Dance as it is now preformed. They are Mr and Mrs Jim Morrison, he being currently National Director of the Country Dance & Song Socicty of America (i.e. the EFDSS in USA).

I gather that my notes and teaching are wrong in a few details and he has promised to send me a detailed list of these later on and I'll send you a copy when I receive them. In the meantime I thought you might like to have George Peterson's address. He was taken into the team when they revived the dance for me and now keeps it alive in the school where he teaches. They give quite a few performances of it every year, I believe. He himself I gather plays the fiddle for it and plays it in the old style with all the "shivers". Tom Anderson of The Forty Fiddlers fame was in this afternoon and gave me the address for George Peterson.

He is deputy head there, so it should get him,

All the best,

Yours as ever,

Pat

A second letter to Ivor on this subject and the full comments about the Dance can be found in Appendix 9.

SGOIL EOLAIS NA H-ALBA
27 CEARNAG SHFORUIS
DUN-EIDEANN EH8 9LD

Fear-stiùiridh agus Ceann-roinne
AN T-OLLAMH IAIN MACUINN

Fòn: 031-667 1011

SCHOOL OF SCOTTISH STUDIES
27 GEORGE SQUARE
EDINBURGH EH8 9LD

Director and Head of Department
PROFESSOR JOHN MacQUEEN

Tel: 031-667 1011

14th June 1977

Dear Eric,

Your letter reached me in the middle of a very unpleasant flu attack and I've been trying to catch up ever since. I did a week-end course with Douglas (Kennedy) last week-end and he's in superb form.

Now about the title – it seems O.K. to me, unless you feel it ought to have the words *Country Dance* at the beginning. (*Country Dance from Playford to P.S.*) Not necessary but possibly clearer.

As regards my own convictions – it's just something I have to do and get out of my system. I've made up dances all my life from the age of 10 onwards. Monica's

Delight which has been fairly widely danced in recent years, I made up when I was 13 (nasty precocious little boy!) Monica was a beautiful blond Edinburgh lass on whom I had a crush at the time. Most of my early efforts were pretty terrible, but one or two have survived. Since those days I have become more critical of my efforts I hope. I have tried various styles, American, English Trad, Playford etc etc and I try not to mix the styles too much. In my Playford type efforts I have tried to extend the style by introducing new figures and new ideas but yet keep a firm foundation in the original style. The hardest thing is to make up a dance that is easy and yet distinctive and interesting and not just a mixture of familiar figures. Many of my efforts are I know over complicated, but in spite of this, some of the best people have found it worth while mastering the difficulties. I flatter myself that a few of my creations have taken their place in the repertoire and people have forgotten they are mine. e.g. Margaret's Waltz, Walpole Cottage, Streets of Laredo, Gipsy's Wedding Day etc. Recently when I was playing

with Ali Bain he said I must hear a waltz he'd picked up from a string band in up-state New York – the Highwood string band I think it was. He then preceded to play me the tune of Margaret's Waltz! (only very slightly different.)

One thing or quirk I have, I do not like any of my dances for which I have written special tunes to be done to other tunes – certainly as regards a public show I know people have to use records at times, but at a club night or something like that I don't mind so much but at a public show I would rather they didn't do something like Leon Jackson's Rag at all than do it to an ordinary English or Scottish Reel or Trad. I think of dance and tune as being very closely allied.

I'm working on another collection to be called "Among the Pines" at the moment. It will have quite a few fairly simple dances in it. I'm not sure when it will be ready. I hope this is enough information for you to go on. Have a good time in USA. Give

my love to anyone I know there: I'm hoping to go out again next year.

Best of luck,
Yours aye,
Pat (Shaw)

In January 1972 **Eric Langford** started the Dartington Hall dance weekends – he was the deputy warden at the Devon Centre at Dartington. He had asked Tom Cook to be the first caller and Tom did it for three years, calling the course "Music Made Visible". Tom suggested that a change of caller might be good so Eric asked Pat who did the weekend of 10-12 January in 1975. Eric asked Pat to come again in 1978 and, you can see by the letter from Pat to Eric, that Pat was trying to think up a different title. Alas, he didn't live to take that weekend and Tom Cook and Marjorie Fennessy shared the calling.

Pat Shaw to **Eric Langford**
14th June 1977
Dear Eric

Your letter reached me in the middle of a very unpleasant flu attack and I've been trying to catch up ever since. I did a week-end course with Douglas (Kennedy) last week-end and he's in superb form.

Now about the title – it seems OK to me, unless you feel it ought to name the words Country Dance at the beginning. (The Country Dance from Playford to PS). Not necessary but possibly clearer.

As regards my own concoctions – it's just something I have to do and get out of my system. I've made up dances all my life from the age of 10 onwards. Monica's Delight which has been fairly widely danced in recent years, I made up when I was 13 (nasty precocious little boy!). Monica was a beautiful blond Edinburgh lass on whom I had a crush at the time. Most of my early efforts were pretty terrible, but one or two have survived. Since those days I have become more critical of my efforts I hope. I have tried various styles, American, English Trad, Playford etc etc and I try not to mix the styles too much. In my Playford type efforts I have tried to extend the style by introducing new figures and new ideas but yet keep a firm foundation in the original style. The hardest thing is to make up a dance that is easy and yet distinctive and interesting and not just a mixture of familiar figures. Many of my efforts are I know over complicated, but in spite of this some of the best people have found it worth while mastering the difficulties. I flatter myself that a few of my creations have taken their place in the repertoire and people have forgotten they are mine, e.g. Margaret's Waltz, Walpole Cottage, Streets of Laredo, Gipsy's Wedding Day etc. Recently when I was playing with Ali Bain, he said I must hear a waltz he'd picked up from a string band in up-state New York – the Highwood String Band I think it was. He then proceeded to play me the tune of Margaret's Waltz (only very slightly different).

One thing or quirk I have. I do not like any of my dances for which I have written special tunes to be done to other tunes – certainly as regards a public show. I know people have to use records at times, and at a club night or something like that, I don't mind so much, but at a public show I would rather they didn't do something like Levi Jackson Rag at all than do it to an ordinary English or Scottish Reel or March. I think of dance and tune as being very closely linked.

I'm working on another collection to be called "Among the Pines" at the moment. It will have quite a few fairly simple dances in it. I'm not sure when it will be ready. I hope this is enough information for you to go on. Have a good time in USA. Give my love to anyone I know there. I'm hoping to go out again next year.

Best of luck,
Yours aye,
Pat (Shaw)

16. PAT'S LEGACY

As I have been collating all this material for this project, I have been conscious that it would be good to have some summation of Pat – both the man and his work.

Two insightful comments were made about the man – the first asked how well did anyone know him apart from the Fleming-Williams and Jean and Nibs Matthews? The second was the feeling that, aside from all his talents, he was always rather a loner.

Colin Hume mentioned that a general legacy was letting people know that it was all right to compose new dances – he mentioned how the writers of "Maggot Pie" came in for a lot of criticism a few years after Sharp's death for doing just that. Colin also feels that Pat let people know that it was all right to look at the original instructions of Playford and other collections and come up with interpretations other than Cecil Sharp's, which was certainly frowned upon when Pat started doing his own interpretations, but is now generally accepted.

Jonathan Cohen wrote –

Pat isn't really known in the choir world but Sing for Pleasure was a great way for people to learn to sing in harmony, with his specially written rounds and his witty arrangements. He wasn't really a "folk" singer as he was classically trained. He was more of the Percy Grainger school but did sing folk songs from around the world, and introduced some of these to this country.

I think it was his enthusiasm and musical knowledge which spread to everyone that came in contact with him that was so infectious and inspiring. He was always experimenting with different musical styles, even encompassing the twelve tone row which was quite trendy in the 60s and used by people like Schoenberg and composers of that ilk. He was also scholarly so it was a great mix of intellect and emotion. For me, it was a quite different approach from the one that I had been used to from my Royal Academy of Music days as his style was so eclectic. He would often use me and my choir, "The Co-operation", to try things out, much in the way Whirligigs would be guinea pigs for his new dances.

Thinking on Pat's legacy, **Robert and Hazel Moir** wrote –

From all that we have read and heard, it is evident that Pat Shaw was a great man, a superb performer and a wonderful composer. He impressed those who met him with his vitality, originality and good humour as well as his versatility in teaching, dancing and singing.

Because of his unique personality he was able to bring together existing traditions and modern ideas to widen the appeal of English Folk Dance. Pat managed to break down the rigidity which had prevailed during the follow on from Cecil Sharp's work.

He introduced and developed different choreography in his interpretations of the old dances and initially this "audacity" was not well received. Pat paved the way for subsequent investigations of original sources, acting as a bridge between the Revival of Cecil Sharp and the post World War II resurgence. He demonstrated that other interpretations could be tried, and many of Pat's versions of the old dances are the accepted ones we use today.

By carrying out his research into the music and dance traditions of the past Pat produced material of considerable value and opened up the way for others to follow suit. This is an important and continuing interest for many in the English Country Dance community today.

Pat's own music and dance compositions have ensured that English Country Dance was and is a living tradition. He developed the idea of using the wider world of music and dance to produce work which has given and still gives encouragement to those who have followed his lead. His music and dances continue to give enormous pleasure to all.

From many of the stories told about Pat he always appears as a larger than life character although his kindness and generosity often shine through too.

We certainly wanted to find out more about Pat, and thanks to the stalwart efforts of Brenda Godrich as editor, and Marjorie Fennessy's inexhaustible store of information about him this wish has been fulfilled.
We hope others will enjoy the book as much as we have.

It is appropriate that **Marjorie Fennessy** should have the last word on this legendary man. She points out that, in his brief autobiography, Pat Shaw characteristically glossed over his immense contribution to the twentieth century folk dance revival. Few people realise how great an influence Pat has had since the Second World War and continues to have today.

He composed music and dances complete with their own tunes in all different styles – "Playford", traditional and American square and contra – he really was a Twentieth Century Dancing Master.

By researching the enormous wealth we have in the Library at Cecil Sharp House and collecting many treasures from all over the British Isles, he also opened and widened the horizon that Cecil Sharp had begun working on.

We all owe Pat Shaw a very great debt.

Marjorie Fennessy at 21

17. APPENDICES

1. PUBLISHED DANCES

	Books	CDs	Date written
Ah! Belinda	New Wine p. 66	NWOB	1971
Albert Memorial Square, The	P.S. book 1 p. 1		1971
All the Young Folk	New Wine p. 68		1971
Amazed Geneticist, The or Ramsay's Reeling	Pinewoods p. 18/19	NQS TF	1976
American Husband, The or Her Man	Pinewoods p. 40	BDF LJ	1977
Another Nancy's Fancy or The Lang Staff	Pinewoods p. 7	D-PS BF-4 TF	1976
Anton's Surprise	P.S. book 1 p. 2	NQS	ca.1964
Arrival from Holland	New Wine p. 14	NWOB2	1971
As I roved out one morning	New Wine p. 34		1971
Avoncroft	P.S. book 1 p. 3	D-PS LJ	1962
Babylon	New Wine p. 10/11	NWOB	1971
Bare Necessities	P.S. book 1 p. 4	ECD TF	1974
Battersea Processional	P.S. book 1 p. 5		1961
Bell of Creation	P.S. book 1 p. 6		1970
Berkshire Tragedy, The	P.S. book 1 p. 7	LLL	1971
Betrayed Lover, The *	New Wine p. 6	NWOB	1971
Buzzards Bay	Pinewoods p. 33	D-PS TF	1977
Camp House Reel	Pinewoods p. 31	LLL	1977
Cardiff Red House (Tŷ Coch Caerdydd)	Welsh p. 68/69	WC	1966
Carillon at Sneek, The	New Wine p. 53	NWOB	1971
Carnival	New Wine p. 32	NWOB2	1971
Cecilia	New Wine p. 44	NWOB	1971
Chigwell Row	P.S. book 1 p. 12	WC	1971
Clarance House	P.S. book 1 p. 8	D-PS TF	1953
Clevedon Sicilian, The	P.S. book 1 p. 10		1965
Clog Dance	New Wine p. 76		1971
Colterom	New Wine p. 8		1971
Country Dance	New Wine p. 64		1971
Cow's Heel (Sawdl y Fuwch)	Welsh p. 72/78	LLL	1960s
Dancing Dutch, The	P.S. book 1 p. 13	D-PS LJ	1973
Dancing the Baby	P.S. book 1 p. 14		1969
Dear Papa and Dear Mama	New Wine p. 78/79	BF-11 NWOB	1971
Delight of the Men of Llay, The (Difyrrwch Gwŷr Llay)	Welsh	LJ	1960s
Donkey Brays, The	New Wine p. 80	NWOB2	1971
Donnie's Farewell to London	P.S. book 1 p. 16		1959
Down in the Nettles	New Wine p. 46	NWOB2	1971
Duchess Sarabande, The	New Wine p. 13	NWOB2	1971
Emperor, The	New Wine p. 52		1971

*   alternative title

English Air, An	New Wine p. 20	NWOB	1971
Errol on the Green	P.S. book 1 p. 17		1972
Farmer, The	New Wine p. 24	NWOB	1971
Farmers' Dance	New Wine p. 59	NWOB2	1971
Flowers of Chirk, The	Welsh p. 64/65	LJ	1960s
Four Winds	P.S. book 1 p. 18	D-PS LJ	1959
Freda's Fancy	P.S. book 2 p. 1	D-PS LJ	
Gay Gaddabout, The	Pinewoods p. 14	NQS TF	1976
Gladys's Galop	P.S. book 2 p. 2	SoS LLL	1974
Greeting, The	New Wine p. 26	NQD	1971
Halsway Sicilian	P.S. book 2 p. 3	D-PS TF	1970
Hamburger Special (McDonald's Reel)	Pinewoods p. 35		1977
Hard Times	New Wine p. 42		1971
Harlequin	New Wine p. 2	NWOB2	1971
Heidenröslein	P.S. book 2 p. 4	LLL	
Helen's Fancy (Hoffedd Helen)	Welsh		
Helwiggery	Pinewoods p. 28/29		1977
Heswall and West Kirby Jubilee	P.S. book 2 p. 5	D-PS NQP TF	1974
I have a Song to Sing	New Wine p. 4	NWOB	1971
Jan Ulrich Christian	New Wine p. 71	NWOB2	1971
Jim Morris-on, The	Pinewoods p. 10		1976
John Raymond	Pinewoods p. 12/13		1976
John Tallis's Canon	P.S. book 2 p. 6	D-PS BF-1 SoS LJ	1965
Johnny's Quadrille	P.S. book 2 p. 8		
Joseph's Jig or Jovial Joc	P.S. book 2 p. 9	SNQP WC	1974
K & E	Pincwoods p. 42	LLL	ca.1969
Katie the Nuisance	New Wine p. 36	NWOB	1971
Kennedys' Rant, The	P.S. book 2 p. 10	D-PS	1964
Kindly Shepherd, The	New Wine p. 16		1971
Kitty Alone	Pinewoods p. 6	WC	1976
Koepoort Galliard, The	New Wine p. 55	NQD BF-11	1971
Leiberts' Wedding, The (A Matrimonial Maggot)	Pinewoods p. 36	WC	1977
Levi Jackson Rag	Pinewoods p. 34/35	LJ HutH	1977
Lindsay Rant, The or Marney's Blarney	Pinewoods p. 11		1976
Little Agnes	New Wine p. 72		1971
Little Hunsdon	Pinewoods p. 30	D-PS LJ	1977
Little Nightingale	New Wine p. 5	NWOB	1971
Long Live London	P.S. book 2 p. 11	BF-1 LLL	1971
Long Pond	Pinewoods p. 5	WC	1976
Lord Thomas of Winchbury		LLL	ca.1960
Lover's Farewell, The	New Wine p. 35	NWOB	1971
Margaret's Waltz	P.S. book 2 p. 12	WC TT	1959
Martial Baron, The	Pinewoods p. 21	NQS TF	1976
Master Jacob	New Wine p. 70	NWOB2	1971
May in The Hague	New Wine p. 12	NWOB	1971

Men of Law*	New Wine p. 9	NWOB	1971
Merrily We Dance and Sing or The Fillip	Pinewoods p. 32		1977
Merry Moment, The	New Wine p. 37	NWOB2	1971
Miss Anderson's Allemande	P.S. book 2 p. 13	D-PS LJ	1962
Miss Avril's Delight	P.S. book 2 p. 14	NQS SoS TF	ca.1970
Miss Bedlington's Fancy	P.S. book 2 p. 16	NQS SoS TF	ca.1970
Miss de Jersey's Memorial	P.S. book 2 p. 18	NQP SoS TF	ca.1970
Miss Fennessy Smiles	P.S. book 2 p. 21		1959
Mr Ganiford's Maggot	P.S. book 2 p. 20	D-PS SoS TF	ca.1970
Mr Shaw's Apologies	P.S. book 2 p. 22	D-PS LLL	1969
Mr Shaw's Canon	P.S. book 2 p. 25	LLL	
Monica's Delight	P.S. book 2 p. 28	WC	1930
Morecambe Bay	P.S. book 2 p. 29	D-PS LJ	1972
Muschamp's Maggot	P.S. book 2 p. 27	WC	1974
My Boy Willey		LLL	1941
My Mother's Geese	New Wine p. 7	NWOB2	1971
Nan's Waltz	P.S. book 2 p. 30	LLL	
Nibs goes West	P.S. book 2 p. 31	LLL	1964
Nightingale	New Wine p. 48		1971
Old Wives' Tales	New Wine p. 22		1971
Pengwern Valley Galop (Carlam Nant Pengwern)	Welsh	TF	
Penniless Soldiers, The	New Wine p. 50	NWOB2	1971
Philida of Utrecht	New Wine p. 56		1971
Phoenix Rejuvenated, The	P.S. book 3 p. 1	D-PS SoS LJ	1975
Pine Cones	Pinewoods p. 43	D-PS TF	1977
Pine Needles	Pinewoods p. 27	NQS WC	1977
Pinewoods Square Eight	Pinewoods p. 16/17	LJ	1976
Planting the May	New Wine p. 28	NWOB	1971
Pride of Newcastle, The	P.S. book 3 p. 2	D-PS BF-11 SoS TF	1963
Prince Consort's Rant, The	P.S. book 3 p. 3		1971
Princess Royal	P.S. book 3 p. 4	LLL	
Quite Carr-ied Away or Joan Transported	Pinewoods p. 20	SNQP BF-1 WC	1976
Rant gone wrong	P.S. book 3 p. 8	TF	1965
Rayleigh Reel	P.S. book 3 p. 9		
Real Princess, The	P.S. book 3 p. 10	D-PS TF	1964
Ronde de l'Amour, La	De Meiboom	WC	1956
Rose of Tankerton, The	P.S. book 3 p. 11	D-PS LJ	1969
Round Pond	Pinewoods p. 22-24	D-PS TF	1976
Sally from Poland	New Wine p. 3	NWOB	1971
Shropshire Galop (Salop Galop)	P.S. book 3 p. 14	WC	1960
Shy Mer-chant, The or Jack's Serenade to Genny	Pinewoods p. 8/9	D-PS LJ	1976
Silver for the Matthews	P.S. book 3 p. 15	LJ	1975
Sleepless Swain, The	New Wine p. 18	NWOB	1971
Slof Galliard, The	New Wine p. 54	D-PS SoS LJ	1971

*   alternative title

Solicitors and Barristers *	New Wine p. 9		1971
Spanish Farmers' Dance, The	New Wine p. 30		1971
Staffordshire Hornpipe	P.S. book 3 p. 16	LJ	1958
Students' March, The	New Wine p. 74		1971
Sweet Rosie Red	New Wine p. 1	NWOB	1971
Sybil's Au Revoir	P.S. book 3 p. 17	D-PS TF	1962
Thames Valley Diamond	P.S. book 3 p. 18		1971
Thora's Surprise	P.S. book 3 p. 19	LLL	
Three Sea Captains, The	P.S. book 3 p. 20	WC	
Treacherous Lover, The †	New Wine p. 6	NWOB	1971
Trip to Orpington, A	P.S. book 3 p. 21	D-PS TF	1959
Troubled Suitor, The	New Wine p. 62		1971
Trumpet Vine			
or Joe Brown's Hornpipe	Pinewoods p. 15		1976
Twelve Reel	P.S. book 3 p. 20		
Twickenham Ferry	P.S. book 3 p. 22	TF	1956
Up on a Lofty Mountain	New Wine p. 58	NWOB	1971
Walpole Cottage	P.S. book 3 p. 24	CSN WC	1963
Waterfall Waltz	P.S. book 3 p. 26	LJ	1966
Waters of Holland, The	New Wine p. 38/40	ECD LJ	pre 1971
Whirligigs' Last Bow, The	P.S. book 3 p. 27	LLL	1973
Winsor Knot, The	P.S book 3 p. 28	LLL	1975
Woeful Lover, The	New Wine p. 60	NWOB	1971

Books
Pat Shaw Collection Books 1 – 3 Dances
Pat Shaw's Pinewoods (Between Two Ponds and Among the Pines)
Welsh – Something old, Something New – A Collection of Pat Shaw's Dances
New Wine in Old Bottles by Pat Shaw (1996 edition)

CDs
BDF ‡	Barn Dance Fiesta – Ring O' Bells Band with Derek Jones BEE011	
BF-1 ‡	Boston Favourites Vol.1	
BF-4 ‡	Boston Favourites Vol.4	
BF-11	Boston Favourites Vol.11	
CSN ‡	Ceilidh Saturday Night – Ring O' Bells Band with Derek Jones BEE004	
D-PS	The Dances of Pat Shaw – The Kenton Ramblers APCD 9802	
ECD	English Country Dances – Bare Necessities	
LJ	Levi Jackson – The Assembly Players APCD 0801	
LLL	Long Live London – The Assembly Players APCD 0201	
NQD ‡	Not Quite Dutch - West Kirby Band with John Stapledon	
NQP ‡	Not Quite Playford - West Kirby Band with John Stapledon	
NQS ‡	Not Quite Shaw - West Kirby Band with John Stapledon	
NWOB	New Wine in Old Bottles – The Assembly Players EFDSS CD01	
NWOB2	New Wine in Old Bottles – Orion's Ring (Recorded live at a dance)	
SNQP‡	Still not quite Playford – West Kirby Band with John Stapledon	
SoS	Shades of Shaw – Dutch Comfort NVS-CD2	

*	alternative title
†	former title
‡	book available

TF   Twickenham Ferry – The Assembly Players APCD 0802
TT   Take Two – John Patrick and Chris Dewhurst CM 106CD
WC   Walpole Cottage – The Assembly Players APCD 0202
HutH   Heatin' up the Hall – Yankee Ingenuity VR 038

Researched Dances – Published

1960s   SIX SIMPLE COUNTRY DANCES
                         from Feuillet's Recūeil de Contredances – 1706
                         and   Essex's Chorography – 1710
                         La Matelotte or The Female Sayler
                         Les Manches Vertes (Greensleeves)
                         Jean qui saute (Jumping Joan)
                         Le Pistolet (Smith's [New] Rant)
                         La Lirboulaire (Lilli Burlero)
                         Le Carillon d'Oxfort (Christchurch Bells)

1960 28 October   HOLLAND as seen in the ENGLISH COUNTRY DANCE
                         1713-1820 (Reprint by NVS 2002 – ISBN 90-805386-4-7)
                         20 Country Dances with references to Holland in their titles
                         taken from various English Sources, selected, edited and
                         described by Patrick Shuldham-Shaw for the Nederlandse
                         Volksdans Stichting

1964 21 September   SIX EASY DANCES (Chwe Dawns Hawdd) c.1760-1813.
                         by Padrig Farfog (Pat Shaw)
                         The Welsh Jig (Y Jig Gymreig)
                         Corris Whim (Mympwy Corris)
                         Tom Edwards
                         Caernarvon Castle (Castell Caernarfon)
                         The Bard (Y Bardd)
                         Lloyd's Whim (Mympwy Llwyd)

1971   FOUR SOCIAL DANCES (Pedair Dawns Cymdeithasol)
                         by Pat Shaw
                         Llanthony Abbey (Abaty Llanthony) c.1825
                         Powell's Fancy (Hoffed Aphywel) Thompson c.1765
                         The Welch March (Ymdaith y Cymry) Wright c.1740
                         Welsh Rabbit c.1750

2000   Something Old, Something New (Hen A Newydd – Casgliad
                         o Dawnsiau gan Padrig Farfog) Welsh Folk Dance Society
                         24 dances researched by Pat Shaw (see Six Easy Dances and
                         Four Social Dances above) and 4 dances composed by him
                         The Flowers of Chirk
                         Waterfall Waltz
                         Tŷ Coch Caerydd (Cardiff Red House)
                         Sawdl y Fuwch (Cow's Heel)

2. Obituaries

Hamish Henderson
1919-2002 singer, collector and poet
"Gang doon wi' a sang, gang doon"

Patrick Noel Shuldham-Shaw – outstanding collector and maker, and 'Admirable Crichton' of the post-World War II English Folk Dance and Song Society – died suddenly on 16 November 1977. He was not yet 60. His loss is a major blow not only to international folk song and folk dance scholarship but also to the still developing and expanding folk revival scene, of which he was a generous and sympathetic if at times shrewdly critical friend.

Pat was in a manner of speaking born into the EFDSS. His mother, Winifred Shuldham-Shaw, was a tower of strength in the Society in its early days, particularly on the dance side, and Pat carried her work forward with quite spectacular virtuosity. After studying music at Cambridge – his preferred instrument while he was an undergraduate was the oboe – he made pioneer collecting trips to the Shetlands in the mid-1940s and noted down a considerable quantity of previously unrecorded fiddle music.

He also "collected" the Papa Stour sword dance, and eventually became so much part of the North Isles scene that he was several times invited to play an official role in the flamboyant Viking ceremonial of Up-Helly-Aa, the Shetland New Year.

His greatest coup in the Northern Isles was, however, his recovery of a version of "King Orfeo" (Child 19) from John Stickle of Baltasound, Unst, in April 1947 (Scottish Studies 20: 124). Bronson expressed the importance of the discovery very well when he wrote (in Traditional Tunes of the Child Ballads Vol. I, p. 275): 'That a tune should in the midst of the twentieth century be recovered for this whisper from the Middle Ages was as little to be expected as that we should hear "The horns of Elfland faintly blowing".' Pat's recording of this rarest of ballads can be heard on Topic LP I2T 160 (Child Ballads, No. 1).

In England itself he went on collecting tours into the Forest of Dean with Maud Karpeles, the principal trophy of their forays being a beautiful version of "The Cherry Tree Carol".

Pat's foremost preoccupation at all times, however, was the dissemination – the "ploughing back" – of what he and others had collected. An accomplished dancer himself – morris, sword, "country" – he carried the standard of English folk dance not only through the length and breadth of the mother country but also as far afield as the USA, where he was a much-loved figure at such institutions as Berea College in Kentucky. He composed dances in the American idiom for the mountain kids in this college, including one "Levi Jackson Rag".

Pat was also a frequent visitor to the Netherlands, where he taught English folk dance to an enthusiastic Dutch society for a quarter of a century. (He was, in fact, due to spend Christmas with these Dutch friends and to celebrate his sixtieth birthday among them. It would have been his twenty-seventh annual visit to Holland.)

It should be mentioned, in this connection, that Pat was a marvellous linguist, and that he was capable of picking up not only new languages but also dialects and *patois* with seemingly effortless ease. (When the cast of *Umabatha*, the zulu "Macbeth", visited the School of Scottish Studies recently, he was heard speaking to them in their native tongue).

Among the English dances he composed were – "Silver for the Matthews" (in honour of the Silver Wedding of old EFDSS friends in 1955); "Margaret's Waltz" and "Walpole Cottage" (in the 1960s); and "Mr Ganiford's Maggot" (1971). He had a truly amazing facility for composing tunes in a variety of idioms; they were mostly catchy tunes and lay as close in to their dances as the skin to the apple.

A year or two ago Pat was invited by Aly Bain to a party in honour of a newly married couple, and there was a good deal of exuberant music making. At one point Aly told Pat he would play him a tune he had picked up in Canada, and he was surprised when Pat immediately joined in on his piano accordion. Aly's find was Pat's own tune "Margaret's Waltz"! (I can personally vouch for the truth of this anecdote which already circulates in folk variants, for I was present at the party).

In 1971 Pat was awarded the Gold Badge of the EFDSS in recognition of his services to folk song and dance, and of his contribution to the overall work of the Society. Nan Fleming-Williams received the award in the same year.

For the past five years Pat had been working on the great Greig-Duncan collection of Aberdeenshire folksong, and it is nothing short of a tragedy that he has not lived to carry this work through to its conclusion – work for which he was uniquely fitted – or even to see the first fruits of his labours in print. His friends at the School of Scottish Studies – and there has never been a more popular adopted member of the School staff – have good reason therefore for an addedly deep and poignant sense of loss.

Pat Shaw knew that he had a serious heart condition, but he went full speed ahead to the end, fulfilling (and enjoying) his manifold self-allotted task. Much love went out to him in many parts of the world. His friends here and elsewhere are bound to grieve for him, but they can be quite sure he would not have wished his death to come in any other way.

Douglas Kennedy

For many years director of the EFDSS, Douglas succeeded Cecil Sharp. A member of Sharp's original demonstration team, he participated in the first English dance schools held at Amherst, MA, during World War I and in the 1920s. In 1950 he and his wife, Helen Karpeles Kennedy, came as staff members to the CDSS summer camp at Pinewoods. He also had several American tours.

Pat's mother, Winifred Holloway, was a talented singing pupil of my father and a contemporary of my sister, Helen, and myself. "Holly" encountered Cecil Sharp when Helen was a pupil at Chelsea PT College, where Sharp was training some of the college students in his recently published English folk dances. Later, during the Great War, Holly, now Mrs Shuldham-Shaw, and Lady Mary Trefusis organised a public meeting to plead for the wider recognition of Cecil Sharp's work while he was actively engaged in the USA collecting songs of British origin in the Southern Appalachian Mountains. Pat inherited not only his mother's musical genius but also her zest for life in every sense.

The Cecil Sharp Memorial Building was opened in the summer of 1930 but alas! Holly was not there to accept the tributes she had earned. She had worked as secretary of the appeal committee for six years and won the praise and recognition of the musical world. The bereft and desolate Pat adopted us and for some years he spent summer holidays with our family. After schooling at Harrow, where he added gymnastics to his quiver of accomplishments, he studied the oboe and took his degree in music at Cambridge.

When at last he entered the portals of Cecil Sharp House as a trained folk dancer and teacher the society welcomed him as a potential future leader. Throughout his life he worked as a free-lance and used that freedom to benefit other musical and national folk societies.

At the time of his death he was completing a scholarly investigation of a folk song manuscript collection in north-eastern Scotland on behalf of the School of Scottish Studies, Aberdeen University, and the EFDSS. Teacher, dancer, singer, composer, Pat Shaw seemed able to play any instrument, pick up any language (even Zulu) and solve any problem or puzzle. Like a poet laureate he was expected to rise to the special occasion and invent an appropriate dance or melody and write verses to suit the needs.

Those of us who worked with Pat acquired the habit of turning to him whenever some problem called for special faculties. A bright light went out of the music world, especially the folk-music world, with his untimely death.*

Nibs Matthews
Artistic Director of the English Folk Dance & Song Society (EFDSS) from 1966, Director 1957-1985

Pat was born in Stratford-upon-Avon on Christmas Eve 1917; his father was a tea-planter in India and his mother (who was an indirect descendant of Sir Francis Drake) was a well-known folk singer and eventually Secretary of the Cecil Sharp Memorial Fund which provided Cecil Sharp House.

He was educated at Harrow where he excelled in gymnastics and first developed his passionate interest in music. He went on to Queens' College, Cambridge, to study music and was at that time a good oboe player and a member of the University Madrigal Society, while developing a profound love of Folk Music from all countries.

After Cambridge he worked for a short period for the EFDSS before joining the National Fire Service in 1942. Four years later, on his release, he decided to take up singing professionally, specialising in Folk Music. Having heard about the traditional music still alive in Shetland, he took a holiday there and was impressed by the players and singers, he went back the following year to collect some of their tunes and songs and notably perhaps the sword dance from Papa Stour. His gift for friendship and sympathetic interest secured him an invitation to take part in the Viking Ceremony of Up-Helly-Aa, which at that time was little known outside Shetland and in April 1947 he recovered a version of King Orfeo from John Stickle of Baltasound, Unst, the importance of which was expressed by Bronson in his Traditional Tunes of the Child Ballads Vol 1. On another collecting tour with Maud Karpeles in the Forest of Dean they found new and interesting versions of "The Cherry Tree Carol" and "The Holly and the Ivy".

About this time Pat took singing lessons from the well-known West Indian actor and singer Edric Connor who helped him to develop his voice. Pat's folk song repertoire was always vast and he had the facility of being able to sing in many languages including Macedonian and Zulu.

On becoming more and more involved with the Society and its work for the general public, Pat learned to play the piano accordion and was always to use it

---

* This was written for the CDS magazine "Pat Shaw Edition" April 1986

and regard it as a real musical instrument – in fact there was hardly an instrument of any sort that he could not pick up and play.

Together with Nan and Brian Fleming-Williams and Jean Forsyth, Pat devised the Concert called "Music of the Countryside", which included songs, solo instrumental items and dance music for listening to – which at the time was unusual. Also in the fifties he was often heard on the BBC West of England radio programme "Country Dancing" as Caller and Singer.

From an early age Pat was a skilled performer of the morris, sword and country dances, but he was also a scholar who studied his facts and he lectured on Folk Music with authority. In the sixties he made a particular study of C17 and C18 Country Dance Collections from which came his new interpretations of figures and movement, though his debt to Sharp for his original work in this field was always acknowledged. He became the Dancing Master par excellence, composing new dances and tunes for countless people and occasions, some of which have already been accepted into the folk tradition. The tune of "Margaret's Waltz" was played to him only last year by Aly Bain who had "collected" it in Canada and thought it beautiful – Pat was overjoyed that one of his tunes had become "real folk" and Aly was surprised to realise that Pat was the composer. Recently "Levi Jackson Rag" has become extremely popular, though it was actually commissioned for a Mountain Folk Festival in the USA in 1976 and was, Pat told me, the one and only time he was paid for composing a new dance.

On the international Folk Scene Pat was also well-known – especially in Holland and America. His ability to make himself understood in many languages was of inestimable value to the many teams he accompanied on tours abroad and he was so versatile he was loved by musicians and dancers alike. He was particularly involved in reviving the Welsh Folk Dance Society where he worked closely with Lois Blake.

Latterly Pat had lived in Edinburgh where he did considerable work on the great Greig-Duncan collection of Aberdeenshire folk songs and it is indeed sad that he did not live to carry this work through to its conclusion and publication.

As well as his work in Folk Music, he was a member of the Executive Committee of the Standing Conference for Amateur Music and he was also a great supporter of Sing for Pleasure, at whose Courses he was recognized as a Composer, Arranger and Conductor. His work for choirs and instrumental ensembles included many of his own compositions, notably carols and rounds.

In 1971 Pat was awarded the Society's highest honour – the Gold Badge in recognition of his service to the EFDSS and his work and devotion to Folk Music.

I met Pat at the first post-war Stratford Festival in 1947 and my memories of him are vivid and various. He always wrote the wittiest rhymes in the Visitors' Book – he never said an unkind word about anybody – he was an entertainer on and off duty (his Nina Sabrina was unforgettable). He was a raconteur, a connoisseur of food and wine and a first class cook. He read, he remembered, he knew his facts and was generous to a fault as well as lovable. He died suddenly in Dorset three days after staying with Jean and me in London, but he had achieved his own stated aim 'to get folk music appreciated and known at home and abroad and to help my fellow countrymen to understand the music of other peoples'.

I am not alone in having lost an unforgettable and irreplaceable friend.

Kathleen Adkins

Kathleen Adkins ("Kattles") and her friend Elsie Whiteman were founding members of the Benacre Band. Pat Shaw dedicated his dance "K & E" to them; "K" played orcon flute, "E" concertina. They were both at Pinewoods dance weeks and can be heard on CDS recordings by the Pinewoods Players.

I suppose I must have been one of Pat's oldest friends; I first knew him in 1925 when he was about eight years old. At that time his mother was the honorary secretary of the Cecil Sharp Memorial Fund, and I used to go to Hampstead several days a week to help her with the secretarial work. Pat was a lively and interesting little boy, very musical and artistic, and always extremely friendly. He used to come tearing down the road to meet me at the bus stop and we walked back to the house together – and Pat then went off to his day school. After a morning's work in the CSMF office, I had lunch with the family and Pat was often there too and we soon became good friends. He took a great interest in the progress of the memorial fund and always asked his mother what *"donions"* [donations] had come in the post that morning. He was a most unusual little boy – and in many ways seemed to be considerably older than his years.

After Pat's mother died, his father, anxious for him to have something special to occupy and amuse him during the school holidays, asked me if I knew anyone who spoke French and who could also help Pat with his music. The only person I could think of was Mademoiselle Yvonne de Coppet, whom I had met through the EFDSS (she was from Switzerland and played the violin). Mr Shuldham-Shaw got in touch with her. The arrangement worked well; later Yvonne became Pat's stepmother.

In 1926 I was invited to join the EFDSS teaching staff. I worked for the Society for many years and often saw Pat at various folk dance functions whilst he was growing up.

After the war, Elsie Whiteman, who had known Pat even longer that I had done, and I worked together for the society in West Surrey and Sussex, organizing square dances, folk-music days, leaders' courses etc. Pat often came to act as caller when we took the Benacre Band to play for the various dance evenings. On one occasion he arrived at the monthly Guildford square dance with the tune "K & E" (Kattles and Elsie) scribbled on a piece of manuscript paper and he told us he had just composed it, wanted to use it that evening and had dedicated it to us! We felt very much honoured. The band did its best with the tune; everyone liked it and it soon became a regular favourite.

By this time Pat's life was totally immersed in folk music, folk song and folk dance and he went all over the country in connection with this. We saw a good deal of him between 1947 and 1960 and were always pleased when he could spare time to come back to our cottage after a local dance evening and spend the weekend with us. We had endless discussions about square dance calls, suitable tunes for them and how to conduct dance evenings.

It was a great shock to hear of Pat's sudden death in November 1977. This occurred only a few days after he had been singing at Cecil Sharp House, to illustrate a lecture/recital given by Mr Douglas Kennedy in memory of Dr Maud Karpeles. We could all see that Pat was not well and we feared he was sickening for influenza, but no one realized he was seriously ill. It was a tragedy that he should die so young.*

---

* This was written for the CDS magazine "Pat Shaw Edition" April 1986

Isabel Bedlington

Isabel Bedlington, a pianist and accompanist, was honoured by Pat Shaw with his dance "Miss Bedlington's Fancy", one of four dances honouring musicians in "Quartet". The other dances being "Miss Avril's Delight", "Miss de Jersey's Memorial" and "Mr Ganiford's Maggot", now published in Pat Shaw Collection Book 2.

I first met Pat Shaw in the mid-1920s. He and his mother (a most distinguished musician) were at the summer school at Cambridge, and I was one of the accompanists.

He was a very musical boy, and showed his talent in those early days. I gave him piano lessons during the school holidays until he went to university, and he was a most rewarding pupil.

His voice developed most satisfactorily during this period and he did a lot of singing at Cambridge. When he came to live in London, he built up quite an interesting connection which led to many concerts. I was fortunate to accompany him at concerts all over the country, and for recitals, a broadcast and a recording of Christmas carols arranged by Vaughan Williams, which were most successful.

He had no trouble with languages; his diction was impeccable and greatly praised by the critics.

His death was a sad loss to all his friends in the musical world.*

---

* This was written for the CDS magazine "Pat Shaw Edition" April 1986

3. Music of the Countryside

Sunday 9 March 1952: 3 p.m.: Village Hall, Bryantspuddle *Nan/Pat/Brian/Jean.*

Sunday 15 May 1953: 8 p.m. Programme of Traditional Songs and Tunes from the British Isles and America. Big school, Tonbridge School, Kent. *Nan/Brian/Pat/Jean.*

Friday 19 February 1954: "Music of the Countryside" 7.30 p.m. Holy Trinity Hall, High Street, Guildford, Surrey. *Nan/Pat/Brian.*

Monday 12 December 1955: "Music of the Countryside" Maidenhead Music Society, 9th Season, 79th concert in co-operation with the EFDSS. *Nan/Pat/Brian/Jean.*

Friday 23 November 1956: "Music of the Countryside" 7.30 p.m. South Park High School, Lincoln. *Nan/Pat/Brian/Jean.*

Thursday 4 April 1957 "Music of the Countryside" 7.30 p.m. Wallingford Grammar School (EFDSS). *Nan/Pat/Brian/Jean.*

Sunday 23 February 1958: "Music of the Countryside" 8 p.m. Cecil Sharp House, London District Committee, in conjunction with St Pancras Arts Festival. *Nan/Pat/Brian/Jean.*

Sunday 9 March 1958: "Music of the Countryside" 3 p.m. St Mary's College Hall, Cheltenham. Presented by The Square Club. *Nan/Pat/Brian/Jean.*

Tuesday 28 October 1958: "Music of the Countryside" The Town Hall, St Alban's (First Bessie Patterson Commemoration (EFDSS Herts. District). *Nan/Pat/Brian.*

Saturday 15 November 1958: "Music of the Countryside" 3 p.m. Museum Lecture Theatre, Bristol (Diamond Jubilee Celebrations, Folk Song Society 1898 – 1958). *Nan/Pat/Brian/Jean.*

Saturday 28 November 1958: "Music of the Countryside" 3 p.m. Museum Theatre, Bristol. *Nan/Pat/Brian/Jean/Denis.*

Sunday 28 February 1960: "The Everlasting Circle" 8 p.m. Emma Cons Hall, Morley College, SE1. *Nan/Brian/Pat/Denis + Isla Cameron, Cyril Tawney, Alan Humberstone.*

Tuesday 25 October 1960: "Music of the Countryside" 7.30 p.m. Town Hall, St Alban's (Bessie Patterson Commemoration). *Nan/Pat/Denis.*

Saturday 10 February 1962: "Music of the Countryside" 8 p.m. Ewell Technical College. *Nan/Pat/Brian/Denis.*

Sunday 18 March 1962: 7.30 p.m. "A Concert of Folk Music" presented and introduced by Richard Wood, Cecil Sharp House. *Nan/Pat/Brian/Denis.*

Saturday 10 May 1962: "Music of the Countryside" 8 p.m. Ewell Technical College. *Nan/Pat/Brian/Denis.*

Sunday 21 October 1962: "Music of the Countryside" The County High School for Girls, Winchester (EFDSS South Hants. District). *Nan/Pat/Brian/Denis.*

Sunday 2 June 1963: (Whit Sunday) "Music of the Countryside" 8.15 p.m. Freshwater Primary School, Isle of Wight. *Nan/Pat/Denis.*

Saturday 28 September 1963: "Music of the Countryside" 2.30 p.m. (EFDSS Eastern Area). *Nan/Pat/Denis.*

Thursday 28 November 1963: "Music of the Countryside" 7.30 p.m. The Assembly Hall, City of Cardiff Training College, Cyncoed Road, Cardiff. *Nan/Pat/Denis.*

Thursday 19 December 1963: "Music of the Countryside" 8.15 p.m. Fenton House, Hampstead Grove, NW3. *Nan/Pat/Denis.*

Tuesday 4 August 1964: "Folk Concert" 7.30 p.m. The Hippodrome, Wood Street, Stratford-upon-Avon. *Nan/Denis + The Spinners, The Ranchers, Alice Brenan, Pauline Hinchcliffe, Rosemary Redpath and Hugh Gentleman.*

Monday 21 September 1964: "Music of the Countryside" 7.15 p.m. The Old Market Place, Shaftesbury, Dorset (S.W.A.A. Tour). *Nan/Pat/Denis.*

Tuesday 22 September 1964: "Music of the Countryside" 7.30 p.m. Shaftesbury Theatre, Dawlish, Devon (S.W.A.A. Tour). *Nan/Pat/Denis.*

Wednesday 23 September 1964: "Music of the Countryside" 7.30 p.m. North Devon Technical College, Barnstable, Devon (S.W.A.A. Tour). *Nan/Pat/Denis.*

Thursday 24 September 1964: 7.45 p.m. "Music of the Countryside" St Luke's College Theatre, Exeter (S.W.A.A. Tour). *Nan/Pat/Denis.*

Friday 2 October 1964: "Music of the Countryside" 8 p.m. The Old Hall, Gainsborough, Lincolnshire. *Nan/Pat/Denis.*

Wednesday 28 October 1964: 7.45 p.m. "Folk at the Winter Gardens" Winter Gardens, Bournemouth. *Nan/Pat/Denis + Steve Benbow and Cyril Tawney.*

Sunday 1 November 1964: "Celebrity Concert" 7 p.m. Compère: Peter Kennedy, Bluecoat Concert Hall, Bluecoat Chambers, School Lane, Liverpool (EFDSS Liverpool Music Festival). *Nan/Pat/Denis + Nadia Cattouse, Rory McEwen, John Doherty (Donegal).*

Saturday 20 March 1965: "Music of the Countryside" Isle of Wight. *Nan/Pat/Denis.*

Wednesday 31 March 1965: 7.30 p.m. Town Hall, Kendall, Westmorland. *Nan/Pat/Denis + Jackie and Bridie.*

Thursday 1 April 1965: "Folk Music Concert" 8 p.m. College of Further Education, Whitehaven, Cumberland. *Nan/Pat/Denis + Jackie and Bridie.*

Friday 2 April 1965: "Folk Music Concert" 7.30 p.m. Assembly Room, Town Hall, Barrow in Furness. *Nan/Pat/Denis + Jackie and Bridie.*

Friday 4 June 1965: 8 p.m. The Royal Festival Hall. Compère *Dominic Behan. Nan/Pat/Denis + Jack Armstrong, Charlie Bate, Dominic Behan, Ian Campbell, The Copper Family, Bob Davenport, Louis Killen, McPeake Family, The Watersons* etc. (Producer: *Roy Guest*).

Saturday 26 June 1965: "Folk Spot" Fingest Barn Theatre, Turville (Len Harman). *Nan/Pat/Denis.*

Friday-Sunday 29-31 October 1965: Liverpool Folk Festival.

Wednesday 3 November 1965: "Music of the Countryside" 8.15 p.m. Fenton House, Hampstead Grove, NW3 (In aid of the National Trust). *Nan/Pat/Denis.*

Thursday 2 December 1965: "Folk Song Concert" 7.30 p.m. Cheltenham Folk Song Club, Town Hall, Cheltenham. *Nan/Pat + Jackie and Bridie and The Watersons.*

Wednesday 11 May 1966: "Concert Spot" 7.30 p.m. Joint Staff Common Room, University College, Gower Street, London (Oxford and Cambridge Musical Club). *Nan/Pat/Denis.*

Friday 20 May 1966: "Music of the Countryside" 8.15 p.m. Kesteven College of Education, Stoke Rochford, Grantham. *Nan/Pat/Denis.*

Saturday 10 September 1966: "Concert" 8.15 p.m. Westfield College, Kidderpore Avenue, Hampstead NW3 (The Standing Conference for Amateur Music, 21st Annual Meeting). *Nan/Pat/Denis + John Beckett (harpsichord).*

Tuesday 13 September 1966: "Folk Spot" Hereford Folk Club. *Nan/Pat/Denis.*

Saturday 1 October 1966: "Folk Spot" Barn Theatre, Turville (Len Harman). *Nan/Pat/Denis.*

Saturday 15 October 1966: "Music of the Countryside" Magdalen College School, Brackley. *Nan/Pat/Denis.*

Saturday 22 October 1966: "Concert" ULIESA Froebel Institute, Roehampton. *Nan/Pat/Denis.*

Sunday 13 November 1966: "Folk Music Concert" 7 p.m. Bluecoat Chambers, Liverpool. Compère *Peter Kennedy. Nan/Pat/Denis + Shirley Collins, Bob Roberts, The Calton Three.*

Monday 14 November 1966 "Folk Spot" The Coach House Club, Liverpool. *Nan/Pat/Denis + Jackie and Bridie.*

Thursday 6 April 1967: "Folk Concert" 7.30 p.m. Whitehaven College Hall (Whitehaven and District Music and Arts Association). *Nan/Pat/Denis + Jackie and Bridie.*

Wednesday 3 May 1967: "The Countryside Players" 7.30 p.m. Old Hall, Gainsborough, Lincolnshire. *Nan/Pat/Denis.*

Saturday 8 July 1967: "Music Gathering" 3 p.m. Queen's Hall, Lairthwaite School, Keswick (Cumberland Music Committee). *Nan/Pat/Denis.*

Friday 3 November 1967: Broadcast "Music of the Countryside" 8 p.m.

Tuesday 7 November 1967: "Music of the Countryside" 7.45 p.m. Primary School Hall, Havant Road, Hayling Island. *Nan/Pat/Denis.*

Sunday 12 November 1967: "Music of the Countryside" 3 p.m. The Youth Centre, Rayleigh, Essex (+ newspaper cutting) *Nan/Pat/Denis.*

Thursday 18 January 1968: "Concert" Whitehaven, Cumberland. *Nan/Pat/Denis.*

Friday 19 January 1968: "Concert" Lancaster. *Nan/Pat/Denis.*

Saturday 27 January 1968: "Music of the Countryside" 3 p.m. Alfred Sutton Secondary Girls School, Green Road, Reading (EFDSS). *Nan/Pat/Denis.*

Saturday 3 February 1968: "Concert", Barn Theatre, Turville (Len Harman). *Nan/Pat/Denis.*

Tuesday 27 February 1968: "Concert / Ceilidhe" 7.45 p.m. Portsmouth Caledonian Society, Porchester Community Centre, Westland Grove, Portsmouth. *Nan/Pat/Denis.*

Saturday 8 June 1968: "Concert" Sheffield Folk Club. *Nan/Pat/Denis.*

Sunday 9 June 1968: "Concert" Manchester Folk Dance Club, Free Trade Hall. *Nan/Pat/Denis.*

Monday 10 June 1968: "Concert" Nottingham Folk Club. *Nan/Pat/Denis.*

Tuesday 11 June 1968: "Concert of Folk Music" 7.30 p.m. The Assembly Hall, Holywell (Holywell Music Festival). *Nan/Pat/Denis.*

Monday-Friday 23-27 September 1968: "Cumberland Tour". *Nan/Pat/Denis.*

Monday 17 February 1969: "The Countryside Players" 8 p.m. Cathedral House, St Thomas's Street, Old Portsmouth (Portsmouth and District Caledonian Society). *Nan/Pat/Denis.*

Wednesday 9 July 1969: "The Countryside Players" present an evening of folk music and songs 8 p.m. Gloucestershire College of Education, Oxtalls Lane, Gloucester. *Nan/Pat/Denis.*

Saturday 22 November 1969: "Music of the Countryside" The Folk House, Bristol. *Nan/Pat/Denis.*

Sunday 23 November 1969: "The Countryside Players" 3.30 p.m. Halsway Manor, Crowcombe (Minehead Arts Society). *Nan/Pat/Denis.*

Saturday 25 April 1970: "Music of the Countryside" 7.30 p.m. *Nan/Pat/Denis.*

Sunday 26 April 1970: "Folk Concert with Music of the Countryside Players" 7.30 p.m. Ladywood Community Centre, Vincent Street (West) Birmingham. *Nan/Pat/Denis.*

Thursday 18 June 1970: Concert "The Countryside Players" 8 p.m. The College Hall, College of Education, Sittingbourne, Kent. *Nan/Pat/Denis.*

Monday 29 June 1970: "Music of the Countryside" 8 p.m. Brambletye School Hall, Forest Row, Sussex. *Nan/Pat/Denis.*

Wednesday 8 July 1970: "The Countryside Players" present an evening of folk music and songs 8 p.m. Gloucestershire College of Education, Oxtalls Lane, Gloucester. *Nan/Pat/Denis.*

Wednesday 24 February 1971: "Folk Night" 7.30 p.m. Assembly Hall, Barking (Barking Arts Council). *Nan/Pat/Denis + Jackie and Bridie and The Yetties.*

Friday 23 April 1971: "The Real Folk" 8 p.m. Avoncroft Arts Centre, Bromsgrove. *Pat/Denis + Fred Jordan.*

Monday 27 November 1972: "Lunchtime Concert" North East London Polytechnic. *Nan/Pat/Denis.*

Tuesday 28 November 1972: "Lunchtime Concert" North East London Polytechnic. *Nan/Pat/Denis.*

Wednesday 29 November 1972: "Lunchtime Concert" North East London Polytechnic. *Nan/Pat/Denis.*

Friday 1 December 1972: Concert "Lancashire Folk Stir".

The Countryside Players

Nan Fleming-Williams
Brian Fleming-Williams
Patrick Shuldham-Shaw
Jean Forsyth
Denis Smith

4. A Pat-turn of Islands

This is an excellent example of Pat's impish humour which has left us dangling. His numbers in the introduction add up to 139 but there are less in the solutions total. So this is a puzzle which we can say contains over 100 names of islands, some from beyond Scotland. How many can you find?

Hidden in the following bit of nonsense are the names of 123 islands from Scotland, fifteen from the rest of the British Isles and a well-known one from further afield. They may be concealed in either of two ways, literally or phonetically, i.e. the usual spelling may be preserved but possibly split between two or more words, or the original sound may be kept but spelt quite differently. An example of the first or literal type might be "She always kept either a cyclamen or camellia growing in a pot in her room." (Menorca); as an example of the second or phonetic type, one might have, "Of course he can't do it" (Corsica). In this second punning type, a few liberties have been taken and it is advisable not to be too pedantic about one's pronunciation! Punctuation is of significance in only one instance. For the rest it can be ignored.

'I'm thinking of spending next week-end in the Highlands', I said to my friend Ronald one day. 'Will you come with me? Please do, then I'll get shown a lot of the beauty spots I might otherwise miss.' 'I'll agree if we go in my car', he said 'yours is owre muckle for yon single-track roads: say ye'll come in mine and the deal's on.' So away we went after lunch the following Friday. 'Papa's touring the Hielands', the kids called after us as we left, and I must admit I kept my fingers crossed as driving with Ron is always somewhat perilous; in fact with his particular kind of conversation one might well call it a risqué business. The car was ancient, held together with string and wire, it wouldn't go in 2nd gear, in fact it was thoroughly unstable and, as Ronald says, it might fall to bits at any moment. As we were about to leave, a policeman on the other side of the road eyed us dubiously. Ronald told me to go across to the cop and say that it was O.K. – it had just passed its MOT.

It was a fine warm day, the sun was shining, the sky was blue, so I took off my jersey and my collar and tie. 'Why no tak aff yer sark as weel?' said Ron, so I did. I sat back mulling over the events of the last few days until I started to feel drowsy. I came to suddenly as the car narrowly missed going into the ditch. I'll make the rascal pay for waking me up like that, I thought to myself, but Ron had stopped and was already out of the car trying to make tea on the Primus stove. He was obviously having trouble with the burner and was getting nowhere. 'Ahoy there, man', he called 'see if ye can fit it; I canna.' By jiggling about with it I managed to get it going and we picnicked on haggis puddings washed down with a dram. 'What's haggis actually made from?' I asked. 'Sheep's liver and lung and oatmeal with a bit o' guid suet', he told me.

As we got back into the car I asked if he would like me to take over for a bit. 'No thanks' he said, 'I feel fine; I dinna tire easily.' So on we went. His car backfired one or twice and I wished we had brought mine since I own a bigger and more reliable one. However it settled down and when warmed up, Ron's car ran really remarkably smoothly.

Later that evening we pulled up at a small hotel. 'We'll see if they've got room for us here' I said. 'It's a nice wee pub. Last time I was here the staff acted in the most friendly manner and the menu is the best for miles around.' They managed to find us a room and after a wash and a change, we had an excellent meal; Rabbit soup, Roast Lamb and 3 veg – none of your synthetic soya protein stuff – then their famous Apple Amber for a sweet. We both refused the cheeseboard and drifted off to the lounge for coffee and a smoke. 'That was really an excellent meal,' said Ron as we went along, 'guid enough for Lord Macdonald's table. No wonder they get a good mention in Egon Ronay's guide.' When we had settled down in the lounge, Ron offered me a real Havana. 'O.K. for Castro maybe,' said I, 'but I prefer my old briar.'

After half-an-hour or so, we went along to the bar. Rab, the barman, welcomed us and asked what we wanted. Perhaps it would be better to draw a veil across the remainder of the evening. I stuck to a decent malt, a Glendronach I think it was, but my friend, as "guid a Scot as aye ye'll find", insisted on mixing his drinks. He always was a fool about this. He started with a double whisky, Bell's I think, with a half-pint of Bass to wash it down. This was followed by several more and then someone suggested he should try a special kind of rum, about 120° proof I think it was. It was supposed to have been bottled specially for the Seaforth Highlanders – a likely yarn! – but Ron went crazy on it. He started to get very high and I got very worried. When sober, he wouldn't injure a fly, but I knew that Ron, normally an absolute saint, killed a chap once when really drunk and he seemed far nearer that state now than at any time since I had known him. 'I say, old man, take it easy. You risk a helluva hangover if you go on like that,' I pleaded with him. 'What ails a chap that he has to drink himself silly? O Ron, say you'll come to bed now.' He took exception to that and started to fight me. Fortunately someone hit Ron, dragged him off me and sent him flying with a punch on the nose. 'I'll fix ye, you idiot,' he said and hurled a piece of rock all the way across the room. 'Who next?' he said. Suddenly the alcohol took over and he dropped unconscious to the floor. We carried him up to his room and put him to bed.

He awoke the next morning full of remorse and with a terrible headache. 'I dinna ken why I fell for yon muck they gied me. It was awfu'. Ach, the foulness o' it. I'll hae to pay for ony damage I caused.' 'It wasn't as bad as all that,' I said, 'come on down and have some breakfast.' After three cups of strong black coffee he seemed to feel better and managed a good plate of bacon and eggs.

After breakfast we went on our way again and owing to his headache he let me drive. I noticed that we were getting low on petrol and said that we'd better get juice before long. 'Gie her a fill at the next garage,' he said. We were going along a valley with a steep escarpment on one side and a more gentle slope covered with ling on the other. Suddenly Ron said 'Gae alang a wee bittie an' I'll show ye a thing there's few people ken aboot. Noo, d'ye see yon muckle stane? Yon's whaur Saint Mungo met Ranald the Hermit.' I said I couldn't see where he meant. He said 'Ay, yon trees are in the way. Drive around the corner whaur the angle's easier an' ye'll see it fine.' I didn't like to show my ignorance by asking about Ranald and I have a nasty suspicion he was pulling my leg.

Round another corner I nearly ran over some cyclists. They were riding four abreast, the fools. They weren't children too young to know better; they were at least fifteen or sixteen years old anyway. Fortunately I was taking my corners slowly, as I'd had a similar experience once before near Ulverstone in the Lake District. The fuel gauge was now showing empty, but by coasting downhill as much as possible, I managed to reach the first garage and we filled up with Texaco. Nearby was a cairn to mark the spot where the Macdonalds won a victory over another clan centuries ago. It made me want to shun any Macdonald I ever met, but then I have got Campbell blood in my veins, so I suppose I am prejudiced. We had our picnic lunch on a sandy beach and spent the whole afternoon there. We packed up about six o'clock, when we saw to the west rain clouds gathering. There was sand all over everything which we quickly shook off and just got into the car again before the rain started. 'It's suddenly turned cald, ye ken,' said Ron with a shiver. By good luck we soon came across a guest house that could put us both up and after a good supper we felt fine and warm again.

Next day Ron took over the wheel again and he drove along the narrow roads rather like the pilot of a jet who forgot to take off. He told me that a lot of what looked like paths on the hillsides were in fact made by sheep who trod, day in and day out, over the same tracks. We stopped once and had a race to the top of a hill from where we had a superb view. Being out of condition, I was puffing and blowing by the time I got to the top, but Ron charged up like a herd of rhinos seeking food or the elephants of Hannibal tackling the Alps, and won easily. 'It's not fair,' I sleepily said and lay back exhausted and went fast asleep for the next twenty minutes.

There is little left to tell. We had a leisurely drive back home, stopping only to visit a stately home containing several portraits ascribed to Raeburn and a garden famed for its sub-tropical varieties of shrubs and trees. About six o'clock Ron dropped me at my door and I asked him up for a drink. He eyed the chaos of my sitting room with horror and said 'Can ye really live in this pig-sty?' 'Yes,' I said, 'I know it's a terrible place, but none the less I call this flat home.' 'Weel,' he said, 'there's nae accountin' for tastes,' and turned and went out of the door.

Pat Shaw 1917 – 1977

List of Islands

Ailsa (Firth of Clyde)
Anglesey (N. Wales)
Aran (Ireland)
Arran (Firth of Clyde)
Ascrib (Highland)
Balta (Shetland)
Barra (Uists)
Bass (Firth of Clyde)
Bell (Newfoundland)
Berneray (Uists)
Bigga (Shetland)
Bottle (Summer Isles)
Bryher (Scilly Isles)
Bute (Firth of Clyde)
Caldy (Pembrokeshire)
Calva (Highland)
Canna (Orkney)
Cara (Islay)
Carna (Mull)
Colonsay (Islay)
Coll (Mull)
Copinsay (Orkney)
Cross (N. Ireland)
Eday (Orkney)
Eigg (Small Isles)
Erin (Ireland)
Eriskay (Uists)
Ewe (Ross and Cromarty)
Eye (Ireland)
Fair Isle (Shetland)
Farne (Northumberland)
Filla (Shetland)
Flat Holm (S. Wales)
Foula (Shetland)
Foulness (Essex)
Fora (Madeira)
Gigha (Islay)
Gometra (Mull)
Handa (Highland)
Herm (C.I.)
Hoy (Orkney)
Huney (Shetland)
Iona (Mull)
Isay (Skye)
Islay (Islay)
Jersey (C.I.)
Jethou (C.I.)

Jura (Islay)
Kaff (?)
Lamba (Shetland)
Langa (Shetland)
Linga (Shetland)
Long (U.S.A.)
Longa (Highland)
Loos (Guinea)
Lord Macdonalds Table
　　　　　　　　　(Skye)
Luing (Slate Islands)
Lunga (Slate Islands)
Malta (Mediterranean)
Man, Isle of (Irish Sea)
Mew (N. Ireland)
Mousa (Shetland)
Muck (Small Isles)
Mull (Mull)
Noss (Shetland)
Oldany (Highland)
Oronsay (Islay)
Papa Stour (Shetland)
Puffin (Bristol Channel)
Rabbit (Sutherland)
Rhode (U.S.A.)
Risga (Loch Sunart)
Rockall (North Atlantic)
Rona (North Atlantic)
Ronay (Uists)
Ronsay (Orkney)
Round (Poole Harbour)
Rum (Small Isles)
St Kilda (North Atlantic)
Sanda (Firth of Clyde)
Sanday (Orkney)
Sark (C.I.)
Scalpay (Skye)
Scarba (Islay)
Scarp (Lewis and Harris)
Scilly (Scilly Isles)
Scotasay (Outer Hebrides)
Seaforth Island (L. & H.)
Seil (Slate Islands
Sheep (Cumbria)
Shona (Loch Moidart)
Shuna (Slate Islands)
Skye (Skye)

Soay (Skye)
S. Ronaldsay (Orkney)
Soyea (Outer Hebrides)
Staffa (Inner Hebrides)
Stroma (Highland)
Swona (Orkney)
Texa (Islay)
Thera (Cyclades, Greece)
Tiree (Mull)
Trodday (Skye)
Trondra (Shetland)
Uist (Uists)
Ulva (S. Hebrides)
Unst (Shetland)
Uyea (Shetland)
Vaila (Shetland)
Vallay (Uists)
Westray (Orkney)
Wyre (Orkney)
Yell (Shetland)

Pat's solution

'I'm thinking of spending next week-end in the Highlands', I said to my friend Ronald one day. 'Will you come with me? Please do, then I'll get shown a lot of the beauty spots I might otherwise miss.' 'I'll agree if we go in my car', he said, 'yours is owre muckle for yon single-track roads: say ye'll come in mine and the deal's on.' So away we went after lunch the following Friday. 'Papa's touring the Hielands', the kids called after us as we left, and I must admit I kept my fingers crossed as driving with Ron is always somewhat perilous; in fact with his particular kind of conversation one might well call it a risqué business. The car was ancient, held together with string and wire, it wouldn't go in 2nd gear, in fact it was thoroughly unstable and, as Ronald says, it might fall to bits at any moment. As we were about to leave, a policeman on the other side of the road eyed us dubiously. Ronald told me to go across to the cop and say that it was O.K. – it had just passed its MOT.

It was a fine warm day, the sun was shining, the sky was blue, so I took off my jersey and my collar and tie. 'Why no tak aff yer sark as weel?' said Ron, so I did. I sat back mulling over the events of the last few days until I started to feel drowsy. I came to suddenly as the car narrowly missed going into the ditch. I'll make the rascal pay for waking me up like that, I thought to myself, but Ron had stopped and was already out of the car trying to make tea on the Primus stove. He was obviously having trouble with the burner and was getting nowhere. 'Ahoy there, man', he called, 'see if ye can fit it; I canna.' By jiggling about with it I managed to get it going and we picnicked on haggis puddings washed down with a dram. 'What's haggis actually made from?' I asked. 'Sheep's liver and lung and oatmeal with a bit o' guid suet," he told me.

As we got back into the car I asked if he would like me to take over for a bit. 'No thanks' he said, 'I feel fine; I dinna tire easily.' So on we went. His car back-fired one or twice and I wished we had brought mine since I own a bigger and more reliable one. However it settled down and when warmed up, Ron's car ran really remarkably smoothly.

Later that evening we pulled up at a small hotel. 'We'll see if they've got room for us here' I said. 'It's a nice wee pub. Last time I was here the staff acted in the most friendly manner and the menu is the best for miles around.' They managed to find us a room and after a wash and a change, we had an excellent meal; Rabbit soup, Roast Lamb and 3 veg – none of your synthetic soya protein stuff – then their famous Apple Amber for a sweet. We both refused the cheeseboard and drifted off to the lounge for coffee and a smoke. 'That was really an excellent meal,' said Ron as we went along, 'guid enough for Lord Macdonald's table. No wonder they get a good mention in Egon Ronay's guide.' When we had settled down in the lounge, Ron offered me a real Havana. 'O.K. for Castro maybe,' said I, 'but I prefer my old briar.'

After half-an-hour or so, we went along to the bar. Rab, the barman, welcomed us and asked what we wanted. Perhaps it would be better to draw a veil across the remainder of the evening. I stuck to a decent malt, a Glendronach I think it was, but my friend, as "guid a Scot as aye ye'll find", insisted on mixing his drinks. He always was a fool about this. He started with a double whisky, Bell's I think, with a half-pint of Bass to wash it down. This was followed by several more and then someone suggested he should try a special kind of rum, about 120° proof I think it was. It was supposed to have been bottled specially for the Seaforth Highlanders – a likely yarn! – but Ron went crazy on it. He started to get very high and I got very worried. When sober, he wouldn't injure a fly, but I knew that Ron, normally an absolute saint, killed a chap once when really drunk and he seemed far nearer that state now than at any time since I had known him. 'I say, old man, take it easy. You risk a helluva hangover if you go on like that,' I pleaded with him. 'What ails a chap that he has to drink himself silly? O Ron, say you'll come to bed now.' He took exception to that and started to fight me. Fortunately someone hit Ron, dragged him off me and sent him flying with a punch on the nose. 'I'll fix ye, you idiot,' he said and hurled a piece of rock all the way across the room. 'Who next?' he said. Suddenly the alcohol took over and he dropped unconscious to the floor. We carried him up to his room and put him to bed.

He awoke the next morning full of remorse and with a terrible headache. 'I dinna ken why I fell for yon muck they gied me. It was awfu'. Ach, the foulness o' it. I'll hae to pay for ony damage I caused.' 'It wasn't as bad as all that,' I said, 'come on down and have some breakfast.' After three cups of strong black coffee he seemed to feel better and managed a good plate of bacon and eggs.

After breakfast we went on our way again and owing to his headache he let me drive. I noticed that we were getting low on petrol and said that we'd better get juice before long. 'Gie her a fill at the next garage,' he said. We were going along a valley with a steep escarpment on one side and a more gentle slope covered with ling on the other. Suddenly Ron said, 'Gae alang a wee bittie an' I'll show ye a thing there's few people ken aboot. Noo, d'ye see yon muckle stane? Yon's whaur Saint Mungo met Ranald the Hermit.' I said I couldn't see where he meant. He said, 'Ay, yon trees are in the way. Drive around the corner whaur the angle's easier an' ye'll see it fine.' I didn't like to show my ignorance by asking about Ranald and I have a nasty suspicion he was pulling my leg.

Round another corner I nearly ran over some cyclists. They were riding four a-breast, the fools. They weren't children too young to know better; they were at least fifteen or sixteen years old anyway. Fortunately I was taking my corners slowly, as I'd had a similar experience once before near Ulverstone in the Lake District. The fuel gauge was now showing empty, but by coasting downhill as much as possible, I managed to reach the first garage and we filled up with Texaco. Nearby was a cairn to mark the spot where the Macdonalds won a victory over another clan centuries ago. It made me want to shun any Macdonald I ever met, but then I have got Campbell blood in my veins, so I suppose I am prejudiced. We had our picnic lunch on a sandy beach and spent the whole afternoon there. We packed up about six o'clock, when we saw to the west rain clouds gathering. There was sand all over everything which we quickly shook off and just got into the car again before the rain started. 'It's suddenly turned cald, ye ken,' said Ron with a shiver. By good luck we soon came across a guest house that could put us both up and after a good supper we felt fine and warm again.

Next day Ron took over the wheel again and he drove along the narrow roads rather like the pilot of a jet who forgot to take off. He told me that a lot of what looked like paths on the hillsides were in fact made by sheep who trod, day in and day out, over the same tracks. We stopped once and had a race to the top of a hill from where we had a superb view. Being out of condition, I was puffing and blowing by the time I got to the top, but Ron charged up like a herd of rhinos seeking food or the elephants of Hannibal tackling the Alps, and won easily. 'It's not fair,' I sleepily said and lay back exhausted and went fast asleep for the next twenty minutes.

There is little left to tell. We had a leisurely drive back home, stopping only to visit a stately home containing several portraits ascribed to Raeburn and a garden famed for its sub-tropical varieties of shrubs and trees. About six o'clock Ron dropped me at my door and I asked him up for a drink. He eyed the chaos of my sitting room with horror and said, 'Can ye really live in this pig-sty?' 'Yes,' I said, 'I know it's a terrible place, but none the less I call this flat home.' 'Weel,' he said, 'there's nae accountin' for tastes,' and turned and went out of the door.

5. Calling the Goats

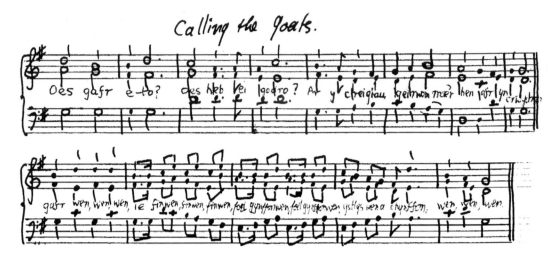

6. PAT SHAW – Singing and playing mainly Folk Songs

These are mostly private recordings from master records and tapes c.1947 and are to be found in the Pat Shaw archives in the VWML at Cecil Sharp House. In the past few years recordings in the Library have been put onto 3 CDs – as listed here. There are also some tapes which are listed at the end

CD1   Records

1.	Blow the Wind Southerly The Black Nag Derbyshire Reel	Accordion	16 July 1947
2.	The Gay Gordons Scapa Flow Atholl Highlanders	Accordion	16 July 1947
3.	Nina Sevena, The Queen of (the Russian) Ballet A Tune from King Arthur by Purcell (Southwind) Trumpet Tune	Song Oboe Oboe	
4.	Lavender's Blue Heilani Vars A Kangaroo A Jig (Purcell dance tune)	piano accompaniment piano accompaniment piano accompaniment oboe & piano accompaniment	
5.	Bold Fisherman She's like the Swallow	piano accompaniment piano accompaniment	
6.	Chanson de Quête Det gingo tud Mae'r esgid fach yn gwasgu	piano accompaniment piano accompaniment piano accompaniment	
7.	Coming in on a Wing and a Prayer Thinking tonight of my Blue Eyes Johnny Hero	piano accompaniment piano accompaniment piano accompaniment	
8.	Gama falon Dat du min leevrten biist Bí bí og bláha Quand la miejo mine	piano accompaniment piano accompaniment piano accompaniment piano accompaniment	
9.	Raslo droo Ich habe mir sines erwählet Per agnet torrent aval	piano accompaniment piano accompaniment piano accompaniment	
10.	A Brisk young Widow Ecoutez donc la complainte Von Luzen auf Weggin zu	(missing)	

10.	This is the truth sent from above	unaccompanied
	Wake up darling it rains (The Crowfish Man)	
	Cripple Creek Girls	
11.	I met her in the garden where the praties grow	piano accompaniment
	Bonny wee thing	piano accompaniment
	The Sailor Home from the Sea	
	Poor Old Horse	
12.	O Waly, Waly (HMV B 9965)	
13.	Searching for Lambs (HMV B 9965)	
14.	Abroad as I was walking (HMV B 9965)	
15.	Yo ba (Children's Hour folk-songs from Switzerland) piano accompaniment	
16	Four Mary's	piano accompaniment
	I will give my love an apple	piano accompaniment
17.	Wake up darling – The Crowfish Man (see No.10)	piano accompaniment
	If I had a Ribbon Blue	piano accompaniment
	Cripple Creek Girls (see No.10)	piano accompaniment
18.	Kiss me (Besame moucho)	piano accompaniment
19.	Kella Bukk	piano accompaniment
	The Garden where the praties grow	piano accompaniment
	Bingo	piano accompaniment
20.	The Twa Sisters (Hedinbro)	
	Down in yon Forest	piano accompaniment
21.	I once loved a boy (Irish)	piano accompaniment
	Go find my true love – There was an old Woman	piano accompaniment

CD2   Records

1.	The Riddle Song – I gave my love a cherry	piano accompaniment
	The Deaf (Old) Woman's Courtship	piano accompaniment
2.	The Lord's Prayer	piano accompaniment
3.	Down in yon Forest (CD1 – No.20)	piano accompaniment
	Zogt zhe Rebbenju	(missing]
4.	Lemady (see Tapes – No.8)	piano accompaniment
5.	Jesus, Jesus, Rest your Head	piano accompaniment
6.	O Waly, Waly (see CD1 – No.12)	unaccompanied

7.	The Brisk Young Widow	unaccompanied
	Dance to your Daddy (see Tapes – No.11)	unaccompanied
	The Lark in the Morn (The Ploughboy)	unaccompanied
8.	Hold On	piano accompaniment
9.	Does you call that Religion	piano accompaniment
10.	Lord Rendell	unaccompanied
11.	Searching for Lambs (see CD1 – No.13)	unaccompanied
	The 12 days of Christmas	unaccompanied
12.	Queen Jane (see Tapes – No.4 with guitar)	piano accompaniment
	The Deaf (Old) Woman's Courtship (see No.1 above)	piano accompaniment
13.	Were you there?	piano accompaniment
14.	The Crucifixion	piano accompaniment
15.	1.(Welsh)	piano accompaniment
	2.(Welsh)	piano accompaniment
	3.(Welsh)	piano accompaniment
16.	1.(French)	piano accompaniment
	2.(French)	piano accompaniment
	3.Au clair de la Lune	piano accompaniment
17.	Going to Shout	piano accompaniment
18.	The Riddle Song (see CD1 – No.16)	piano accompaniment
	The Robin	piano accompaniment
19.	Boom, why does my heart go boom (Sung in French)	piano accompaniment
	1.(Finnish)	piano accompaniment
	2.(Finnish)	piano accompaniment
20.	The Truth sent from above (see CD1 – No.10)	unaccompanied
	The Holly and the Ivy	piano accompaniment
	(This is the usual version, not the one he collected in the Forest of Dean)	
21	I wish I were on yonder hill (Subhail a ghrach?)	
	Black is the Colour of my True Love's Hair	
	Welsh Song	

CD3 Records

1.	The Unquiet Grave	piano and violin accompaniment
	The Seeds of Love (missing) (HMV B 9775)	piano accompaniment

2.   Bushes and Briars (see Tapes – No.12)   unaccompanied
         (HMV B 9775)

3.   King Herod and the Cock (see Tapes – No.10)   piano accompaniment
         (HMV B 9776)

4.   On Christmas Night (HMV B 9776)   piano accompaniment

5.   The Cherry Tree Carol (HMV B 9776)   piano accompaniment
      (This is the usual version, not the one he collected in the Forest of Dean)
                        piano accompaniment by Isabel Bedlington on Nos. 3 – 5

6.   The Evening Prayer –
         Matthew, Mark, Luke and John (HMV B 9964)   piano accompaniment

7.   Gloucestershire Wassail Song (HMV B 9964)   piano accompaniment
                        piano accompaniment by Gerald Moore on Nos. 6 & 7

8.   (But) Black is the Colour   unaccompanied
         (Cecil Sharp Appalachians see CD2 – No.21)

9.   Hi, Hi, Ho (Calling the Cattle into the Farmyard) piano accompaniment
         (one of CD2 – No.15, Welsh)

10.   The Sailor home from Sea – As I was walking   piano accompaniment
         (see CD1 – No.11)

11.   Poor old Horse (see CD1 – No.11)   piano accompaniment

TAPES

1.   Farmer's Wife and the Devil   guitar

2.   O Waly, Waly (more verses than usual)   guitar

3.   My Boy Willy (word missing)   guitar

4.   Death of Queen Jane   guitar

5.   Froggy would a-wooing go   guitar

6.   Branch of May   unaccompanied

7.   The Trees they do grow high   unaccompanied

8.   Lemady (One Midsummer's morning)   unaccompanied
      (see CD2 – No.4.) (one word missing)

9.   Lord Dunwaters   unaccompanied

10. King Herod and the Cock (started twice)   unaccompanied

11. Dance to your Daddy   unaccompanied

12. Bushes and Briars (more verses than usual)   unaccompanied

13. (empty)

14. As I walked through the Meadows   unaccompanied

15. O Sally, my dear   piano accompaniment

16/17. A Wassail, A Wassail   unaccompanied

18. It was one Summer's morning (spider)   piano accompaniment

19. King Pharim   unaccompanied

20. As I walked out one Summer's morning (one verse) unaccompanied

There is a CD **Come and Join the Dance – Songs for Children** which features Pat Shaw with Mary Rowland and Esmé Lewis with instruments played by James Blades, Alf Edwards and Joan Rimmer.

Tracks are –
>Oh, come and dance with me
>Marietta
>Sur le pont d'Avignon
>Mango Walk
>Aiken Drum
>Ground Hog
>Down by the River
>Peanuts
>The Surprise
>Mister Banjo
>Jinny Crack Corn
>When you beat on the Drum
>One, two, three, a'lary
>Toady
>There was a Pig went out to dig
>Mistress Brown
>The Bells
>Three Little Pigs
>Husho, sleepy-head
>Fire down below
>The Death of Admiral Benbow
>The Keys of Canterbury
>There was a Man of Thessay
>Little Mohee
>The Song of Creation

One More River
Tom, the Piper's Son
The Coasts of High Barbary
Bruton Town
Stanley the Rat
I had a Hippopotamus
The Derby Ram
My Heart's in the Highlands
Yankee Doodle
Sunny Bank
The Huron Carol
The Twelve Days of Christmas

There is a copy of this CD in the VWML.

Other private recordings have been made over the years. Two we know about are –

1948 – Pat arranged a recording (see Pat in Shetland Chapter 8) with Nan Fleming-Wiliams (violin), Pat (piano-accordion) Brian Fleming-Williams (guitar) and Geoffrey Ginn (drums) comprising Jackson's Escape from the Trows (composed for Mr. Robertson of Tresta, Fetlar), Da Herra Boys and m.v. Earl of Zetland composed aboard that vessel during one of the food relief trips in March. On the other side the Traditional Players play three jigs for the American dance "Portland Fancy".

1974 – Pat Shaw Live at Levi Jackson.

2002 – the NVS produced a recording which includes Pat teaching some of his dances as well as singing recorded during the Christmas Course 1973.

Others could well have been made. It would be good to know of them and to have copies deposited at the VWML.

Please contact Marjorie Fennessy if you have any information of other recordings.

7. How to Sing a Folk Song *

I. WHAT ACCENT?

"Folk-songs with a BBC accent? Anathema! Horrible! These people should never touch folk song – if he wants to sing let him sing something else."

It would be just as logical to try to prevent the working man singing Handel, Schubert or Brahms. Folk song belongs to us all and we will all sing it in different ways. Percy Grainger points out in an article in the Folk Song Journal that rarely does the traditional singer sing in dialect. He sings in what is to him straight English. It will inevitably be coloured by his dialect but this is what is natural to him. Some people don't believe that BBC English is natural to anybody, but it is, and when it is, it is to my mind preferable on the whole, to a phoney country accent and certainly to the phoney American accent one hears applied to so much English Song these days. I say "on the whole" because there are exceptions where a touch of dialect seems to be essential. Generally the more serious the song, the less dialect seems to matter. It is as if the import of the song transcends dialect, and BBC if that is natural to the singer sound less affected than an assumed dialect. (There is such a thing of course as "affected BBC" which is not really natural to anyone and it is this which so often gives offence in the performance of folk song by singers trained in other kinds of song.)

Too often have I heard singers in their teens and twenties imitating not only the accent but also the cracked voice of some singer in his dotage and by "cracked voice" I do not mean ornamentation. I have known well-known folk-singers so busy giving a replica of the style of the person from whom they learnt the song that the song itself gets lost and is deadly dull to listen to. "Ethnic" once quoted me as saying 'It's the song itself that matters – not the way it is sung'. I probably expressed myself badly. What I really mean is it is the song that matters and the way in which you sing it must be made to serve the song and not be an end in itself.

The trouble with trying to lay down rules about this sort of thing is that there are almost always so many exceptions that the rule is not worth laying down, but I think the above one has few exceptions.

One difficulty is that what sounds affected to one person seems natural to another. I found that during my service as a fireman during the war, when it was only when my fellow firemen knew me well enough to realise that my accent was natural and that I wasn't putting it on, that they looked on me as one of themselves. It is the same with folk song.

My aim with most songs is to find a pronunciation which will not call attention to itself but leave the listener to get on with his task of listening to the song.

II. ACCOMPANIMENT AND PRESENTATION

The guitar is no more traditional to English folk song than the piano. It is however a pleasant instrument for accompanying the voice and, if used with discretion, need not get in the way of the song and can even perhaps enhance it. But American folk guitar style to me (and even more so the banjo) immediately makes the song sound American. 'At least it's a folk style' people tell me 'which is more than yours is.' True, but being a completely foreign style that to me doesn't make

---

* First published (in two parts) in English Dance and Song Vol. XXIV (Nos. 4 and 5 – March and September 1961).

it any more valid. It forces itself so often on songs, completely destroying the natural character of the song, whereas an accompaniment that is in no particular style but is discreet leaves the song to speak for itself.

What about orchestral accompaniment? This (like so much else) is largely a matter of personal taste. The orchestral accompaniment to the records of Stella Yapapa (Greek Folk Songs) and Germaine Montero (Paseando por España) is first-rate. (So is the singing of these two artistes: one feels it is personal, will appeal to the general public, and yet has grown out of a tradition). On other records, possibly because the style of singing is antagonistic to folk song and one feels that the artist has no real interest in the subject, however much he likes the songs themselves, the orchestral background seems too symphonic. It all depends on how it is done. So many "classical" singers seem to sing words – not sense. They over enunciate. I've been guilty of this myself I know. One has to learn by experience what consonants to leave out, exactly how much extra to give for a big hall, etc., etc. On the other hand some singers, particularly those who come to folk song from more popular fields of music are often lazy about their words and although they may be singing "sense", the sense does not come across to the listener. It is as bad to under-do as overdo.

This leads on to the question of how to get a song across to an audience. After I had been singing in a school once, the music teacher came up and said 'Thank you so much, you actually made them listen'. On the other hand I've known such humorous songs as "The Man at the Nore" (Eddystone Light) fall completely flat on the sort of audience that simply does not realise that a song may tell a story— the sort of person who has to have music the whole time as a background, but never really listens. This sort of audience – generally urban – is the performer's nightmare, and one has to resort to all kinds of tricks to try to get across. Perhaps this is one reason why certain artists – particularly teams of artists, use so many gimmicks in their performance that the song itself is lost. A folk song should be able to get across to an audience in a straightforward manner and not have to rely on gimmicks, though an occasional gimmick can be fun on occasions. The fault lies largely with the audience who are not accustomed to listening. But who is responsible for this state of affairs? Is it education that has failed to teach people to listen? Is it singers in the past whose diction has been so poor that people couldn't hear the story anyway? Is it that songs (this applies to other forms of song as well) are forced on people when they want to be doing something else, e.g. talking to each other or dancing or eating. This, I think is frequently true of cabaret. I take my hat off to all who sing at all those occasions only to be talked and whispered through. They may get quite a good hand. People will say afterward 'Oh yes they were very good', but ask them what a particular song was about and – 'Oh yes! That one about the er – Well, oh yes, he married her in the end'. Sometimes people don't even remember that much about it. Children, if properly handled will always listen and are probably the best audience of all.

Is folk song precious? Or are folk song enthusiasts precious? Some certainly are, and the worst offenders are those who are intolerant of anything except the traditional singer and the slavish imitation of it. We all, I think, respect the real tradition and what is good in it and it must always be the fountain head or root (whichever you like to call it) of our own approach.

But most of the people who practically genuflect at the term "traditional singer", fail to realise that among traditional singers there are good and bad, and there are a lot of things which some (but not all) traditional singers do that are certainly best left uncopied. Heaven preserve me from the traditional singer that does nothing but glory in the sound of his or her voice and just doesn't care about the song, except as a vehicle for it. I have heard many. These people are, surely, far more precious in their outlook than the pre-war school or as they are sometimes called "The Wildflower" school. There are various other "isms" in the folk song world today. some more precious than others. Everyone is entitled to his own opinions but should realise that there may be others who hold folk music in just as high esteem, and who may be equally knowledgeable on the subject, who disagree. My remarks must be taken in this way. They represent my own opinions and conclusions and are not to be taken as laying down the law. Frequent discussion and friendly argument between people of widely different opinions can tend to widen the gap but frequently tends to make both sides a little more tolerant of each other.

As an example I would quote the supporters of two different styles of arrangement. One, the sort of close harmony arrangement that is evolved by many of the folk song "groups" to-day; the other, choral arrangements by a composer such as Vaughan Williams or Holst. They are both equally far removed from the real thing but nonetheless valid for that.

Finally, there is the question of the microphone. Has its influence been to emasculate our English folk song style? This is too big a question to argue here; but listen to some of the full-blooded traditional singers from the continent, before you decide!

8. King Orfeo

This is from notes made by Pat Shaw for an article in the FMJ. The texts of the songs can be found in that article.

During one of my early collecting trips to Shetland, it was either July 1946 or April 1947, I happened to be visiting Mr J. Barclay of Mid Yell. I had been told that he was interested in Shetland music and Shetland lore in general and he showed me a number of items of interest which he kindly allowed me to copy. Among these was the accompanying version of the text of King Orfeo preserved as a cutting from the "Shetland Times". There was no date on the cutting but, I remember, it was yellow with age and my guess is that it was published either late last century or early this.

At that time my knowledge of balladry was minimal. I had heard of King Orfeo and knew of the one version published in Child, but this find, though I did take a copy of it, did not strike me as being of particular interest as it had no tune.

Some while later, at the end of April 1947, I was visiting my old friend John Stickle of Hoy Villa, Baltasound, Unst. We were chatting away and he asked me what I had collected recently in other parts of Shetland. I sang him the little Hylta-dance jingle I had just noted a day or two before from Jimsie Laurenson, Aithbank, Fetlar, remarking what a curious bit of nonsense it was. He said that he could sing me something every bit as nonsensical as that and at once started to sing. As I listened and took the tune and words down on paper, (there were no tape recorders in those days), I realised that what I was listening to was a fragment of King Orfeo. Had I not copied the Shetland Times version previously, I doubt very much whether I would have recognised it for what it was; of course I would have found out eventually. You can imagine how thrilled I was; here, for the first time on British soil, I was noting the tune for a very rare ballad. Now the ballad could be brought to life. On looking through the Shetland Times text and comparing it with the Child version, I soon realized that the Cape in the story of the latter were largely if not entirely filled out by the former. John Stickle only had a fragment of four verses – those about being invited into the "Haa" and playing the "notes o' noy" and the "notes o' joy". These I kept along with John Stickle's version (even though possibly a bit corrupt) of the chorus and from the other two versions of the text, I was able to build the ballad up into a singable whole which I eventually recorded at the request of Douglas Kennedy who wanted it as an illustration to a lecture on ballads. Somewhat later, Francis Collinson collected another version of the tune in a different part of Shetland.

The tune and text I noted and later recorded from John Stickle were first published in the English Folk Dance and Song Society's Journal for 1947, subsequently in the Shetland Folk Book (Vol II – there given without Stickle's text) and in professor Dronson's encyclopaedic work on the tunes for the Child Ballads. The recorded version may be found in the archives of the RP library of the BBC.

Although this "Shetland Times" version was referred to in my article in the EFDSS Journal for 1947, it caused no comment. Not only does it fill some of the gaps in the Child text, but it is considerably different in style, having little trace of Shetland dialect. With the interest generated by the publication of the version discovered by Marion Stewart in the last issue of "Scottish Studies", I feel this little-known text should become better known, The note that prefaced it in the newspaper cutting ran as follows:

"The following old song was procured and written down from oral recital at Gloup fishing station in 1865, by the late Mr Bruce Sutherland of Turf-house, North Yell." From this I would assume that it was recited and not sung.

9. Papa Stour

11 Ettrick Road,
Edinburgh, EH10 5BJ
3rd May 1976.

Dear Mr Allsop,

Many thanks for your letter. I am delighted to hear of your Papa Stour project. I had vaguely heard that a group of people from Leeds University was attempting an "in depth" study of the Papa Stour Sword Dance. Is this your group, or is this still somebody else? If it is, I think you ought to get together with them.

Before I tell you my own personal contacts, reminiscences etc. about the dance let me tell you that there is recording of the complete dance with the prologue, the Trip, and the dance itself recorded by Peter Cooke on behalf of the School of Scottish Studies as well as a separate recording of the tune played by a different fiddler. The team recording the whole performance was led by Geordie (G.P.S.) Peterson who, if I remember correctly, was taken into the team for the first time on the first occasion that I saw the dance. The recording of the tune on its own was from John Fraser, who used to play for the dance until he emigrated to New Zealand. I also got a recording from him in about 1953 after I had recorded a complete performance of the dance in 1951 when it was played by Laurie Fraser, a nephew of John Fraser. Laurie was also the musician the first time I saw the dance in 1949. So in addition to two recordings of the tune made by myself which are now at Cecil Sharp House (with copies at the School of Scottish Studies) there are two further recordings in the archives at the School of Scottish Studies. If you want further details of these with such other information as he has, I suggest you write direct to Peter Cooke, School of Scottish Studies, 27 George Square, Edinburgh, EH8 9LD.

In your letter you mention "A Voyage round the Coasts of Scotland and the Isles" by James Wilson. What about Hibbert's account of his journey to and round Shetland (Hibbert's first name and the exact title of this work unfortunately I have forgotten *) which, if I remember rightly, is what Sir Walter Scott copied for "The Pirate". To get specific details of this, I would suggest a letter to the Shetland Folk Society or the Librarian at the public library in Lerwick. While on the subject of letters, a note to Tommy Anderson (mention my name), 7 Queen's Place, Lerwick, Shetland, might produce some interesting information. He is the leading authority on Shetland Fiddle Music and is employed by the Education Authority to teach Shetland Fiddling in the schools. (Have you ever heard of such an intelligent Education Authority?) Geordie Peterson also should still be alive. He's only about in his mid-40s. Perhaps you could get him down to go through the whole thing with you. Tom Anderson or Peter Cooke would tell you how to get in touch with him. I've just tried to get Peter on the phone, but could not.

As regards my own connection with the dance the story is somewhat as follows. I went up to Shetland for a holiday first in 1946.

While up there, I realised that there was a lot of interesting traditional music to be got and I got a few items on that trip and decided to go back for a long stay and to try to collect as best as I could in a serious way. I already knew of the

---

* "A Description of the Shetland Islands: comprising an account of their geology, scenery, antiquities and superstitions by Samuel Hibbert or Hibbert-Ware (1782-1848)" – Ed.

dance as I had seen the pamphlet by Alex Johnston in the library at Cecil Sharp House. I had also read an article on it, I think in an EFDS magazine of way back, by Sybella Bonham-Carter. This could be traced and found, I expect, but honestly I don't know if it is worth taking the time to do so. On my early visits to Shetland I visited Norman O.M. Cameron, of Gardie, Bressay. He was an early member of the EFDS and a founder member of the Greensleeves Morris Men. He had, I think with the help of Sybella Bonham-Carter, noted the dance and he showed me his notation. One of the enclosures you will see is my own shortened version of this. Norman Cameron died a few years ago, but his widow is still alive. She was much younger than he was, but whether she still lives in Bressay or not I don't know. Greensleeves revived the dance many years ago using Cameron's notes. The figures were reasonably accurate, but the style bore little resemblance to what I was to see later and because of the difficulty of everybody getting over their neighbours sword simultaneously, they used long swords as flexible as rappers and bent them downwards for that particular bit. They were so floppy that the Shield (lock) would scarcely hold together! Gordon Neil or one of the older Greensleeves men (perhaps Willie Ganiford?) might still have a copy of Norman Cameron's notes if you want to chase this up.

On my first visit to Shetland I was shown a copy of the Scotsman of April 21st, 1928, which contained the Papa Stour tune along with one called the Day Dawns. This I copied and I enclose a Xerox of my copy.

In 1948 I visited Papa Stour, I think only for one day. My memory for this is a little hazy. Here I met Laurie Fraser from whom I noted some fiddle tunes, including his way of playing the sword dance tune. I found it extremely difficult to note with any accuracy – this was before the days of tape recorders. I enclose a copy of this notation too. If my memory serves me correctly, it was not until August 1949 (though it may have been 1948) that I actually saw the dance performed. I had gone to spend five days on the island, and on arrival asked Alex Johnston who was then post-master on Papa Stour, if there was any chance of seeing a performance. He said that they might be able to get it up for me and they would have a dance in the local school which they used for all social get-togethers, to celebrate the occasion. Accordingly about three or four days later the whole island gathered for a social evening and fairly early on they performed the dance for me. They had rehearsed all that afternoon and took the opportunity to bring in a couple of eighteen year-old boys on the island so that they might be able to pass it on later. Geordie Peterson was one, I think, and Ivor Isbister, son of the local schoolmaster and a native of Foula, was the other. Ivor, sad to say, died very young of some dread tropical disease while at sea in the Merchant Navy.

Needless to say I watched hawk-eyed, particularly as they told me that they were going to do it again later in the evening and I was to take the place of one of them. This happened and I am proud to say that I went through it without making a single mistake. What I gained from this was not only a knowledge of the figures which I found coincided with Cameron's description pretty exactly, but a realisation of the feeling and style which I could never have got from the outside or by just relying on either Johnston's or Cameron's descriptions. At this point in time, they still had the custom of the fiddler giving the signal to go into the next figure by drawing his bow twice across the strings on the wrong side of the bridge. (They had stopped doing this when I next saw them two or three years later.) They kept what I usually call the "Tunnel" figures going a long time. The whole dance, I remember lasted nearly twenty-five minutes without the prologue. The other point I remember with great clarity was the very slow, vigorous, heavy step. I have since found it very difficult to get English sword dancers to get this. They always speed up and if they try to dance to the recording I made of the whole thing on the second occasion I saw it, they cannot manage to keep in time with it. The whole weight of the body was behind every single step however short. In open figures like rings, the step was extremely vigorous with a bit of a spring from foot to foot, but when it quietened down there was still this feeling of weight behind each step. It was nothing like anything I have seen in the Yorkshire dances, though Grenoside is possibly nearer than any of the Cleveland dances. Another thing I remember on this first occasion was the way they ducked when going under arches. I had always been taught never to duck, but it obviously didn't apply here! Again, particularly in the "Tunnel" figures, when a man entered the tunnel, he ducked and gradually raised himself as he passed through the tunnel. This gave a curious effect that people were always walking up-hill. On this first occasion there was no "Over your neighbour's sword" figure done one by one, individually. Both times everyone got over the swords together. I was so delighted that on my first attempt I got over without stumbling, as it is really the hardest bit of the dance. The second time I saw the dance some years later they did this figure, individually the first time and all together the second. On this first occasion there was no definite timing of any figure and perhaps as a performance it was a bit ragged round the edges. As the second performance was definitely for a show, they had polished it up quite a bit. (See my fairly complete notes on the figures of the dance enclosed.) I was thrilled at the whole experience as you can well believe and remember sending a telegram to Douglas Kennedy about the event. Very shortly after that, I taught the dance while it was still very fresh in my mind to a group of men who were at the EFDSS Staff Conference. From Nan Fleming-Williams and Jean Forsyth (now Matthews) I get the right sort of wildness into the music and when we performed it to the rest of the staff one evening, it was one of those rare occasions when there was really magic abroad. The music really took hold of the dancers in an uncanny way and they gave a remarkably good performance. One of the dancers, John Armstrong, now headmaster of a special school for emotionally deprived children at Standlake, Oxfordshire, was so bitten with it that he went to Shetland for his next holiday and learned the dance first hand. It had changed a little in the meantime as I found out the next time I saw it.

On his return to London John got some Scots together to work it up. He abandoned the costume actually worn in Papa Stour which consisted of a white shirt, dark trousers, (the trousers of each individual's best suit in fact), and a coloured sash worn over one shoulder (right, I think), fastened at the waist on the other side. John put his team into fishermen's sweaters, dark trousers and Wellies! (The Papa men wore their ordinary shoes.) They also used to take it much too fast. They danced it once for me to illustrate a lecture and I wanted them to dance it to my recording made on the second occasion that I saw it. They found it quite impossible to maintain the slow speed and we had to abandon the project. John might have something to add to this if you wrote to him.

On a visit to Shetland in 1952, I saw the dance again, this time performed at a concert in the hall at Sandness (the d is silent) on the evening of the Sandness regatta. I slung a mike on the tilley lamp (the hiss is quite audible in the background of the recording) and let it run for the whole performance. The original tape has disintegrated but copies were made in time and may be heard at the Library at Cecil Sharp House or at The School of Scottish Studies. The BBC made a 78 record of the prologue, the opening and closing of the dance, (enough to get a pretty good idea of the tune and style of playing) and the epilogue. This was taken directly from my tape. There is a copy of this too in the Sound Library at Cecil Sharp House. On this occasion I noted that they omitted the drawing of the bow on the wrong side of the bridge, as I have already mentioned, and they had made one or two alterations to the dance and that they had shortened it, not by omitting any particular figure, but by not letting each one go on for such a long time. It also had more polish but was still, I think, without definite phrasing.

Sometime later I saw a performance on telly. I was appalled as the dancers wore a ghastly sort of "fancy dress" and the thing completely lacked guts. I afterwards learnt that this had been done by a team that had tried to work it out for themselves and had no connection with Papa Stour or anybody in Shetland; so I discount everything I noted on this performance.

I have taught it as best as I could on various occasions, with varying results. I have always tried to keep the style as close as possible to that which I so vividly remember from the first time I saw it, but sometimes the influence of other sword dances was too strong and time too short to counteract it. I think now you have the complete story from my angle. May I wish you luck in your researches and studies on it. It is a dance like nothing else; I find it tremendously exciting and worthwhile, equal to and tremendously different from any other British sword dance. I hope you may find the foregoing and the enclosures of use. Let me know please if I can be of further assistance, (I occasionally stay with friends at Cawthorne, near Barnsley), and please let me know if you discover any new and valuable information about it. I am always interested in this particular dance and always shall be, so please let me know how you get on. All best wishes.

Yours sincerely,
Pat Shaw

P.S. I forgot to tell you that ... * Uncle, John Frazer who was the old fiddler for the dance and who had returned from New Zealand where he had lived most of his adult life. He played it rather differently. This too can be heard at C# House or at the School of Scottish Studies.

---

* The hand-written PS was partially illegible on our photocopy.

10. Publications

Pat Shaw in EFDSS Publications

English Dance & Song

1941 Vol 5 No.3 p.30	A Note on Siding
1942 Vol 7 No.1 p.6-7	Music Notes 1 Jigs and Strathspeys
1942 Vol 7 No.2 p.17	Music Notes 2 Reels and Hornpipes
1943 Vol 7 No.3 p.28	Music Notes 3 Playing the Tunes
1943 Vol 7 No.4 p.42	Music Notes 4 usic for Squares
1944 Vol 9 No.2 p.20	Jazz
1947 Vol 11 No.5 p.71	Tunes from Shetland
1950 Vol 15 No.3 p.80	Christmas Day i da Moarnin
1951 Vol 15 No.4 p.115	Arrangements for Haymakers Band
1955 Vol 19 No.6 p.217	The Gipsy's Wedding
1955 Vol 20 No.1 p.29	The Gipsy's Wedding
1959 Vol 23 No.2 p.53	Up With Aily
1959 Vol 23 No.3 p.66	Margaret's Waltz
1959 Vol 23 No.3 p. 67-68	The Hair's Maggot
1960 Vol 24 No.1 p.11-12	The Fair Quaker of Deal
1961 Vol 24 No.4 p.108-109	How to Sing a Folk Song
1961 Vol 24 No.5 p.144-145	How to Sing a Folk Song 2
1961 Vol 25 No.1 p.11-12	Jubilee Dance Competition
1963 Vol 25 No.6 p.186-187	Captain Macintosh
1964 Vol 26.No.2 p.37	Walpole Cottage
1965 Vol 27 No.5 p.153	Holborn March
1965 Vol 28 No.2 p.50 –52	The English Country Dance Part 1
1966 Vol 28 No.3 p.66-68	The English Country Dance Part 2
1966 Vol 28 No.4 p.100-102	The English Country Dance Part 3
1967 Vol 29 No.2 p.53	Freda's Fancy
1967 Vol 29 No.3 p.83	More Figure Eights from Herefordshire
1969 Vol 31 No.4 p.133	The Holly and the Ivy
1969 Vol 31 No.4 p.140	Nan's Waltz
1971 Vol 33 No.2 p.59	Two Dances on the Occasion of the RAH Centenary
1971 Vol 33 No.3 p.102	The Thames Valley Diamond
1975 Vol 37 No.3 p.102	Silver for the Matthews
1977 Vol 39 No.2 p.67	Bray's Dances

Folk Music Journal

1947 Vol 5 No.2 p.74-80	Folk Music and Dance in Shetland
1948 Vol 5 No.3 p.156	The Old Hoss
1949 Vol 6 No.1 p.13-18	Folk Songs Collected in the Shetland Isles
1953 Vol 7 No.2 p.96-105	7 Songs Recorded by B.B.C. from Mrs Costello
1958 Vol 8 No.3 p.178	E. J. Dent 1876-1958
1959 Vol 8 No.4 p.213	Review "Twelve Manx Folk Songs"
1960 Vol 9 No.1 p.59	Review "Songs of the Irish"
1961 Vol 9 No.2 p.109	Review "Canada's Story in Song"
1962 Vol 9 No.3 p.129-147	A Shetland Fiddler and His Repertoire. John Stickle

1962 Vol 9 No.3 p.159-161	While Shepherds Watched
1963 Vol 9 No.4 p.180	Transcription of 11 Songs of George Maynard
1965 Vol 1 No.1 p.60	Review "Now is the Time for Fishing" FG 3507
1966 Vol 1 No.2 p.67-91	The James Duncan Manuscripts Folk Songs
1967 Vol 1 No.3 p.181	Further Notes on the James Duncan Manuscripts
1967 Vol 1 No 3 p.182	Review "The Traditional & National Music of Scotland"
1969 Vol 1 No.5 p.366-367	Edric Connor 1915-1968
1970 Vol 2 No.1 p. 48	Review of "European Folk song"
1972 Vol 2 No.3 p.250	Review of "Folk Music & Dances of Ireland"
1975 Vol 3 No.1 p.94-95	Mrs Lois Blake 1890-1974
1975 Vol 3 No.1 p.95-96	Frank Howes 1891-1974

Other Publications

1928 1st Edition EFDS	Cecil Sharp and English Folk Dance
1971	The Social Dance in England, in Sixty Years of Folk
(undated)	A Round for my Friends
(undated)	Two Rounds for Christmas

DAWNS – the magazine of the Welsh Folk Dance Society

1961 No.2 p.17	Ymdaith y Cymry
1977 p.10-13	Staging Dances for Competition

NVS

1960 1st Edition, London	Holland as Seen in the ECD 1713-1820

Country Dance and Song

1991 Issue101 p.6-7	The Punch Bowl

18. CHRONOLOGY

1917	24 December	Patrick Noel Shuldham-Shaw born at Stratford-upon-Avon Father – Henry Shuldham-Shaw Mother – Winifred "Holly" Holloway/Shuldham-Shaw
1920s		Isabel Bedlington gave Pat piano lessons
1923		Pat started day school in Hampstead
1923		Pat started English folk dancing
1925		Kathleen "Kattles" Church-Bliss (Adkins) met Pat
1926-31		St. Aubyn's (pre-prep School) Rotttingdean
1930	7 June	Cecil Sharp House opened. Pat danced in team
1930	14 August	Pat's Mother died
1930		Pat, aged 13, special grace to become EFDSS member
1930		Kathleen Church-Bliss suggested Mademoiselle Yvonne de Coppet, who spoke French, to help Pat with his music and French in school holidays. She later became Pat's stepmother.
1931		Pat, aged 13, composed **Monica's Delight**. Pat said 'Monica was a beautiful blond Edinburgh lass on whom I had a crush at the time.'
1931-36		Harrow School
1936		Nan Fleming-Williams met Pat at Christmas School in Chelsea, London
1936-39		Queens' College, Cambridge – studying music and played oboe. Sang regularly in the University Madrigal Society
1939-42		EFDSS Midland Area Organiser
1942-46		National Fire Service in Birmingham and later in Cardiff Folk Song Recital in aid of NFS Benevolent Fund
1942-46		Pat started to write tunes in his small Ms books, the first being **My boy Willey** for Bernard Willey, a policeman in Birmingham

1943		Recitals of Folk Songs
	8 August	EFDSS Summer School, Reading University
	28 September	London
	9 October	Recital of Folk Songs, Royal Society of Artists, Birmingham
	27 October	Recital of Folk Songs, Overseas Club, Birmingham
	21 November	Recital of Folk Songs, accompanist Isabel Bedlington, for EFDSS Members at Cheyne Walk, London
	30 November	Recital of Folk Songs at Dulwich Road Girls School, Kingstanding, Birmingham

1944		Recitals of Folk Songs
	29 August	London
	29 September	Music Lovers Club, Cardiff
	25 October	Yugo-slav House, London
	31 October	Cecil Sharp House, London
	4 December	National Fire Service Benevolent Fund, Cardiff

1945		Recitals of Folk Songs
	11 April	Council for Education in World Citizenship, Sheffield
	18 April	Barry
	25 April	Council for Education in World Citizenship, Sheffield
	14 December	County School, Penarth

1946 — Decided to sing professionally. Holiday in Shetland Isles.

1946   19 February — Recital of Folk Songs with Esmé Lewis, Barry Music Club

1946   17 April — Pat recorded folk songs (Boosey & Hawkes)

1946   19 April — Recital at Rhiwtina

1946   13 June — Broadcast Children's Hour. Folk Songs from Czechoslovakia

1946   30 August — Pat recorded Children's Hour – Folk Songs from Switzerland (Boosey & Hawkes) and other folk songs

1946 — Pat wrote **Nan's Waltz** tune for Nan Fleming-Williams. Much later (c.1970), he composed a dance to this tune.

1946-48 — Pat composed a number of tunes for people and places in the Shetlands, finishing with **Lord Curzon**.

1946		Recitals
	19 February	Barry
	19 April	Rhiwtana
	13 June	BBC Children's Hour
	30 August	BBC Children's Hour
	20 November	The Lodge, Llandaff (in aid of Llandaff Church Schools)
	25 November	Dulwich Road Girls School, Kingstanding, Birmingham

1947		Spent 5 months collecting folk music and songs in Shetland. Pat collected Papa Stour sword dance
1947	April	Pat collected "King Orfeo" (version) from John Stickle
1947	25 April	Recital of Folk Songs, Lerwick Town Hall, in aid of Gilbert Bain Hospital.
1947	4 September	Pat collected songs from James Laurenson of Fetlar
1947	5 September	Pat collected a song from John Stickle of Baltasound, Unst
1947	22 July	Grosvenor House Hotel, Park Lane. EFDSS HQ team demonstration. Helen Kennedy was ill, so Marjorie Fennessy danced with Pat in her place and was sewn into her skirt!
1947	August	Stratford-upon-Avon Festival. Nibs Matthews first met Pat
1947	21 October	Folk Song Evening
1948	5 March	Recital of Folk Songs, accompanist Isabel Bedlington, at Cecil Sharp House in aid of International Folk Music Council
1948	1 May	National Coal Board – National Colliery Music Festival – Haringey Arena – Pat in Band
1948	May/June	Spent two months in Shetland collecting music. Also songs from James and Bruce Laurenson
1948	11 May 8 June	Collected songs from James Laurenson of Fetlar Collected a song from Bruce Laurenson of Bressay
		A private record was produced "Shetland Isles", which in fact was three of Pat's tunes. The Band was Nan, Brian, Pat and Geoffrey Ginn, who played an excellent drum roll on one track
1948	December	Pat first visited Holland as a Musician and shortly afterwards as a Teacher. He visited Holland annually for over 25 years.
1948	12 July	Recital at Wigmore Hall
1948	August	Stratford-upon-Avon Festival?
1949	22 January	Recital.
1949	11 February	Pat, Nan Fleming-Williams & William Ganiford – Marjorie Fennesy's 21st Birthday dance at Cecil Sharp House

1949		Pat composed **Freda's Fancy** with a second tune **Hope for South Africa** for Freda Pash when she went to South Africa as EFDSS Representative on Mrs Barney Heffer's return to this country. (2 December)
1950	13/15 Jan.	Folk Song weekend Westham House, Barford, Warwick
1950	29 March	A Concert of Folk Music, Beveridge Hall, Senate House, University of London, by Ralph Vaughan Williams, Clive Carey, Pat Shaw (tenor), Everal de Jersey (piano) with a small Choir and Orchestra.
1951	6 June	British Music at Wigmore Hall, London, including Pat singing six folk songs, unaccompanied.
1951	8 June	Pat Shaw "do" at Russell Square
1952	18 August	Pat Shaw and Maud Karpeles collected in Forest of Dean "The Cherry Tree" and "The Holly and the Ivy" both different versions from the well-known ones.
1953	Whitsun	Pat composed **Clarance House** (Thaxted) with second tune **Whit Monday** for Mrs Jones, wife of first Warden on her retirement.
1953	25 July/ 1 August	Bangor University Summer Course
1953	1 August/ 15 August	Stratford–upon-Avon Festival
1954	15/16 Jan.	Attingham Park weekend Pat & Nibs Matthews
1955	11 February	Attingham Hall weekend (Pat?)
1955	31 March	Shetland Music – Pat, Nan Fleming-Williams. John Armstrong and team danced Papa Stour sword dance at CSH.
1955	5 November/ 10 December	EFDSS HQ Team to South Africa for the Pretoria Centenary Celebrations and then 5 weeks travelling round South Africa by train (Pietermaritzburg, Durban, Port Elizabeth, Cape Town, Kimberley and back to Pretoria)
1956	8 March	Pat composed dance to **Twickenham Ferry** song tune for Mrs A. M. Foxley and Twickenham Group
1956	10-12 August	EFDSS team and Pat – GENEVA

1956	23 September	Pat attended second Square Dance Callers' Get-together at United States Air Force Service Club, RAF Station, West Drayton, Mddx. Marjorie Fennessy went as his partner (Taw)
1957	3 January	Council for Education in World Citizenship – Concert by Young North American Musicians in Central Hall, Westminster. After the Interval "A collection of American Square Dances. Presented by EFDSS. Caller Mr Pat Shaw, musician Mr Frank Hawkins."
1957	10 January	Pat Shaw MC at Seymour Hall – Ball evening before RAH Festival 11 and 12 January
1958	7 March	Concert at St Pancras Town Hall?
1958	22 March	Pat composed dance to **Staffordshire Hornpipe** tune (Knot of Rope – emblem of Earl of Stafford 1444)
1958	16 July	Pat went to see South Africans off at Southend Airport (Marjorie Fennessy accompanied him)
1958	4/18 Aug.	EFDSS Team and Pat – PORTUGAL
1959	Spring	Pat composed the dance **Donnie's Farewell to London** for Donnie McBain, leader of McBain's Band, on his retirement to Lochinver. Pat had composed the tune earlier under the name **Monica's Maggott**
1959	25 March	Pat composed the dance **Margaret's Waltz** with a second tune **Farewell to Devon** for Margaret Grant on her retirement as EFDSS Representative in Devon. In 1977 Aly Bain, a Scottish fiddler, heard the tune of **Margaret's Waltz** (only – not **Farewell to Devon**) in Canada from Jean Carignan and told Pat that he had heard this wonderful tune. Pat was delighted that his tune had become "traditional". However in Scotland the tune was erroneously thought to be for a Scottish lady at the time!
1959	11 April	Pat at Streatham with six couples Whirligigs
1959	circa	Pat composed **Four Winds** ("Mollie's Fancy") for Mollie Du Cane – it being the name of her house. The movement in the dance with two couples dancing a double figure of eight round a standing couple later became known as "four winds"
1959		Pat composed the dance **A Trip to Orpington** for the Kent Folk Dance Club

| 1959 | 2 October | First "Another Look at Playford" at CSH |

| 1960s | | Welsh Folk Dance Society. Pat became involved when Lois Blake took him to a course at Pantyfedwen, Borth. He became a member of the Executive Committee for a number of years and researched Welsh dances, as well as composing **The Flowers of Chirk** for Jack Salter, **The Delight of the Men of Llay** (Dyfyrrwch Gwŷr Llay) for Betty Davies and **Helen's Fancy** (Hoffedd Helen) |

| 1960s | | Pat researched Feuillet's Recüeil de Contredances 1706 and Essex's Chorography 1710 and edited "Six Simple Country Dances". (La Matelotte or The Female Sayler, Les Manches Vertes (Greensleeves), Jeanne qui saute (Jumping Joan), Le Pistolet (Smith's [New] Rant), La Lirboulaire (Lilli Burlero) and Le Carillon d'Oxfort (Christchurch Bells)) published 1964 |

| 1960 | | Pat Shaw composed the dance **The Shropshire Galop** (known as **Salop Galop**) |

| 1960 | 29 April 10 June | South African tour (2nd – 1st tour November/December 1955) |

| 1960 | 28 October | "Holland as seen in the English Country Dance 1713-1820" twenty dances with references to Holland in their titles researched by Pat Shaw for Nederlandse Volksdans Stichting (reprinted 2002 by NVS – ISBN 90-805386-4-7) |

| 1961 | | RAH – Dancers finished in Sword Lock, choreography by Pat. |

| 1961 | 2 April | Easter Parade Battersea Park – **Battersea Processional** was composed by Pat for the occasion for The Whirligigs |

| 1961 | 30 June | Whirligigs danced at 21st Birthday Party for Rupert Caporn at Hampton Court Palace with Pat as musician. |

| 1962 | 4 January | Pat composed **Sybil's Au Revoir** for Sybil Lightfoot's retirement from CSH |

| 1962 | 10 February | Music of the Countryside – Ewell Technical College |

| 1962 | 11 April | Whirligigs illustrated a talk that Pat was to give. He was ill so his talk was read. Jimmy Coleman played |

| 1962 | 22 April | Easter Parade Battersea Park. The Whirligigs with Pat and Vi Le Maistre as musicians |

1962		Pat composed **Avoncroft** for a young group of dancers
1962	7 June	Bishop's Park, Fulham (Pat in Band)
1962	9 July?	Pat composed **Miss Anderson's Allemande** for Ethyl Anderson, EFDSS Organiser in Liverpool
1962	July/August	Macedonia tour
1963		The Show "Wait a Minim" at the Fortune Theatre, London, was of South African music. Andrew & Paul Tracey, the sons of Hugh Tracey (an expert in African music) were the lead players – one of whom could play eighteen instruments – the kalimba being one. It was Pat's association with this family, which led to Pat getting us all to buy and play the kalimba.
1963		Recording by The Purcell Singers (RMC CM46) with Pat singing folk songs.
1963	20 April	Pat composed **The Pride of Newcastle** (upon-Tyne) for the Newcastle Group while on the train on his way to take a dance at Ainwick Castle
1963	24 May	Pat composed **Walpole Cottage** the home of Grace Meikle and Leonie Morris at Chipstead, Surrey. Commissioned for a Farewell Party at CSH
1963	27 June	Pat Shaw on Welsh Television at Cardiff with Whirligigs (Dawnswyr Chwyrligwgan) dancing Welsh dances!
1963	12 July	Hampstead Garden Suburb – Pat & The Whirligigs
1963	3/11 Aug.	Bangor Summer School
1963	12 December	Anglo-Welsh Folk Song in CSH Library with Esmé Lewis and Pat swapping songs – Lullabies in Wales and songs about horses in England
1963	19 December	Music of the Countryside – Fenton House, Hampstead (Winifred (Holly) Holloway's piano/harpsichord were bequeathed to Fenton House on her death)
1964	circa	Pat composed **Anton's Surprise** for Anton van Renssen – Dutch accordion player from The Hague
1964	14 April	Easter Parade Battersea Park – Tuborg Lager float for musicians, Pat and Vi Le Maistre. The Whirligigs danced.

1964	5 June	Concert in Christ Church, Hampstead
1964	June	Pat composed **Nibs goes West** with second tune **Jean's on the Fiddle** for Nibs and Jean Matthews for their first visit to USA, where Nibs worked for a year with CDSS. First presented on BBC West Region broadcast.
1964		Course at Bangor University with dance at end of week at Llanrhaeadr ym Mochnant
1964	12/13 Sept.	Whirligigs danced at Bagneux (Paris) with Pat, Nan, Vi and Jonathan Cohen (the only time he played an accordion!) as musicians
1964	21 September	Pat researched and published as Padrig Farfog (Patrick with the beard) "Six Easy Dances". (The Welsh Jig, Corris Whim, Tom Edwards, Caernarvon Castle, The Bard and Lloyd's Whim)
1964	6 November	**The Real Princess.** Pat composed this dance for Princess Margaret, but she did not come!
1964	December	Pat composed **The Kennedys' Rant** with second tune **The Deck House** Reel (the name of their house) for Douglas and Helen on their retirement from the EFDSS to Waldringfield, Suffolk
1964	December	Pat presented the Christmas Carol Concert at CSH
1965	April	Pat composed **John Tallis's Canon** for the Treasurer of Manchester District of EFDSS. The tune is based on Thomas Tallis's famous hymn tune, which is in canon. This was composed for the first weekend taken by Pat Shaw and Ethyl Anderson.
1965	May	Pat was commissioned by David Fleming-Williams to compose a dance for a ballet "Dark to Dark" he was producing for the…
	23 October	London District Festival at CSH. It was called **Rant gone wrong**
1965	11 August	CCPR Festival – Crystal Palace. Pat there?
1965	November	Pat composed **The Clevedon Sicilian** or **Doreen's Delight** for The Clevedon Group's 21st Birthday and for Doreen Gregory, sister-in-law of Dr Leonard Luckwill. (**As Luck will have it**)
1965	20 November	Ashford Day of Dance. Pat Shaw MC
1965	December	Pat presented the Christmas Carol Concert at CSH

1966	4 February	The Overseas Student Friendship Association. Singing with Pat Shaw. Dancing with The Whirligigs.
1966	7 May	Pat and Whirligigs – Chingford
1966	August	Pat composed **Waterfall Waltz**, when he visited the falls at Llanrhaeadr ym Mochnant. This dance won 1st Prize at the National Eisteddfod (Port Talbot) Competition for a Twmpath Dance.
1966		Pat composed **The Delight of the Men of Llay** (Welsh Betty's Dance) Betty Davies
1966		Pat composed **Pengwern Valley Galop**
1966	9 October	Pat's Party at Abernethy House for Pellissiers from South Africa, who were our "hosts" in November/December 1955 when EFDSS team toured South Africa, starting with the Pretoria Centenary Celebrations.
1966	December	Pat presented the Christmas Carol Concert at CSH
1967	1 February	Polka Rehearsal – Shetlands – Pat Shaw. This was for a television show.
1967	27 March	Pat composed **Cardiff Red House** to the tune **Tŷ coch Caerdydd**
1967	27 March	Pat's **Waterfall Waltz** (Dawns y Pistyll) (Caerdroea Troy) was published in "Four Welsh Barn Dances" (see August 1966)
1967	December	Pat produced the Christmas Carol Concert at CSH
1968	When?	Recital in Lerwick in aid of a local hospital
1968	16/17 February	Pat Shaw – Producer of RAH Festival
1968	December	Pat produced the Christmas Carol Concert at CSH
1969	April	Pat composed **The Rose of Tankerton** for Miss Agnes (Cissie) Gloyne for her 80th Birthday. She was the EFDSS Representative in Kent. The dance was performed at the Cliftonville weekend
1969	April	Pat composed the dance **Dancing the Baby** for June Wilson/Lay when she was dancing both English and Scottish dances

1969	pre-May	Pat composed **K & E** for Kathleen "Kattles" Church-Bliss/Adkins and Elsie Whiteman of The Benacre Band.
1969	December	Pat produced the Christmas Carol Concert at CSH
1969 1970 1970	December January 19 September	Pat composed **Mr Shaw's Apologies** for the Devon District Playford Club, as he had double-booked the date and could not go to Exeter. Marjorie Fennessy taught the dance when she went to the Devon County Club.
1970	18 March	"In an English Country Garden". Concert in memory of Percy Grainger at St Pancras Assembly Rooms. Pat was compère and sang folk songs accompanied by Jonathan Cohen. The Co-operation sang Pat's arrangements (Jonathan Cohen's Choir)
1970	circa	Pat composed the dance **Bell of Creation** to Sydney Carter's tune.
1970	circa	Pat composed the dance **Halsway Sicilian**
1970	December	Pat produced the Christmas Carol Concert at CSH
1971	January	Pat composed **The Albert Memorial Square** and **The Prince Consort's Rant** for the centenary of The Royal Albert Hall, The two tunes may be played together to the harmonies of the first. Pat produced the EFDSS Festival at the RAH that year.
1971	17 September	Pat composed **Long Live London** for a London District Dinner Dance at Derry & Toms, Kensington High Street, London. M.C. Pat Shaw. Band: The Journeymen.
1971		Pat researched and published "Four Social Dances" (Welsh) (Pedair Dawns Cymdeithasol) (Llanthony Abbey (Abaty Llanthony), Powell's Fancy (Hoffed Aphywel), The Welsh March (Ymdaith y Cymry) and The Welsh Rabbit.)
1971	27 September	Pat composed the dance **Chigwell Row** for the Club's 20th Anniversary
1971		Pat composed **The Thames Valley Diamond**. It was commissioned by Kingston-Thames Valley District for the Diamond Jubilee of the EFDS 1911-1971.
1971	November	Pat received the Gold Badge of the EFDSS. Douglas Kennedy said in his citation that if you wanted to know anything 'Ask Pat'. Pat's "thank you" was sung to the tune of "Searching for Lambs".

1971 or 1970	1 November	Pat published **Quartet** – (**Miss Avril's Delight** (violin) for Miss Elsie "Ruby" Avril. **Miss Bedlington's Fancy** (piano) for Miss Isabel Bedlington. **Miss de Jersey's Memorial** (piano) for Miss Everal de Jersey and **Mr Ganiford's Maggot** (violin) for Mr William Ganiford.)
1971	15 December	"Music of the Countryside" (Nan Fleming-Williams, Pat, Denis Smith) at CSH
1971/2		Pat published a book **New Wine in Old Bottles** of 54 dances (his age) to books of Dutch tunes of 17th/18th centuries he had been given some years before. (This was edited and reprinted in a bound book in 2004 by the NVS – ISBN 90-9009249-8)
1971	December	Pat produced the Christmas Carol Concert at CSH
1972	10 April	Last "Another Look at Playford" taken by Pat Shaw. The series did continue for some time afterwards.
1972	April	PAT SHAW to SCOTLAND to live and research Greig-Duncan Collection of Aberdeenshire folk songs
1972		Pat composed the dance and the B music for **Errol on the Green**, when he went to live in Edinburgh.
1972	8 November	Pat composed **Morecambe Bay** for Pat Wilkinson and Club for the Annual Ball of the Lancaster & Morecambe Club.
1972	December	Pat produced the Christmas Carol Concert at CSH
1973	15 March	Pat composed **The Whirligigs Last Bow** (Maggot) for the Final Fling of the Club (formed by Marjorie Fennessy in 1951). Unfortunately Pat Shaw could not be present at the dance at Cecil Sharp House, London.
1973	December	Pat produced the Christmas Carol Concert at CSH
1973	Christmas	Pat composed **The Dancing Dutch** – for his 25th Annual visit to Holland.
1974	April	Pat composed **Muschamp's Mushrooms** for Joe and Gladys Muschamp. **Muschamp's Maggot**, **Gladys's Galop**, **Joseph's Jig** and **Bare Necessities** (the name of their shop)
1974	August-Oct.	Pat went to teach at Pinewoods, USA, and toured round as well.

1974	2 November	Pat composed **Heswall & West Kirby Jubilee** for their Club.
1974	December	Pat produced the Christmas Carol Concert at CSH
1975	27 February	Pat composed **The Winsor Knot (of Ruby hue)** for Joan (pianist) and Jack Winsor's Ruby Wedding
1975	18 April	Pat composed **Silver for the Matthews** for Jean & Nibs Silver Wedding at London District's Dinner & Dance at Rembrandt Hotel. M.C. Pat. Band: The Ranchers
1975	October	Pat composed **The Phoenix Rejuvenated** for the 21st Birthday Party of The Phoenix Club. Based on "The Phoenix" (D.M. 1670)
1975	December	Pat produced the Christmas Carol Concert at CSH
1976	7/9 May	A Pat Shaw weekend at Halsway Manor, taken by him.
1976		Pat composed fourteen dances and published them in **Between Two Ponds** in aid of Pinewoods Fund (USA). It was hoped that **Among the Pines** a second book would have been ready by August 1977. Unfortunately it was not. **Pat Shaw's Pinewoods** of all dances was published in 1985.
1977	25 July	Pat composed **The American Husband** or **Her Man** for Al Herman's 60th Birthday. In Pat Shaw's Pinewoods.
1977	October	Pat composed **Little Hunsdon** (a cabin for a single person) which is published in Pat Shaw's Pinewoods.
1977	11 November	Maud Karpeles Memorial Concert by Douglas Kennedy and Pat Shaw. The last time Pat sang at CSH
1977	16 November	Pat died at Weymouth, Dorset, and was cremated there.
1977	9 December	Pat Shaw Memorial Service at St. John's Church, Hampstead, London.

****

| 1978 | Calan | Clwt y Ddawns 2 (A Selection of Welsh Dances) stereo record was published. Pat had been very involved in this. He played accordion, guitar and flageolette and sang. The band played his arrangements of tunes he had collected "Sweet Richard", "Miss William's Fancy" and "Milford Haven" and his own "Richard's Wife" and "Mince Pies", as well as the rest of the music on the record. |

19. CONTRIBUTORS

Contributors to Pat Shaw Memories

Where no page number is given it means that the contribution has been included in the editorial text rather than being directly attributed.

OBITUARIES AND PRE1990 REMINISCENCES

* Contribution sent in by someone else.